Dinner's in the Freezer!

More Mary and Less Martha

Jill Bond

Illustrations by Reed Bond

GCB Publishing
a division of
Great Christian Books, Inc.
229 S. Bridge Street
P.O. Box 254
Elkton, MD 21922-0254

Excerpts reprinted from <u>You and Your Child,</u> © 1877 by Charles R. Swindoll, used with permission from Thomas Nelson Publishers, Nashville, TN.

Excerpt reprinted from <u>Air Assault and Pepper</u> © 1982 by Ft. Campbell Officers' Wives' Club, used with permission.

The author would love to hear from you, write to her at:
Jill Bond c/o GCB Publishing
229 S. Bridge Street, P. O. Box 254
Elkton, MD 21922-0254

Acknowledgment and Dedication:

With special acknowledgment to our proof readers: Jacqueline J. Howe, Vicki Morrison, Clella K. (Nelson) Sleigh, Martia DeMore, Kay Black and Zoe White for all their time, effort, skill, encouragement, and love. Thank You.

Without the wonderful stories, anecdotes, recipes, tips, and illustrations given to me from my family and friends, this book would be impossible. I thank each person mentioned in this book for their touch on our lives. We made much effort to contact everyone to thank them personally and to acknowledge their contribution.

My children, Bethany Kay, Trent, Stuart, and Reed are my full-time job. I praise the Lord for making me the richest woman in the world. They are my true wealth.

The Lord has blessed me with the most handsome man I've ever met in my life for my husband. It's with joy that I thank him for the hours and hours that he has spent wading through my drafts, correcting my horrible spelling and logic glitches. Not only has he been the main editor of this book, but he lives the program. I dedicate not only this book to him, but the rest of my life. He makes it a joy to submit.

Contents

Part I - Getting Started

Quiz
Introduction i
Chapter 1: More Mary and Less Martha 1-1

Part II - The Economics

Chapter 2: The Logic Behind the System 2-1
Chapter 3: Benefits Worth Considering 3-1
Chapter 4: The Recycling Revolution 4-1
Chapter 5: C.O.R.D. 5-1
Chapter 6: Equipping the Professional: You 6-1
Chapter 7: A Word or Two on Nutrition 7-1

Part III - The System

Chapter 8: A Fast-Forward Look at the Program 8-1
Chapter 9: Personalizing Your Plan 9-1
Chapter 10: The Mega-trip: Shop — pppiiinnnggg 10-1
Chapter 11: The Mega-cook 11-1
Chapter 12: Storing It All Away 12-1
Chapter 13: Atypical or a Typical Day 13-1
Chapter 14: Applying the Principles 14-1
Chapter 15: Hospitality 15-1

Part IV - Recipes

Chapter 16: Freezer Recipes 16-1
Chapter 17: Quick and Easy Recipes 17-1
Chapter 18: Extras and Whole Home Management 18-1

Part V - Who, What and Where

Chapter 19: Graduation 19-1
Appendices:
    A: A Source of Hope A-1
    B: Educational and Homeschooling Resources B-1
    C: Miscellaneous Resources and Suppliers C-1
    D: Miscellaneous Reading D-1
Endnotes Endnotes-1
Form Masters
Registration and Order Forms

To help put yourself in the proper mindset for the budget-helping and time-easing techniques of this book, honestly ask yourself some questions before you continue reading:

1. Take a look at your calendar. Do you have days filled with field trips, lessons, errands, and/or activities? Is there just no time to cook?   ☐ YES   ☐ NO

2. Have you ever come home after a day of outings too tired to cook, only to find you didn't thaw out anything for dinner?   ☐ YES   ☐ NO

3. Last month did you have to "run-through-the-drive-thru," call the pizza man, or pick up that convenience meal from the grocer on the way home?   ☐ YES   ☐ NO

4. Have you ever wondered how much "convenience" costs?   ☐ YES   ☐ NO

5. Would you love to have a graceful evening out with your husband in a "real restaurant" (one that has cloth napkins)? Can you remember the last time you dined out (in contrast to catching a bite)?   ☐ YES   ☐ NO

6. When you entertain, would you like more time to spend with your guests? Would you like to spend less time in the kitchen?   ☐ YES   ☐ NO

7. Are you committed to your job? Do you consider yourself a professional?   ☐ YES   ☐ NO

8. Are you willing to re-organize, learn some new management techniques to help your family? Are you teachable?   ☐ YES   ☐ NO

9. Would you like some more disposable income? Do you have any month left after the end of the money? Do you need to stretch your income to meet all the needs of your family?   ☐ YES   ☐ NO

10. Would you like more time with your husband when he comes home from work?   ☐ YES   ☐ NO

11. Could you use an extra 30 to 60 minutes a day (for reading aloud to your children, prayertime, one-on-one with each child, some handwork, or _____)?   ☐ YES   ☐ NO

12. Do you need HELP in your home?   ☐ YES   ☐ NO

So if you want to be more Mary and less Martha, then let's learn some techniques and ideas that will help . . . .

Introduction

"Just a cookbook?" was the response. "Oh, well."

"Yes, a cookbook, if that's what <u>you</u> want to call it," was my reply.

As if a "cookbook" is somewhat less of a book than a novel. It figures. I'm used to it.

But I still don't like that attitude.

It's the attitude that a book which assists ladies in one of their functions in the home doesn't qualify as a real book.

Other books — texts giving doctors academic tools for their art, books giving professors guidance, manuals giving businessmen information to operate more efficiently — are heralded. But, books that in the same style give women tools for their trade are given little acknowledgment.

The issue isn't cookbooks.

It's the image of home-making skills that gives me passion to speak out.

This particular book, which I refer to as a "working book" can sink or swim — it is not in my hands. It is in the Lord's.

But what must not sink is the role of motherhood/wifedom/home-making.

I believe our role is one of the most **important** ever ordained by God.

Before there was the first farmer, there was a wife. Before there ever was the first industrialist, there was a mother.

My heart sinks when I hear home-making belittled.

Whenever I fill in a form asking for "occupation" I write <u>Professional Mommy</u>. Receptionists look at it. Some laugh. One even marked through it and wrote "housewife." I said, "No, I'm Alan's wife, not our house's. If it helps, write 'Home-maker.'" She accepted that.

I'm proud of what I do! I could have written "author," "speaker," "businesswoman," or . . . , but I thought they wanted my full-time job.

Writing, speaking, and assisting with our home business are all just part of my job description as "home-maker." Just as changing diapers, washing windows, decorating, and hostessing are all part of the same job description.

i

Why are we treated as second-class citizens? Why are only "paid" vocations valued?

What have I done to contribute to this lie?

There was a time when asked what I did for a living, I'd answer, "I'm a computer systems designer; but right now, I'm not formally employed." I was battling within myself between what I knew was right — staying home and rearing my own children and what the world was hammering into me daily — "you're wasting a perfectly good mind."

Eight-year olds (especially one going on 68) challenge your intellect. They ask questions that keep you on your toes. They don't accept pat answers.

Six-year olds challenge your creativity. What can we make with an old sock, some glue, a cardboard box, and some tacks?

Three-year olds challenge your personality. If I ever needed leadership ability it's with my three-year-old.

Babies and children learning to crawl challenge your organizational ability. How do you run a home with everything placed two feet from the ceiling?

And husbands challenge all your "interpersonal skills." Any top executive must be able to work with people and be submissive to their bosses.

Not only does professional mothering keep every quality I'd put on a resume in top form, but I can be in love with my boss.

When I hear on newscasts someone's outcry for women's "rights," all I can think of is that what she's crying for are "wrongs" — we don't need to be liberated OUT of the kitchen, we need to be liberated IN the kitchen.

There are many reasons I've written this book. The most important reason is that I believe the Lord has called me to it — I certainly don't have the wherewithal to do it without His help. My family encourages me daily, even to the point of being willing guinea pigs with the products from my test kitchen.

But I want to offer **you** encouragement and I want to give you tools to help you in the best job in the world. Yes, we are called to do manual labor sometimes, but we are certainly allowed to do it the best, quickest, and most efficient way possible. Why spend more time doing a job than is necessary?

Rocking a child is just as important as preparing a feast.

In the text of this working book, I explain why I looked for better ways to prepare our meals. I developed "Dinner's in the Freezer!" which is basically a method of shopping, cooking, and storing many meals (weeks or months) worth of food in just a few days. But why do I want to share it with you?

This book started with the encouragement of friends, especially one dear friend, Robin Scott, now residing in California.

Friends would ask me how I accomplished as much as I did. I'd answer, "I have one and one half more hours in my day than you do."

They'd ask, "How do you manage on just one salary?" I'd answer, "I spend about half as much as you do on groceries."

They'd ask, "How come your kids love good food?" My reply, "I only serve them good food — fresh, healthy food."

"How?"

So, I'd spend hours on the phone explaining the steps I used to stock numerous dinners in the freezer. Robin asked if I'd teach her and some other friends how to do this. I offered my first workshop to some friends in our homeschool support group in the summer of 1990. I was going to type up some hand-outs. Those "few" handouts became the first edition of this book (more than eighty pages).

That book, though I sold many copies separately, made sense to ladies who would attend my workshops. It became apparent that I needed to expand the book so that it could stand alone and make complete sense apart from the workshop. This is the result of that expanded work.

I've taken from the experiences the Lord has given me to teach you some tools that are used daily by industry. Businessmen everywhere and every day use economies of scale, inventory management, quality assurance, optimal production quotients, and labor negotiating skills. They use those "professional" sounding words. We do the same things everyday, too. We just call it "buying the big jar of peanut butter," "our pantry," "mold control," "let the dishwasher do it," and "getting the kids to help."

Writing this book has been fun and my hope is you'll enjoy reading it. I know if you've had a toddler, you'll identify with my "typical days."

We chose this layout for you to write in this book. It's yours. Please jot down memory joggers, hints, reminders, or notes on the side panels. If any of my anecdotes remind you of a funny story around your home, a memory from your own upbringing, or a tip, write it down in the side panel. Would you also write it on a note and mail it to me? I'd love to hear it. It might appear in the revised edition or in our newsletter. But, most of all, it's to encourage you and to make this household management system more personal. It'll be your book, not just mine.

Reed, our eight-year old son, has received many compliments on his drawings. I've been encouraged by the positive response we've gotten on such a "bold" move as to print a child's rough drawings instead of hiring a professional artist. We believe children have merit. We don't believe that they have to wait until they're of legal age to contribute to their family or to His kingdom. Many of these drawings were done when Reed was six. I feel he has talent and I want to encourage him. If God is calling him in this way, I want to train him up in the way he should go. Besides, I personally feel it's just the look I want this book to convey — pro-family, pro-motherhood, pro-children, pro-LIFE.

Since I'm frequently asked for my opinions and my recommendations concerning products and supplies, we decided in this edition to list some of these products and/or companies by name. As a service to you, we've written to a few of these companies asking if they'd offer you an incentive. The ones that we have heard from as of this printing are included in the back of the book. **Please, whenever you contact these companies mention us.** That will help you. If the companies see that we are referring customers to them, then they will be more likely to continue or to upgrade their incentives. Please note that we contacted companies that we would recommend anyway. Their incentive did not buy our endorsement.

(I also want to state that the tone of this book is focused on your role as homemaker, no matter what you do full-time. I realize that not all ladies have the opportunity to stay home full-time. Please don't accept this focus on housekeeping skills as an attack on anyone's situation. I don't feel called to accuse anyone or to make anyone feel guilty. I'm trying to encourage you and I'll leave it with the Lord to convict those He will one way or the other on their options. Many ladies don't have the choice to stay home. BUT, if you are trying to stay home, perhaps this book will give some financial assistance. Most of my readers are wives and mothers. If you aren't married and/or don't have children, please disregard my prejudice in word choices and illustrations. This system can definitely be adapted for singles and for couples, as well as single mom families and extended families.)

If this book encourages you and helps you in the "mundane" tasks of mommyhood, then I've done my job because you're just as important as a doctor, a professor, or an industrialist.

Yes, it's just another cookbook from just another professional mommy.

Jill Bond
Central Florida
January 1992
(Updated December 1992)

Clarification: During the final editing of this book we moved from Texas to Florida. Ninety percent of this book was written in Fort Worth, Texas.

> ❧ *"The aged women likewise, that they be in behavior as becometh holiness, not false accusers, not given to much wine, teachers of good things; That they may teach the young women to be sober, to love their husbands, to love their children, to be discreet, chaste, keepers at home, good, obedient to their own husbands, that the word of God be not blasphemed."*
> *—Titus 2:3-5*

CHAPTER ONE

More Mary and Less Martha

"Darling, what do you want for dinner? Hot dogs or cold cereal?" my sweetheart husband asked while I lay incapacitated, unable to even sit up. He had a lengthy repertoire of feasts — two. Thus, my system of meal management — of **having** dinner already in the freezer — came from **wishing** dinner was in the freezer.

I still don't understand why anyone calls it "Morning Sickness." Must have been some man joking around. I would have gladly opted for it to be just morning sickness instead of the afternoon, evening, midnight, 24-hour-sickness that I had. To add insult to injury, every book I read said that "morning sickness" usually only lasted for the first three months. Why then did I have it for the entire 40 weeks?

When every fiber of your being is ill, you don't feel like slicing, dicing, stirring, and broiling you and your loving spouse a feast. You feel like crawling into bed. But he's hungry; plus you must feed the baby you carry.

So after three days of cold cereal and hot dogs, I realized I needed *HELP*. Not many young couples can afford to dine out through 40 weeks. We couldn't. Alan was a lieutenant in the Army, so we definitely didn't have money to spare.

Necessity mandated action. I couldn't look at another bowl of cold cereal. Fortunately, the next day, I was not as ill. Since I couldn't predict when another good day would come, I made enough spaghetti sauce to feed Alan's entire platoon. We ate our meal and froze the remainder. The next good day, I made meatloaves. The concept was no longer on the back burner.

Alan didn't know how to cook, but after four years of West Point, he knew how to follow orders. So we scheduled our first "cooking weekend." I'd sit, lean, or stand, depending on the swelling of my feet, and we'd chop, slice, "guosh" (as in blending meats), mix, bake, store and freeze meals.

What a joy when Reed Christopher arrived. We could spend the time with him, recuperate, and not worry about shopping, finances, or dinner, because . . .

"Dinner was in the freezer!"

My little "baby" turned eight years old recently, and we're still using this method — learning and improving it each time. The Lord has blessed us with two more sons, Stuart and Trent, and, as I type this, our fourth, a girl, Bethany Kay is teething. No, I wasn't visited with morning sickness again; it was only with the first one — praise the Lord. But with each child, there were different "happenings" that greatly impeded my ability to meet the hunger demands of my family (a fall down a flight of stairs, a three-month restriction to bed for a serious illness, a sprained hip, complete bed rest for the first three months of this last pregnancy and a six-month recuperation after near-fatal blood clots brought on by childbirth complications).

So, one advantage that we definitely appreciate about this method is the alternative we have for those "sick days." Even though Mommy may feel worse than mud, the family still needs to eat. Church members and friends are wonderful helps, but for those long illnesses, injuries, or the one-day flu, we have a wonderful peace since "Dinner's in the Freezer!"

In my favorite Book there's a story that, if it happened today, might go like this:

> Tonight is the big dinner party Julie and June had looked forward to for days. Finally their special guest of honor arrives. Julie runs to the front door to greet him and begins to fawn all over him. He is so fascinating that she forgets all about the hors d'oeuvre tray she was preparing. She is enthralled with the anecdotes that her guest is telling, for they are stories with emotional word pictures that are reaching her heart. She doesn't even think about adding the finishing touches to the table setting she had previously spent so much time designing.

> Then June storms through the dining room door. As she wipes her hands on her apron, she looks among her guests for her sister, her flighty sister. Rage develops in her as she sees Julie sitting on the floor (how unladylike!) listening to their guest of honor.

> "The nerve! Here I've been in the kitchen 'slaving over a hot stove,' juggling the preparations for five courses. All Julie was responsible for was two courses and the table setting, and she couldn't even get that right. Well, that girl always had her priorities mixed up. I mean, what would people think? There might be spots on the china!"

"It's a good thing at least one member of this family keeps a check on proper etiquette or our standing in this town would be ruined," June's thoughts race as she politely acknowledges her guests. As she greets her guest of honor, "Oh, darling, I'm so glad to see you. I hope you don't mind if I borrow my sister for a minute." June grabs Julie's arm tightly, though giving all appearances of civility. Talking through clinched teeth with a forced smile on her face, she hisses, "I'm trying to put on a nice dinner party and you're in here acting like a guest. Get in the kitchen this minute and help get this meal fixed."

Julie has star dust in her eyes, and is only half-listening to her older sister, "Oh, June, he's wonderful. We've never had such a fascinating guest before. No wonder he's the talk of the town. Why he just was telling the most fascinating story about —."

"Are you going to come in the kitchen and help me NOW or not?" June said, losing all semblance of a calm demeanor.

"In a minute. I want to hear how this story ends," Julie says as she strains to hear the guest's compelling voice.

That was the straw that broke the proverbial camel's back. "Well, if he's so wonderful and wise, then maybe a word from him will help set your priorities straight," June warns Julie.

June interrupts the speaker, "Excuse me, sir, but with all your expertise in dealing with people, I'd like your help on a little matter. You've met my adorable sister, but you see, she's left all the work in preparing this little shindig for me to do. And we have all these hungry people to serve. Obviously, it isn't fair, now is it? Would you kindly tell my sister to get her act together and help me with getting dinner on the table?"

"June, my dear friend, I'm sorry to disappoint you, but Julie does have her act together, it's YOU that needs to rethink your priorities."

1 - 3

Can't we all identify with both of these sisters? That's why this timeless story of Jesus' advice to Mary and Martha is so full of meaning for us today. It is so terribly easy to be a Martha. Have you ever given a dinner party and finally "met" your guests during dessert?

Or later?

Have you ever been to the home of a Martha?

It is an easy trap for the unprepared. It is hoped some tricks and methods in this book will help you avoid some of the trap's allure. These methods have been helping me for years. They work when I let them. I often need to relearn some things, especially how to be more like Mary and less like Martha.

If one of your goals is to be more Mary and less Martha, too, then perhaps this book will help — as long as it's preceded and accompanied by prayer.

You've decided you need help in the kitchen, in the laundry room, in the . . . well, everywhere. But you're wondering if you're qualified. Even more so, you're wondering what makes me qualified to help you? Read on. . . .

Qualifications

The "Dinner's in the Freezer!" program developed from two characteristics:

1) NEED — I needed *HELP!*
2) EXPERIENCE — I've spent eight years shaping the plan.

The only qualifications you must have are need and desire. Do you need help? Admittedly, it would be easier to hire a cook and a maid, but most of us can't afford one. So what's the next best thing? A desire to get snappier in your homemaking skills.

Now that you qualify, why should you listen to me? What are my credentials?

I hesitate to write my "resume" because my qualifications are not needed to save yourself time and money using this method. But, since you must "employ" me to the position of helpful friend with believable, useful advice, I need to sell myself.

One of my favorite anecdotes comes from Charlie Shedd.[1] He tells of how for years he trained parents on child-rearing, and then he had kids of his own. . . needless to say, his whole strategy changed. It's easy to be an armchair quarterback, isn't it?

Well, I assure you, I'm right there hunkered down in the trenches with you. As I write this, my eight-month old baby is playing at my feet; my two-year old son, who we fondly refer to as "The Rhi-monk-eros" (half rhinoceros, half monkey) is napping; my five-year old is watching a "McGee and Me"[2] VCR tape; and my seven-year old is drawing cartoons[3] at his table. Right now it's peaceful and quiet. My dinner is out of the freezer and in the oven. Ah, but there are those days when I have to mop the floor three times. In other words, I am for real. I'm not looking back fondly remembering the way it was, I'm living it today.

Taking a peek at my worldly resumes, you'd see I have several degrees. The certificates are framed and stuffed in a box in the attic. I'm a graduate of Florida State University and the University of Central Florida. My FINAL major was marketing (more on this later). I toyed with nine other majors before settling on marketing (so I could graduate one quarter sooner). They were computer science, international affairs, math, economics, business administration, finance, government, statistics, and another I can't remember (it is that important). If you ask my father, he'll tell you I majored in Alan — the most rewarding of all my college studies. With so many credits in unfulfilled majors, I graduated with enough hours for one and a half degrees.

I have half a master's degree in Systems Management, out of the Industrial Engineering Department of Murray State University. A military transfer out of the country prevented me from completing that degree.

I've completed graduate level courses at Southwestern Baptist Theological Seminary towards a Masters in Communications.

For me, the degrees are not important; but the lessons I learned have helped me to put some things in perspective. As our God never wastes anything, He reminds me of lessons learned that apply to the best occupation in the world . . . Professional Mommy.

I also remember always wanting to learn to cook. I watched my mother and grandmother, and as I grew older they'd allow me to help more and more. In contrast, a dear friend was going to marry a millionaire and hire cooks. So when she married a wonderful man (but not a millionaire) she put a long cord on her phone, and called her younger friend (me, at age 16) who walked her through preparing dinner. "Now go to the frig and pull out the milk. Measure out one cup. . . ." She learned quickly and is now an expert cook. The reason I mention this is to point out what a difference our attitudes can make. Our world doesn't applaud homemaking skills. What a shame! But then the world does a lot of things wrongly.

When I was in the ninth grade, I received several citations during the school's award ceremony. Afterwards, when I was interviewed, I proudly showed my award for being "valedictorian" (highest G.P.A. in Jr. High), my Journalism award, and my award for being top Home Economics student. The first two were highly regarded, the third, joked about. I still hold it in high regard, even if the rest of the world doesn't.

Before I married Alan, I had a dream job that exposed me to high-caliber professional cooking. I referred to it as the best job in the world — Walt Disney World, that is. I trained the sales staff at the resort complex. For two weeks, I'd have to tour the complex, sampling the wonders of the World with four new trainees. And they paid me! We'd have to do such painful, unattractive things as spend a day at the Fort Wilderness campground, a day at the different hotels, a day shopping at The Village. . . . It was so tough. We should all have such cushie jobs.

I certainly did learn from all my tours through the various hotels and restaurants. I asked questions and observed the activities in those professionally designed, equipped and managed kitchens. The methods those chefs used in the four-star restaurants were fascinating. The convention kitchens could simultaneously serve 1,000 meals. It didn't just "happen." They were organized! They planned ahead. They were professionals.

We don't have to have million dollar budgets and hundreds of hungry patrons to be motivated to serve a quality meal. We have a stronger incentive. We're serving loved ones. We have the best clientele in the world — our families. We, too, are professionals.

What do you do?

"What does your daddy do?" the testing administrator asks the 5-year-old.

"He works in the garden. He takes me to the store. He plays ball with me. He takes us to church . . ." the wide-eyed boy fondly focuses on all the great times he's spent with his daddy.

"No, no, no! What does he DO?" says the administrator becoming frustrated after a few rounds of this.

"Oh, he also watches football and . . ." he searches his mind for all the things that daddy does.

"I'm afraid your child is just not ready for kindergarten. He doesn't even know what his daddy does," the "expert" informs the interested mother.

"I don't understand. What do you mean he doesn't know what his daddy does? And what does that have to do with kindergarten?" his curious mother asks.

"He should be able to say 'Daddy works for the Acme Widget Company as the Vice-President in charge of corporate hieroglyphics.' And your child said he gardened, played ball, etc. He obviously doesn't have an adequate command of the English language," this "Gate-keeper of Higher Learning" rattles off.[4]

It sometimes amazes me the importance placed on what someone DOES. The point is that "DOES" only refers to paid positions outside of the home and that all else is unimportant, uninteresting, and unprofitable.

Can you identify with my next story?

"And this is Alan's wife, Jill," the boss introduces me to his wife. Then in a whisper, "She's a housewife."

Mrs. Boss turns to me, obviously searching her mind for something to say. She asks with a very slow, punctuated voice, adopting a speech pattern that you might use with someone in their English-as-a-second-language introductory class, "Ah, . . . how. . . are . . . your . . . chil . . . dren?"

The natural me wants to level her intellectually. I want to ask her if <u>she's</u> ever been invited to join Mensa. I want to . . . but then, wonderfully, the Holy Spirit nudges me to love her in His name.

Leaving the corporate social gathering, Alan gives me a hug. "I overheard how the other women were attacking you for being a full-time Mom. Wow, were they ever prejudiced. What horrible images they had of the housewife as dumb, boring, ignorant and incapable of a polysyllabic utterance." He opens my car door, adding "I hope, after talking with you tonight they won't be so wrong again. I'm proud of the lady-like way you convinced them."

It was nice of him to say, but he didn't know how my insides were raging with "how dare they's."[5]

Housewives certainly have been victimized by some lousy public relations.

The world has misjudged the occupation. I remember all my marketing courses (advertising, surveys, research, strategies, etc.). They informed me of what the housewife is thought to be and the hooks to get her (and her money) every time she walks in a store, watches an ad, or hears a "hype." She's not nearly as pliable as Madison Avenue would like to believe. She's smart. And she does care. We'll be discussing more marketing concepts throughout the book.

It's a standing joke in my family about all my many majors. Not that I'm fickle, but because I enjoyed so many pursuits, I couldn't decide. Yet none was inclusive of all my interests. I'm a "Jill of all trades," and a mistress of none. Our Lord knows what he is doing, and I surely don't. I now realize He's given me a job that uses all my interests, yet is never boring or monotonous. I'm a teacher, chef, systems analyst, dramatist, writer, marketing whiz, and economics forecaster, plus new roles every day. I'm just another professional mommy.

A professional is one who has an assured competence in a particular field or occupation, and/or is engaged in a specific activity as a source of livelihood. It is also a manner, an attitude of perceiving yourself. Professionals are committed. They strive for excellence in their work. We stay-at-homes qualify on all those accounts.

Newspaper interviews of me in high school, back when I was going to "conquer the business world," stated my goal of going into International Law. The Lord's plan is so much better: International Grace. We're the only profession that gets to take our work WITH us. My life's work is eternal: my husband and my children.

Likewise, your life's work is eternally significant. So let's get motivated to make the most out of our Divine calling. One aspect of our job description is turning a portion of our husband's earnings into meals that not only are healthy and filling, but that our children will eat.

Martha and George

One of our field trips was a tour of the U.S. Currency Mint in Fort Worth, TX. The tour was fascinating as we watched the tight security and the thorough controls on the production of one dollar bills. The meaning behind the term "green back" became clear as we saw from a large vat, custom green ink being applied to the printing presses rollers for the back side of the bill only. One section of the mint had a static display of U.S. currency of our nation's history. I was very encouraged with one of our first "bills." Not only is George Washington on the face, but he's accompanied on the engraving by his wife, Martha. In the very first days of our country's formation, the woman's role was esteemed.

Now that you've waded through some of my background, think about your background. You are the most eminently qualified woman in the world to be the mother of your children and the wife of your husband. Of all the possible ladies in the world, the Lord gave you the unique set of talents, skills, and background that He desires for you to use in developing your child into His plan. No one else can do it as well.

You have experiences, bents and tendencies that (used in love) will bring the very best out of your family. And that's what we're all after. Your temperament is matched with the needs of your husband. Your style is perfect for creating the right atmosphere in your home.

Not someone else. You.

Isn't that concept humbling?

Yet, as stated earlier, the Lord wastes nothing. Dig down inside the reservoir of your soul and bring to the surface those abilities He's granted you. This isn't being conceited, it's recognizing your calling with His Provision. He never calls us to do anything for which He doesn't equip us.

To give you some ideas, here are the experiences of some friends who:

- learned how to grade meat as a 4-H project, now she is a pro at dealing with butchers.
- developed a flair with interior decorating. Her table-settings seem to even make the food taste better.
- waitressed for years and now is a consummate hostess.
- helped plan the meals for her sorority.

He's called you to be the "bread-maker" in your family. Take a few moments and praise Him for His very personal work in your life and ask yourself these questions. Then you'll always have an answer for the question, **"And what do you do?"**

1) How has God been training me for where I am today?

_____

_____

_____

_____

_____

2) Am I qualified? ☐ Yes ☐ No
(For the program, you only have to have NEED and DESIRE.)

3) Do I need help in the kitchen? ☐ Yes ☐ No

4) Would the Lord have me be more conscientious in the kitchen?

☐ Yes   ☐ No

5) Am I willing to re-organize some of my current methods?

☐ Yes   ☐ No

6) Would my family benefit from healthier food?

☐ Yes   ☐ No

7) What is my "resume" for my position as wife and mother?

_____

_____

_____

_____

_____

_____

8) What unique talents has He given me that help me serve my family?

_____

_____

_____

_____

_____

_____

Don't ever compare yourself with anyone else. Everyone's situation is her own. For instance, we all attempt to serve healthy meals to our families. However, if you're looking outside, you'll always find someone doing a better job than you. For example, if you're making your own sandwiches, instead of junk food, there's someone who's . . .

- using whole-wheat bread; then there's someone who's . . .
- baking her own whole-wheat bread; then there's someone who's . . .
- baking her own whole-wheat bread from fresh ground flour; then there's someone who's . . .
- baking her own whole-wheat bread from flour she ground herself; then there's someone who's . . .
- baking her own whole-wheat bread from flour that she ground herself from fresher grain; then there's someone who's . . .
- baking her own whole-wheat bread from flour that she ground herself from organic grains, then there's someone who's . . .

. . . from organic grains she grew herself.

. . . from better seeds,

. . . with better soil,

and on and on.

I'm not here to look in your oven and point a finger. I'm here as a neighbor to share with you some concepts, tips, and recipes that have worked for my family and others. If the Lord is convicting you to tighten the food budget, revamp your time demands, and head toward better nutrition, then glean through the rest of the book. Incorporate what is useful. But don't get discouraged, as if you're not doing enough.

I also don't believe the "Super Mom" myth. Don't let trying to live the myth rob any sunshine from your day either. Remember, the Lord is working with you, in you, and through you.

Recognizing the value in "old, mundane, frumpy" household chores is a step in the right direction in appreciating your "lot" in life. Personally, I've never had an old, mundane, frumpy day, just moments when I'm looking at the grungy sink, paint-stained counter, and jellied chair through earthly eyes. Ah, but when I try to look at the same things through His eyes, I see the sink mess as the remnants of a plaster creation my son just made, the counter colors as a remnant of a masterpiece now hung on the refrigerator, and the chair as an opportune lesson for a five-year-old on following through. Whenever you get discouraged, try looking "down" on the situation and I'm sure you'll rethink the old "I hate housework" mental tape.

Now you know you're uniquely qualified to serve your family. Trust me to give you some suggestions as we examine the logic behind the program.

Behold that which I have seen: it is good and comely for one to eat and to drink, and to enjoy the good of all his labour that he taketh under the sun all the days of his life, which God giveth him: for it is his portion. Every man also to whom God hath given riches and wealth, and hath given him power to eat thereof, and to take this portion, and to rejoice in his labour; this is the gift of God. For he shall not much remember the days of his life; because God answereth him in the joy of his heart. Ecclesiastes 5:18-20 (KJV)

CHAPTER TWO

The Logic behind the program

We have been looking forward to this trip for months — our sorority "Weekend" to North Carolina for snow skiing. This is going to be fun. I am confident. I have been an excellent water skier since I was five. So, this should be a breeze.

Within minutes of arriving at the ski resort, I am raring to go. I have snow skis on for the first time and all I want is directions to the slopes. I bypass the bunny slope, saying to myself, "too simple. The beauty of the mountains is spectacular, so why not ride that long ski lift? The view ought to be fantastic from up there." So I jump on the bench and chat with my co-passenger. The ride ends all too soon, and it starts to hit me. All the lift benches on the way back down were empty. It isn't a round trip — I am going to have to SKI down this monster of a mountain. Its former beauty starts to turn grotesque. I swallow and ask my new friend, "By the way, how do you get off this lift?" "Just jump as it starts to loop around," comes the helpful reply.

"That was easy enough. Nice level ground up here," I think. But as I begin to ski, I realize the stark difference between snow skiing and water skiing: gravity verses a friendly boat-driver.

How do I get started? There aren't any "Hit it" signals up here. So I watch the other skiers and give a heave on my poles.

As my skis glide through the soft powder, I think, "Hey, I'm enjoying this." THEN . . .

I look up at my first life-or-death situation. The trail disappears and heads 180 degrees in the other direction. That's another distinction between water and snow skiing — no rope for getting through turns. I look down at those big, long, skinny wooden slats, then I holler to a skier in front of me, "How do you turn?"

She hollers back, "Just fall down and get up in the other direction!" "Logical. . ." I guess. I watch and she falls down. I'm getting too close to the edge of the mountain so I don't have many choices. I fall down, too. The other skier gets up and heads in the new direction. "O.K.," I mumble as I crawl up, lose my balance, sink back down, and madly grab at a ski that's getting away. Finally, I manage to get back up and off of the snow that's sopping my clothing, and pop my Frankenstein-boots into those two slimy, wooden sticks (I mean skis).

I "shove off" again and just as I start to like it, there's another one of those hairpin turns. "There's got to be a better way," I think to myself as a little child glides by and sprays me with snow. Insult to injury! It isn't long until, by observing other skiers, I learn basic leaning techniques. I never get used to two skis, though. I have my best control when lifting one ski and slaloming, which is another term that means totally different things in the two sports.

At the next curve, there's my friend the "Just-fall-down" lady, and sure enough she deliberately falls over and gets up in the other direction. Every time!

The second day there, I am thoroughly enjoying myself and learning all the new jargon, styles, and tricks of this sport. When I see "Mrs. Just-fall-down" again, I asked her if this is her first time out on the slopes, too. She starts to fall down again at the next turn, "Oh, my, no. I've been skiing for years!"

For some of my readers, the techniques in this book will be akin to falling down and getting up in the other direction. For some of you, it'll be simply a slight deviation in your current path. And for some of you, it'll be straight down-hill racing all the way.

So let's take a look and find out if we're starting on the advanced or the bunny slopes.

Old Methods

What method are you using now?

Check all that apply:

☐ Go to the grocer's once a week and browse, spending $200 for lack of a plan.

☐ Use a menu plan, but still cook in small quantities, buying only a one-week supply of groceries at a time. Are you a victim of what the grocer over-stocked?

☐ "What am I hungry for?"

☐ Open the refrigerator/freezer and stare — maybe dinner will jump out?

☐ Put it off — maybe Hubby will take us out to dinner.

☐ Clip coupons, but spend all your "savings" in gas driving around town?

☐ Attempt long-range cooking, but not really serious about it?

☐ Pouring money into someone else's organizations? (Like a Fortune 500 Corporation)

☐ _____
_____
_____

(fill in the blank)

Did you discover yourself in any one of these methods? I know I've been a little of each of them at times.

What are these methods costing you?

Let's Look at the Hidden Costs

There are obvious costs in those old methods of food preparation, plus some "hidden costs." The obvious ones need little explanation, but it's the hidden costs that confound us.

Opportunity Costs

One way of looking at some of these hidden costs is through an economics term called Opportunity Costs.

> **Opportunity Costs:** The value of alternatives given up in choosing what to buy.

What does that mean exactly? Since you can only spend a ten-dollar bill one time, it's all the things you could have bought, but didn't, with that same ten dollars.

Example: You see a beautiful blouse for $40. The opportunity cost of that blouse is two video tapes, 35 pounds of ground meat, a love offering to the foreign missionary visiting Wednesday night, or. . . .

A real-life example of this concept is played out every day as families choose what is most important to them. One of my brothers' companies sells and services televisions. They've remarked about receiving calls for T.V. repairs at homes in which the only "furniture" in the room was the T.V. The children would be in rags and obviously underfed, but this family had chosen to spend its first dollars on fixing the "entertainment" device instead of on a bed, clothes, or food.

We don't shop in a vacuum. Each spending decision we make is related to each opportunity we didn't take.

You may already have been thinking in terms of opportunity costs, but you may have called it "I only have $____." Most mothers already know they can only spend the budgeted amount one time, but it does make you stop and reconsider a "sale" item if you first think of what you're **not** going to be able to do with that money if you buy the item. Even if it looks like a great deal, your money might be better spent elsewhere.

When you apply this concept of opportunity costs to the old method of food preparation, you'll find new motivation to try the approach from this program.

Stewardship R Us

We endured an exercise in good stewardship instilling the concept of opportunity cost for one of our sons. Stuart's birthday was coming up and Reed had saved $10 for a gift. Though we rarely go the retail toy store route, we suffered through for this experiment.

Reed had only one ten dollar bill. He could only use it once at the register. He would chose an appropriate gift then see something else. He'd have to take the first item back. After an hour of criss-crossing the store choosing and replacing, Reed understood opportunity costs. Stuart's new birthday gift didn't cost just $10, but it cost 4 sets of Viewmaster® slides, 2 sets of books for his learning computer, and that game he wanted. Not to mention hundreds of other options available outside of the toy store. But for this experiment, we stayed within a given boundary of the toy store. It worked. Reed has a new appreciation for budgets and why we spend our money as we do.

It might be an experiment in stewardship you'd like to adopt with your children.

More Hidden Costs

Time: Time is a precious commodity around our house. What about yours? Could you "spend" (as if it were cash) the hour to an hour-and-an-half on something more worthwhile than cooking and shopping?

Peace of Mind: Are you spending your mental energy in preparing (or in avoiding preparing) dinner? Could that emotional drain from figuring out what in the world you're going to fix for dinner be redirected?

Quality: Could you refocus the work you've been doing to produce a better (healthier, fresher) product (meal)?

Funding World System: In the world of marketing, the jargon centers around the "Four P's:" Price, Place, Package, and Promotion.
- Price: What are you really buying? Is it a good value?
- Place: Is there a better place in which to pour your resources? Do you have to shop at the nicest store?
- Package: Do you want to waste money on fancy packaging?
- Promotion: Are you being bought by advertising?

Promoting Materialism: Do you have the "in" things? Do you want to support world materialism? Read Revelation 18:23b.

Paying for Rotten T.V.: I don't know about you, but if I buy a heavily advertised laundry detergent for $10 a box, I'm not too thrilled with the idea that as much as $2.10[1] of that could be going to keep a sin-riddled soap opera on the air.

Chemicals/Sugar: Is there an alternative that doesn't have so many chemicals, preservatives, sugar, etc. ? My children have enough energy. I don't need them to get "juiced" with red dye.

"God" of Convenience: Have we been paying higher prices for the convenience of worshiping at the altar of "instant total gratification?" What, then, are we teaching our children?

Over-Head: I know I'd rather spend our money on my own freezer than to buy one for the local grocer. Mark-up on grocery items can go over a hundred percent.[3] That translates into 50¢ out of every dollar you spend going to the store for their equipment, building, etc.

It is difficult to avoid some of those costs. We're commercialized. How many children know product jingles by heart? It is like the story of the little boy showing his little sister Santa's reindeer, "See? There's Dasher and Dancer, Comet and Cleanser . . . ."[4]

Preservatives:
Warning: This story is shocking. While recovering our soldiers that had paid the ultimate price for our country, medics in the Vietnam War discovered that the bodies were already "embalmed." The men had so much preservatives in their systems from their diets that they themselves were –"preserved"

The Vietnamese, in contrast, discovered that their casualties' bodies were already decomposing. Their diets were radically different from our men's.

I know that is a graphic illustration. It upsets me. It makes me think twice about feeding my children preservatives. Preservatives are chemicals designed to preserve what it comes in contact with— even your digestive tract.[2]

Brand Loyalty

Brand Loyalty is a very real force in consumerism. Advertisers are trying either to break your brand loyalty toward the competitor's product or to build it for themselves. The "successful" ones do both.

Countless psychographic studies prove that Americans are creatures of habit. I've heard this story in many sermons because it is a visual word picture[5] that we can identify with. We've all done it to some extent.

> The new bride serves her husband a ham dinner. He looks at the ham and notices that the end is cut off. "Honey, why'd you cut the end off the ham?"
>
> "That's how Mom always did it," she answers.
>
> So the next time they have dinner at her parents' home, he asks his mother-in-law about the ham cooking technique.
>
> "That's how my mother always cooked it," she answers.
>
> When Christmas rolls around and all the family is together, he asks his wife's grandmother about the end of the ham.
>
> "Oh, that's the only way I could get it to fit in my pan," she answers.

Ask yourself if any of your habits are costing you more than you'd like. Breaking them isn't easy, but since you're qualified for your role (see your answers in Chapter 1), and you're concerned about the cost to your family, you are half-way there to throwing out those bad habits.

Do you use the same brand of tomato paste your mother uses? It's natural to do so. Hopefully it's the best brand. But what if it isn't? Could you force yourself to grab for that other can — the one without added sugar, with less salt, or without a major brand name? It isn't as easy as you'd think.

In the Notes column, jot down some habits you're going to re-examine.

The opportunity costs of bad habits are expensive. And there are other economics to consider.

Passive Income

Passive income might also be called "unearned income." Even so, it is still a real consideration in your family's financial health. The way to calculate this income is to figure what you'd have to make in the out-of-the-house job market to equal the monetary impact you can make by reducing spending.

For illustration purposes: You are savvy and "save" a dollar in purchasing a needed item for your home. You would have to earn $1.75-$2.50 (depending on your tax bracket and taste in peripherals) with an outside job to bring home that same dollar.

This may seem far-fetched until you consider that dollar saved was tax-free. You didn't have to have an expensive wardrobe. You didn't have to hire a babysitter or pay a daycare facility. You didn't have the extra expense of commuting. You didn't have the education bills of continued training. This list could continue on and on as you start to realize the **expenses** associated with earned income. If you want to really examine this in detail, look at some of the business expenses that the Internal Revenue Service (IRS) considers as costs of earned income.

Don't ever under-estimate your worth in your job as equipper of the family's well-being.

For instance, a family thought they needed only $100 more a month to break-even. So, the mother took a job at $12,000 a year (part-time). Besides the expenses of moving into a higher tax bracket, and hiring a stay-in-their-home childcare giver, she was so tired when she came home from work that they ate out in restaurants more often. She "earned" extra treats for herself, and soon found that even with the new income, they were still in the hole financially. She quit and then, with money-saving techniques, made up the difference and more. Peace and calm have again entered their home.[6]

Real Dollars

Now we're getting into the nuts and bolts — real dollars you can see. What are the savings in noticeable figures?

Recently, when we used the "Dinner's in the Freezer!" system, the total of all our receipts was under $200. That made enough entrees for over four months worth of dinner meals. The last time we cooked, as of this writing, I "splurged" and spent $378 for over six months worth of dinner entrees.

That figure beats the "Auburn Drive" grocery bill average. I did a "scientific" marketing survey on my street: I asked some neighbors how much they spent a week at the grocery store. I knew I was saving, but I didn't realize by how much. Admittedly, we live in what the local marketeers describe as a YUPPIE (Young

Dining Out Every Meal

I know several families that dine out at restaurants every day.

When I visited one friend's home, I noticed a darkened alcove off the living room, it was a "kitchen." She didn't even have a stove — she knew she'd never use it. She had eaten every meal of her married life in restaurants.

On the next page I state a figure of $27,375. It may seem farfetched to some of us, but that is what it would cost our family of six to eat in restaurants for one year.

There are families, and singles that do dine out more than dine in.

I love to go out to eat, but it's a planned dinner not a last resort because we're hungry and there's no food in the refrigerator.

With this program, we're able to dine out in quality restaurants, not just fast food joints. We especially enjoy going to ethnic restuarants as field trips for our children to learn more about other cultures.

The mathmetics to correspond to the text:

Yuppie average: $200/ week means $867/month
My average: $150/month
Thrifty average: $300/month

My spending compared to Yuppie average:
$150:$867=1:5.8

$1800 (my yearly budget) compared to $27,375 (cost of convenience meals for a year, see below) = 1520%

Mathematical calculations:

Calculations of my "hourly wage"
16 (hours) x 3 (sessions a year) = 48 hours a year
$150 (savings between thrifty shopper's budget and my budget) x 12 (months a year) = $1800
$1800 ÷ 48 = $37.50

$717 (difference between my budget and Yuppie budget) x 12 (months a year) = $8604
$8604 ÷ 48 = $179.25

When we dine out, we average $20-$50 per meal. For frozen dinners for our family we'd average $15-$20 per meal. So taking a average on those two and using $25 per meal, the calculations would be:
$75 (medium range of **three** convenience meals) x 365 (days a year) = $27,375
$27,375 ÷ 48 (hours worked) = $570.31 an hour.

These figures were calculated for a family of six. Again, this study was NOT scientific.

Use your own budget figures to calculate your savings.

Urban Professionals) neighborhood with some DINKS (Double Income, No Kids) but the results shocked me — $200 a week![7]

You should contrast this with what it would have cost you to buy and cook with the one day/one meal method. This means I spent less than 1/5 that of my neighbors.

Or to be more precise, since you are making convenience meals, contrast the new grocery figure with what it would have cost you to buy these meals as a frozen dinner (convenience item) or at a restaurant. The savings can be as much as a thousand percent.

Of course, your savings will vary on how well you work the program, your food tastes, and your ability to purchase bulk items.

One way I considered my savings, to give you an example, was very encouraging. Not using my neighbors' figures ($200 a week), but a thrifty shopper's budget of $300 a month, I calculate I average $150 a month on our food. (I still buy fresh produce, etc., in addition to the food prepared in the freezer). That's a savings of $150 a month (conservatively). Calculating that out:

I spend four hours shopping, two hours planning, and ten hours cooking. That's a total of sixteen hours per session. Or a very conservative $37.50 an hour comparing my method to a thrifty shopper. Likewise, I save $179.25 an hour compared to my neighbors, and/or $570.31 an hour compared to eating convenience meals. (That's my whole-month budget compared to what we'd spend if we dined out and/or ate convenience meals three times a day.)

That sounds like it's well worth my time. Is your time worth it?

You can approach your food budget from different perspectives:

A. Just making it stretch (You only have X amount of money and it has to feed your family for so many days.)

B. Extra money (You have X amount to spend, and if you can spend below that figure, you can pocket the rest for a special project, treat, or offering.)

C. Free food (You have X amount to spend, and it lasted for an extra month, so that's "free" food for that month)

Here's an example of bulk-size savings:

1.   Tuna in 6 1/8-ounce cans from a thrift store/discount grocer
            17 cents per ounce

2.   Tuna in 6 1/8-ounce cans from a state-of-the-art grocery store
            24 cents per ounce

3.   Tuna in 66.5-ounce cans from a wholesale source
            9 cents per ounce

Now, combining these savings with the three different approaches just mentioned, you'll see that:

A.   If all you can afford is $5.79, then by buying the large cans you have enough tuna for 10 meals compared to 5-1/2 meals with #1, and 4 meals with #2.

B.   By buying the large can you saved $5.51 in small cans for the same volume of tuna (difference between thrift store and wholesale store), or you saved $10.17 (difference between grocery store price and large can price).

C.   You "earned" 32.5 ounces of free tuna (between #1 & #3) or 5 entrees. You earned 42.4 ounces of free tuna (between #2 & #3) or 6 entrees.

Or in other words, you can spend $5.79 for the tuna in large cans (enough for ten meals), or you can spend $15.96 for the same amount of tuna for these meals by only using small cans and cooking one meal at a time. And that's just one ingredient in a casserole. The savings just multiply.

I like to think that we eat 1 to 2 months "free" (from the "extra" food in the larger cans).

Mathematical Calculations:

- A) #1 cost $1.04 a can for 6 1/8 oz. For $5.79 that would buy five and a half cans.
- A)#2 cost $1.46 a can for 6 1/8 oz. For $5.79 that would buy four cans.
- B) #1: 66.5 oz at the 17¢ rate = $11.30. $11.30-$5.79=$5.51
- B) #2: 66.5 oz at the 24¢ rate = $15.96. $15.96-$5.79=$10.17
- C)#1: $5.79 at the 17¢ would buy 34 oz. 66.5 (amount in large cans)oz - 34 oz=32.5 oz.
- C) #2: $5.79 at the 24¢ price would buy 24.1 oz. 66.5 - 24.1 = 42.4 oz.

Husband's Enthusiasm

Recently during a long distance telephone conversation with one of my readers, she told me excitedly that her husband was so impressed with her new adventure into mega-cooking that he pulled cash receipts from the last year and did a real figure comparision between what they were spending before and after mega-cooking. He calculated that they are now saving $400 a month. It would be $500 but they are setting aside $100 a month in their next "mega-cooking account." Your savings will vary on how well you work the system, but I'd like to hear your success story.

Disclaimers

■ Your savings will depend on how you shop, eat, and work the method.

■ Since I like to cook, I still plan at least one meal each week that I cook from the "ground up."

■ Some meals are almost completely "self-contained." You might just need to add a bread and salad at little extra effort.

■ Some meals will require more work for side dishes. Example: for meat-loaf, you'll still want to plan your side dishes ahead of time.

■ Some meals are labeled "some assembly required (sar)." Much of the presentation can be done ahead, but the actual mixing of ingredients is best left until just before heating.

■ It's your choice to suit your needs.

❦ *"He that is faithful in that which is least is faithful also in much: and he that is unjust in the least is unjust also in much. If therefore ye have not been faithful in the unrighteous mammon, who will commit to your trust the true riches? " — Luke 16:10-11 (KJV)*

CHAPTER THREE

Benefits worth considering

I'm constantly having to re-learn Biblical lessons. This story is an example of how the Lord lovingly taught me the meaning of Romans 12:20, *"Therefore if thine enemy hunger, feed him; if he thirst, give him drink..." (KJV)*

The simple notice, "Workmen will be here to work on your roof Monday," didn't seem that ominous. Considering the unnerving effect it had on our home in the ensuing days, the notice should have been typed with headline emphasis on bright red paper, "WARNING. . . ."

We were living in military housing in the Republic of Panama, where Alan was stationed for two-and-a-half years. We were at the mercy of whatever edict the Housing Command wanted to wage. This time it was "remodeling" our roofs. The roofers became my enemies rather quickly.

By Thursday of that week, I was asking for prayers from my Ladies Bible Study group. After four days of hammering and sawing above our heads, my nerves were frazzled and our infant and toddler had screamed all along. Naptimes, lunches, and even my cherished quiet-times were disturbed. I told my sisters-in-Christ of my morning ordeal:

"This morning I had stepped out of the shower to hear the nails, shingles, and wood scraps falling from my once stable roof onto the glass patio table, bikes, and wading pool. I put on something, ran downstairs and out onto our much used patio. The sight was post-war. I returned to my closet and grabbed a pair of tennis shoes, wondering if my husband's army boots wouldn't be better protection. As I darted between the pieces of falling debris, collecting those toys and knocking off the pieces of dry tar that covered them, I thought of getting Alan's field helmet as a hard hat. The workers saw me and momentarily stopped their demolition party for me to fish out the rusty nails from the plastic pool and drain it, then to move the redwood picnic table and toys and put them someplace. But where? The middle of the living room, of course. I thought I had the situation well in hand as my two sons and I squeezed through the stacked furniture to leave for a nice, quiet morning at church. Then I discovered the front yard, which was even worse than the back yard." By then I was in tears relating my ordeal.

I was comforted with my friends' words, "You have every right to be upset, dear." They prayed for me.

Back home, refreshed by our morning of Bible study, I once again tried to put my boys down for their much-needed afternoon nap. Then I tried to seek the Lord in my quiet-time. I felt justified in my attitude and quite self-righteous.

During my systematic Bible study, I read Romans 12. The Lord's words do cut like a double-edged sword. They hacked at my wish for the roofers to just go away and leave me some peace. They cored my righteous indignation. They severed my easy way out. They purged my need for prayer for **my** hardships.

Right then, all I could honestly pray was that I willed to love my enemy roofers. That day, with rivets flying, hammers driving, saws screeching, and chisels ripping, my two pre-schoolers slept for three hours just a few feet below the workers.

Then, the next day, the Lord started pointing out that these Panamanian men were working on metal thirty feet above ground, removing the worn-out shingle-roof and replacing it with eight-foot sections of sheet metal. Each day the Lord would bring to my attention more about their work — hardships and difficulties.

The Lord reminded me that the climate in this tri-canopy jungle area was so humid that my glasses fogged whenever I opened the front door. He reminded me of how hot the cement patio could get by mid-afternoon even when it was shaded. The question stung — how much worse the metal must burn and magnify the hot tropical sun? There was no wind. Our townhouse was so located between two rises that when we once tried kite flying, the only air flow was generated by my husband running across the parking lot.

Not only were these workers climbing up to this height on reflective steel, in a hot, breezeless midday; they were using heavy equipment, and some of it vibrated horribly. The love that the Lord created in me for these low-paid workers amazed me, especially when I realized that they had left their homes in the slums of Panama City early in the morning to ride the military bus to the U.S. Army post to repair my roof, to give me a safe and dry home.

For the rest of the six weeks, the boys had peaceful naps, my dog didn't seem to even want to growl at the intruders much less howl as she did when they first "attacked" our home.

The Lord started making my prayers more personal until He moved me to want to do something. But what? Along with other military wives, I had received many lectures about security around the native labor. We had been advised against opening our doors to them. Some silly housewives had done so, to their regret. Yet, the Scriptures said. . . .

As I prepared an afternoon snack for my sons, in my climate-controlled home, I asked the Lord to show me, to tell me, it was OK to reach out. My dog started sniffing at the front door and whining. I looked out the window and there flat on his back on the gravel, was a swarthy, ill-shaven Panamanian trying to quench his thirst under our low-set water faucet. That did it.

I made a pitcher of lemonade, grabbed the ice, and handed my oldest son a package of cups. I started pouring some cups for the five workers in the crew, when I remembered that we had a gallon of ice cream in the freezer — a staple for us, a rare luxury for them. We went in to get it and a box of cones. By the time I went back out, the roofers from the other buildings in the cul-de-sac came over for something to drink. I made up as much fruit drink as I had containers and dumped every ice cube from the freezer. The gratitude on their faces was real. So was mine. I tried in my limited Spanish to say, "No, no, it is I who am grateful to you." Then Reed, my then two-year-old, thrilled with all this excitement, said, "Mommy, I want to tell them about my friend." I, too hastily, thought he was going to tell them about his three-year-old playmate who had recently broken his toy. Joyously he sang "Jesus loves you, this I know. . . ."

This story illustrates a benefit of the "Dinner's in the Freezer!" system that is worth your considering: the ministry potential. Some other benefits we'll examine are medical reasons, deriving more time for bonding, and getting more munch for your money. In Chapter Four, we'll look at one more benefit: stewardship of the earth. In Chapter Seven, we'll examine the nutritional benefits of this system.

Ministry Potential

» My experience is that often you have little warning of when your neighbor has a need for a meal. If you received a call today from your church secretary telling you that a mother in your church was just admitted to the hospital, how soon could you get a meal over to their family? Would you have to first go to the store and buy ingredients, then come home and prepare it? After looking at your schedule, would you have to ask her to put you down for next Tuesday? Wouldn't it be great if you could open your freezer, grab a complete dinner and have it in the troubled family's home within minutes?

» This program, since it frees you from the hour and a half of dinner-duty each night, allows you the time to minister, to volunteer, and/or to join a witnessing team.

» There are so many wonderful ministries that we'd love to support. But sometimes, there is no money available for offerings. If you work this program well, you'll have that "extra" money for those ministries, missionaries, or missions that you've been praying for a way to support.

» Entertainment itself can be a very fruitful ministry. I'm thinking about a saint who was one of the powerhouses at our church in Panama. Betty Kearney was a tremendous witness, inviting families, singles, and homesick soldiers to her home for some of the best cooking in the world. One of her recipes is on page 16-11. But entertaining frightens some ladies. It's so much work. They can't afford to throw a dinner party. Hopefully, after reading this book, you'll have gained some encouragement, ideas, and the wherewithal to try entertainment as a ministry. With "Dinner's in the Freezer!" a dinner-party is easy.

» Do you have an elderly parent who needs assistance, or know of someone who is facing a long convalescence following an accident or surgery? The prospect of recruiting meals for them for every night for months appears to be next to impossible? Team up with a few ladies (or if it's your parents, bring all the siblings in) and in one day mega-cook for them, leaving their freezer filled with several months worth of ready-to-heat meals.

Medical Reasons:

» You have the opportunity to tailor your menus according to your family's allergies. If you have a child allergic to milk, you can substitute soy milk in all your recipes. You'll be hard-pressed to find allergy-sensitive convenience foods at a reasonable price.

» You can replace fatty meats (pork, beef) in recipes by using leaner meat like turkey.

» You can reduce the volume of meat in the recipes and so decrease health risks.

» Many convenience foods are prepared with standard bleached white flour, but you can control the type of flour your family eats. If you prefer, select whole wheat or oat flours instead of bleached white flour in your breads, gravies, pastries, coatings, fillings, etc.

» Your food will only have the chemicals/preservatives that YOU add.

» Are there certain foods that your children (and husband) won't eat if they can recognize it? For instance, my darling of a husband detests eggplant. I happen to think it's a wonderful nutrient and fiber source, so I run it through the processor and "hide" it in pizza bread.

» Is someone in your family on a special medical diet? Some families prepare two meals every time they eat, one for the medical patient and one for the rest of the family. This can be very time consuming and costly. This program allows you to customize their diet (e.g., salt-free for heart patients, and sugar-free for the hypoglycemic or diabetic) and pre-prepare the meals and store them. Then they're ready to thaw, heat, and serve without the expense of using costly, packaged, supplemental diet programs.

» And speaking of diet programs, some people are trying to lose weight or are on weight reduction regimens. It's easy to give up when you have to weigh and measure your food for every meal. This, too, can all be done at one time and stored in marked containers of exactly the volume you're allowed. You'll be less likely to cheat, or go back to regular eating if you already have weeks left of "diet meals" in the freezer. And some of us need all the encouragement we can get.

More Time for Bonding

» Would you like the time to read aloud to your children, but you can't — you have to stir, chop, slice, and dice? By mega-cooking, you'll have that hour a day for reading through "The Chronicles of Narnia" by C.S. Lewis[1] to your little ones.

» Maybe you call them outings, adventures, or field trips, but have you been limiting where and when you can go because of mealtimes? In the morning, grab a frozen picnic dinner out of the freezer. It'll thaw by dinner. And spend the afternoon at the park. Go ahead and accept that only available time slot for the afternoon program at the museum — you don't have to rush home to fix dinner. Outings are a special bonding time.

» We love to take walks in the evenings, and since you need less time to clean up after dinner (all the pots, processors, etc., were used and cleaned months ago) you only have the plates and casserole dish to clean up. This allows for that special bonding time as a whole family, not with half the family off in the kitchen scrubbing pots.

» The big cook weekend is also a time for bonding. We get the whole family involved and try to make it memorable and fun. More hints on this in Chapter Eleven.

» We're spending less time in stores shopping. I like that. My children aren't repeatedly assaulted with "buy-me" displays. They aren't festooned with the latest craze. We can spend more productive hours playing, riding bikes, reading, helping someone, than pushing a cart up and down aisles of brightly colored temptations. Haven't we all witnessed the grocery store show-down between the tired mommy and the hard-as-nails child threatening a temper tantrum if mommy doesn't buy "Blast-Oh Pops"? In contrast, we've had many people stop us to inquire what we're doing (a family of six with three loaded shopping carts is sort of a spectacle) and comment on how well our children are behaving. For shopping tips and suggestions for turning drudgery into an outing, see Chapter Ten.

» In our discussion of the Mary/Martha (Julie/June) story, we looked at the never-meet-your-company hostessing style. This plan gives you the luxury of being able to greet your guests at the door, and to actually sit down and eat the food WITH them. How's that for bonding?

More Munch for the Money

» I appreciate the work of Christian financial advisor and author, Ron Blue. I've heard him say that our checkbooks are descriptive of our Christian lives. He asks what if our checkbooks would be opened on judgment day?[2] Terrifying thought? I firmly believe that the Lord calls us to be good stewards of His resources. That includes monetary provision.

» Wouldn't it be nice if your budgeted amount did reach to the end of the month? But how much more wonderful if it provided food for next month, too? It can be done.

» O.K. You have $10 dollars to buy some meat and vegetables. Wouldn't it be great if you could also get those new shoelaces you need, plus a bunch of grapes with that same $10? This can be done, too.

Self Quiz

To encourage yourself, personalize the benefits already suggested:

1. Think of what you would do with an extra hour and a half a day....
   - ☐ Spend one-on-one time with each child
   - ☐ Learn a new craft (e.g., English smocking)
   - ☐ Bake your own bread
   - ☐ Start a new ministry (e.g., visit a nursing home)
   - ☐ Have a longer quiet/prayer time
   - ☐ Relax, calm down
   - ☐ Have a conversation with your husband
   - ☐ Write letters, a book, a journal, a family history
   - ☐ Read _____

☐ Play_____
☐ Start an exercise program
☐ Start a home business[3]
☐ _____
☐ _____

2) How will you spend the extra money you'll be saving?

☐ Offering to _____
☐ Scholarship fund for your children
☐ A vacation to _____
☐ We need _____
☐ Special Project _____

3) Your family could benefit from:

☐ lower cholesterol food
☐ lower fat in diet
☐ lower sugar in diet
☐ more fiber in diet
☐ more vegetables/fruit in diet
☐ less chemicals in diet
☐ more _____
☐ less _____

4) Do you have a special medical need?_____

_____

5) Have you been wanting to do more ministry work? Finish this sentence: I think
we'll start/continue _____

_____

_____

_____

_____

I have a distinct purpose in asking you to write down your thoughts as we work through this book. In the middle of the "mega-weekend," or somewhere else along this line, you are going to want to call me names, or wonder why you're involved in something that's so much work. I'll make no apologies. The big cooking session is **work**. It might be different from anything you've done before. And you'll be tempted to quit. I've even wondered at times if it's all worth it. That's when I remember my motivation for this program: time, energy, and money savings. Not to mention how wonderful it'll be when it's all over and that, for the next several months, I'll rest easy because "Dinner's in the Freezer!"

One more mouth to feed

Unashamedly, I love children. If I were physically capable, I'd have ten or even more.

Some families want more, but they just don't know how they can afford another mouth to feed.

If just one family finds they can indeed afford another child by using this system, the Lord be praised and all my work will be worth it.

I'd love to hear your story.

Jacqueline J. Howe, stay-at-home mom and freelance writer, wrote me:

> "I did this in October — and it almost took me a week to do it. The kitchen was a disaster — I seemed to be so disorganized — I thought 'Never again.' But, now that it is over, I'm gladly doing it again. It is just great ... so many times I've been on a roll with writing while children are asleep and I can keep going knowing I don't have to be in the kitchen for dinner. It is a real blessing and I hope it helps others."[4]

I certainly don't want to mislead you into thinking that it's a snap-of-the-fingers operation. It takes planning, organization, and follow-through. But considering all the benefits, I feel you'll agree with me that being a good steward in the kitchen is a worthwhile endeavor.

In addition to all the benefits already mentioned, have you already thought of some of the benefits this program has in relation to our being stewards of the earth? The next chapter should give you even more incentive to re-address some of your old household management habits, adopt some new, and perhaps, suggest some more ways to care for our limited resources.

"Six years thou shalt sow thy field, and six years thou shalt prune thy vineyard, and gather in the fruit thereof; But in the seventh year shall be a sabbath of rest unto the land, a sabbath for the LORD; thou shalt neither sow thy field, nor prune thy vineyard. That which groweth of its own accord of thy harvest thou shalt not reap, neither gather the grapes of thy vine undressed: for it is a year of rest unto the land. And the sabbath of the land shall be meat for you; for thee, and for thy servant, and for thy maid, and for thy hired servant, and for thy stranger that sojourneth with thee. And for thy cattle, and for the beast that are in thy land, shall all the increase thereof be meat." — Leviticus 25: 3-7 (KJV)

CHAPTER FOUR

The Recycling Revolution

Did you know it's O.K. for Republicans to recycle, Democrats to save money, and Independents to get organized? That's right.

Do you picture the typical "environmentalist" as someone in Earth shoes, with stringy hair and glazed-over eyes, driving an old, beat-up van? Is the closest you've ever gotten to one via a Public Broadcasting System special?

Do you think the term "recycler" is a euphemism for a bag lady?

One of the first instructions the Lord gave mankind is stewardship of the Earth.

Genesis 1:28-30 states:

"And God blessed them, and God said unto them, 'Be fruitful and multiply, and replenish the earth, and subdue it: and have dominion over the fish of the sea, and over the fowl of the air, and over every living thing that moveth upon the earth.' And God said, 'Behold, I have given you every herb bearing seed, which is upon the face of all the earth, and every tree, in the which is the fruit of a tree yielding seed; to you it shall be for meat. And to every beast of the earth, and to every fowl of the air, and to every thing that creepeth upon the earth, wherein there is life, I have given every green herb for meat:'and it was so."(KJV)

We have a mandate from the Lord to be wise servants of His property. The passage at the beginning of this chapter, Leviticus 25:3-7, demonstrates the Lord's wise counsel to us over the use of His creation. Modern terminology applies the words ecology and environmentalism to this concept. I choose the word stewardship to differentiate what the Bible says from what the world systems are ballyhooing. This precept of stewardship has been polluted with anti-Christian philosophies and has been linked with New Age tenets. This is a shame. As Christians, I feel we can do much to bring back a Godly perspective.

Have you heard the "Mother Earth," "Father Sky" arguments? Or the "harmonic convergent" dribble? The New Agers are verbose and receive ample media coverage. We're told to save the whales, but not our unborn children. We're told to worship "Mother Earth" and "Father Sky" and not our Father in Heaven.

Some Christians so dislike this trend that they run away from the issue altogether. We should be on the forefront, demonstrating our appreciation for His creation by our wise use of it.

These two ways of looking at environmental concerns are at opposite ends of the spiritual realm. Let's be careful, watchful, and discerning.

With that in mind, let's take a positive look at what we can do to improve this area of our lives.

We are all pilgrims in our *walk*. Some are farther along than others. I personally know I'm just starting out and learning new applications of Truth everyday. Here's an example:

I had a bad attitude.

While living in military housing, we had "free" utilities. The bases provided water and electricity as part of the housing programs. As a form of rebellion and protest of what I considered below common decency wages that the government paid my husband and sub-standard housing, I deliberately wasted energy.

I saw no value in turning lights off when I left home. I ran the heat and air at extremes. I sent gallons and gallons of water down the drain needlessly.

I was wrong.

Then, in love, a Christian sister, Pam Doering, presented a Bible study on God's calling us to be wise with His world. A light flashed on in the muck of my soul. I had always viewed it as me against the Army system, never as me against the Lord's system. That day I became frugal with water. I started viewing my gluttony in energy consumption as a sin — a denial of Scriptural precedent.

I still have a long way to go. How about you? If the Lord has been working with you in this area, and you've been asking for ways to apply His Word, then some of these tips, suggestions, and ideas might help.

"Dinner's in the Freezer!"
System Advantages

This system has many advantages when it comes to wise use of His creation's resources:

Less garbage/waste products:

By purchasing food in large containers you cut down on the amount of packaging being thrown away. Let's look back at the example of tuna, but this time at the cans themselves: One large can (just the metal) weighs 7 ounces while a smaller can weighs 1 1/2 ounces. For the same amount of tuna meat, that's a 233% reduction in the amount of metal used in packaging. Also, consider the paper, ink, etc., used in the labeling, and the environmental impact increases.

Some municipal waste collection systems charge citizens by the number of trash cans they fill a week. If you can cut down on your volume, you save dollars. That adds even more incentives.

Less water used:

You can either use one gallon of water once to cook two pounds of noodles, or, using the round robin approach, cook ten pounds of noodles.

You also save water in the clean-up stage. You're dirtying all your pots and pans at one time and washing them on that big-cook weekend, rather than every night.

Less electricity:

By cooking in multiples, you use your electrical equipment to their fullest. You aren't wasting heat. To illustrate you can either

1) heat your oven to 425° and place in one loaf of banana bread six separate times for three hours of baking (30 minutes each); OR

2) heat your oven to 425° and bake six loaves of banana bread at one time for 40 minutes using only a little more energy than to bake one.

Less waste:

You're using all the food in a container. You're preparing YOUR family-size portions, so, you're not wasting food. Convenience foods are portioned for the "average" family, or "average" eater. I don't know about your family, but there is very little that's "average" about mine. The way my family eats, an "average" adult portion is only a "snack." Not only can you cut down waste, but with the C.O.R.D. approach (explained in Chapter Five), you won't be throwing away as many leftovers.

Mathmetical Calculations:
66.5 oz (volume of large can) ÷ 6.125 oz (volume in small can) = 10.9 cans

10.9 x 1.5 oz (weight of small can's metal) = 16.35 oz (this is what the small cans would weigh for the same amount of tuna.)

7 oz (weight of large can's metal) compared to 16.35 oz = 233%!

Buying in season:

"To every thing there is a season, and a time to every purpose under the heaven." Ecclesiastes 3:1 (KJV). Buying produce when it's in season and at its best price just makes sense. With our global market place, you can purchase strawberries year round, but at up to ten times the cost of buying them in season.

Buying locally:

This might not seem obvious at first, but perhaps an example from the Argentine economy will shed some light on this concept. One of my college professors pointed out that Argentines are literally starving for lack of food. Yet, the wealthy entrepreneurs are getting richer by exporting some of the native fish to the U.S. for use in catfood. Does this strike you as unreasonable?

Buying from a local farmer benefits the farming industry, and reduces his costs for shipping.

Certainly much of our food has to be shipped in. Often, we have no choice. I'm just suggesting that when you have the choice of buying locally, do so. For more information on the health implications of shortening the time from the plant to the plate see page 12-4.

Re-usable containers:

In the section on storage, page 12 - 2, I suggest that you re-use containers as often as they remain safe. It makes sense to use a container more than once before you throw it away. Or, in some cases, one storage container can be used thousands of times and even then be melted down for recycling. Compare that to containers that you use once. Compare that to containers that will biodegrade after "millions" of years (e.g., styrofoam).

Incorporating little choices here and there adds up to make a big impact.

Coming around full circle

Hopefully we're in a recycling revolution — not a revolution as in revolt, overthrow, or an assertedly momentous change in any situation — but a revolution as in coming around full circle.

Recycling is not a new idea, no matter what all the press hoopla says.

Honey

Local honey can be used as a sort of immuno-therapy. By eating a tablespoon of local honey each day, you can reap some of the same rewards as seen with allergy shots. You are accustoming your body to the allergens in the area.

I think some of us are simply re-discovering principles that our grandparents considered common sense, a way of life and good stewardship. In our current day, we live in a disposable society. We use everything once and it "disappears" weekly into the garbage truck.

Grandmother wouldn't have dreamed of throwing out her flour sack after each use. No, those flour sacks became dish cloths, curtains, wall hangings, and even clothing.

Grandfather didn't get his oil in a new plastic container with a convenient pouring spout. Each time it was empty he took his glass jar to the store and had it filled from the reservoir.

Our grandparents or perhaps our great grandparents (depending on your age) reused or recycled just about everything.

What would our American heritage be without quilts? Quilters created this art form by finding new uses for the scrap material after they made clothing.

Speaking of our American heritage, aren't you delighted that Abraham Lincoln "reused" that envelope as notepaper to write down the Gettysburg Address?

To get a feel for what we've lost in recent years, I interviewed my mother, Zoe White, of Haines City, Florida, to find out how waste was handled way back then in the "olden days" of the nineteen fifties and sixties. I learned quite a bit, for instance . . .

When my parents were living in Ohio in the early fifties, residents of their community were required to separate all their trash into glass, cans, and paper. They each were "issued" a round wire basket to burn all their paper products themselves. She said it became a social time as all the neighbors would gather and talk while they burned their garbage. The city would pick up the glass and cans for recycling.

While my dad was in the Air Force we lived in Germany. The Germans were very resourceful and considered some waste control methods to be merely sensible. At first my delicate "sensibilities" winced with my mom's next illustration. Regularly the "honey wagon" would come and pump out the septic tank and spray it on the gardens. The gardens thrived. The major consideration was that all garden food had to be washed in chlorinated water. Families were issued tablets of disinfectant to add to one gallon of water to clean all produce.

As a child during World War II, Mom took great pride in the fact that she had perfected peeling off the waxed paper of gum wrappers so the aluminum foil would remain all in one piece and could be used toward the war effort. Tin foil HAD to be re-used. She had to turn in her old toothpaste tube before she could purchase a new one.

Wind Chimes

Attractive windchimes can be made from the lids of your tin cans by collecting different size lids. Using a nail and a hammer, punch a hole in the exact center of each disk(lid). Then with pliers, start twisting the lid so that it has pleats and resembles a bell. You'll be making five or six twists in the lid to make it turn down and into a bell shape. Use ribbon to string the "bells" together. A variety of about ten bells make a lovely chime. Depending on the ribbon you use you can make these for year round enjoyment or as a Christmas decoration. BE VERY CAREFUL with the sharp edges of the tin. This is NOT a craft project for small children.

Make your own paper:
This is a fun and educational project for adults and children.

Tear or cut paper into small (less than 1") pieces. Using colored paper makes for beautiful finished projects.

Pour 2 cups of water and a cup of small paper pieces into the blender. Process on high until all the pieces have turned to mush.

Pour out paper mush onto a screen or fine colander. We use one of our window screens. We've had no problem with clean-up. You might want to test it first. Let all the water drain off. Repeat these steps until you've made as much mush as you need.

Then you can take this paper mush and form it into all kinds of shapes or leave flat. For instance, we cover the bottom of a bowl with plastic wrap. Then layer on mush. When it dries you have a beautiful paper bowl for dry flower arrangements, decorative pieces, etc.

We like to save used construction paper and old bows and ribbons to make colorful baskets, bowls, and containers.

If you let it dry flat, you can use it for beautiful note cards, and artwork.

People made rugs out of rags. It's a craft that is now experiencing a revival. The German ladies would unravel a sweater that a child had outgrown and reknit it into a larger size. Additionally, feather pillows and beds are simply an attempt to use something that might otherwise be waste.

Growing up in central Florida was idyllic. We always were surrounded by orange groves with citrus trees in our yards. It's fascinating all the ways that orange pulp, peeling, etc. are used. The University of Florida research station[1] in Lake Alfred has developed 23 products that are made from the orange pulp that most of us throw away after juicing the fruit. One example is that the pulp can be used as feed for cows.

In other words, we haven't invented a new concept with the current interest in recycling/re-using. We're just coming around full circle to what our grandparents and parents have already known. And it has never been easy. We've, as a people, struggled with several things when it comes to recycling:

- affluence,
- no perceived need to conserve,
- apathy,
- divorced from seeing/hearing the problems,
- failure to recognize our Scriptural mandate,
- perception that recycling is difficult.

Yes, recycling can take up some of your valuable time. I consider it time well spent.

Many common household products can be re-used or recycled:

Paper:

1) Use the back. Lists don't have to be written on clean sheets.
2) For art projects, use newsprint as a floor cover. Colored paper can be re-used in a paper-making lesson (see side box), and try paper mache' with old newsprint or paper. (Caution, newsprint stains, especially when wet.)
3) Use in unconventional ways: cards and wrapping paper being used on home-made cards, paper, decoupage, etc.
4) Use as shipping material.
5) Roll up newspapers into fire place logs.
6) Sell to the paper recycler. Examples of recycling policies are on page 4- 9.

Wood:

1) Scrap wood is a delight for children's creativity.
2) Fuel for your fireplace.
3) Secondary use. For instance: One day in the trash pile for our cul-de-sac, I spotted a wooden shipping crate. It just took a coat of paint to transform this discarded 3' x 3' crate into a colorful cube that we're still using five years later as a table/container.

4) Even sawdust is being creatively used as a packaging material.

Plastic:

1) Use your garbage bags (before you fill them with trash) as drop cloths on the floor and spill protection under your baby's highchair.
2) Use grocery store plastic bags for carry-alls/totes until they're worn out, or as trash bag liners. Our trash service will only pick up garbage that is bagged in plastic. So instead of spending money on new bags, we re-use the ones we receive from shopping.
3) Re-use plastic containers as often as they still seal.
4) After you use a bread bag, shake it out, then store it in the freezer for re-use for the next time you bake your own bread, or need to store more food. By storing them in the freezer you stop the growth of mold, etc., from the food residue in the bag. This works with many other types of food storage bags.

As a mission project, our Good News Clubbers[2] collected, washed, dried, and sent bread bags to some missionaries in Africa. These missionaries make all their own bread on their compound and desperately need storage containers.

Old prescription bottles can be turned in for re-use; some hospitals have collection centers.

Send old prescription bottles to mission hospitals. While we were in Panama, the mission doctors received medicine in large quantities and were desperate for little containers in which to give patients their dosages.

5) Be creative, fill that bleach bottle with sand for an exercise weight, carve it out to bail water out of a boat or _____(fill in the blank).
6) Recycle plastic bags for re-processing. Many grocers have a bin to put them in. Some stores encourage re-using by refunding customers five cents each time we bring our own bag in for our groceries, either plastic or paper. They even accept it when I use my string bags.
7) Many recycling centers accept certain plastic, especially milk cartons.

Glass:

1) Reuse to hold something else.
2) Make into craft/art projects.
3) Donate old eye-glasses to Christian Blind Mission International, 450 East Park Avenue, Greenville, SC 29601. For more information call them at 1-800-YES-CBMI (937-2264).
4) Sell to the glass recycler.

This list is certainly not exhaustive. I'd love to hear your ideas and experiences. Write me and your ideas might appear in another edition or in our newsletter.

Bread Bags

Do **NOT** turn the bags inside out. The ink used for labeling could contain lead or other dangerous chemicals.

Clearing House:

As a service to you, I will gladly act as a clearing house for ministries, information, and requests.

If you know of a ministry that has needs that ladies across the nation could fill, please write me with the information regarding the group.

If you would like to know of ministries that might need some of your "scrap" material write me with your question.

A prime example of this is the Christian Blind Mission International.

Recycling Guidelines

Formal recycling, the actual "turning in" of your waste material for it to be used by someone else (after you've done all the recycling you can with it) is becoming easier and easier.

Here are some general guidelines:

First, call your local recycling center for their specifics. Every center has its own rules and regulations. Different centers specialize. Save time and money by calling and asking questions. (Look up "Recycling Centers" in the Yellow Pages®.)

Second, design a system for separating your waste into major categories. There are fancy recycling bins you can buy, but why not "recycle" an old box, drum, or torn-up laundry basket in which to collect your items.

Third, start "collecting." Think before you throw anything away. Ask yourself, "Could we re-use or recycle this in any way?"

Fourth, rinse or wash out all containers. You don't want to turn your garbage cans and recycle bins into "hazardous waste" disposal sites.

Fifth, every family has a trash compacter. Mine comes in size 9-1/2 regular — my foot. For tin cans, open both ends and mash the sides flat. For milk cartons just "dance" on top of them. For aluminum cans, a heavy step will mash them every time. Paper is best left flat. Don't wad it up like we're so apt to do.

Sixth, sort and put it in the designated bin.

Seventh, when the bin gets full, take it to your closest recycling center, charity collection point, or neighborhood pick-up point.

Eighth, enjoy that feeling of accomplishment and count your new change (honestly, there's not big money in this at the family level).

Ninth, start all over again.

Your center will have its own restrictions, but here are some rather "generic" rules:

Aluminum cans: Must be ALL aluminum. Keep aluminum trays, foil separate. Different centers will take them flat or whole. Most all require that they be dry. Going price: 30 cents per pound. (Some churches now have two trash cans side-by-side, one for aluminum cans and one for all other trash. Are you in any organizations that could start this?)

Glass: Bottles and jars accepted. Some will only accept clear glass, not colored. Some centers require you to sort out by colors, while some let you mix it all together. Some centers only allow container glass and refuse dishes, window glass, and light bulbs. Some will take any glass. Some require that lids, caps and labels be removed. Some do not. Some accept broken glass. Going price: 1 to 2 cents per pound.

Plastic: Some places only accept milk, water, and soda bottles, while some will accept almost any type of plastic, including bags. Most all require that the plastic never held any oil. Check with your center to find out if lids must be removed. Some places will accept all types of plastic, but only pay for certain types. Going price: 1 to 2 cents per pound.

Aluminum Trays and Foil: These must be clean and soft-type aluminum like T.V. trays, pie plates and foil. (Be sure you've gotten all the use out of them you can, see page 12-3.) Going price: 2 cents per pound.

Steel Cans: Usually must be dry. Policies vary on whether they are accepted whole or flat. Some require the magnet test. These must be separate from the aluminum cans. If you can find a place to take these, great. If you can find a center that will pay you, wow!

Paper: For the best price, separate paper into four types:
1) White paper with or without printing — computer printouts-green, blue, multicolor bar copy paper
   Top dollar — $8 per 100-pounds.
2) White paper printed on laser printer, fax paper (or thermal paper) — $2 per 100-pounds
3) All other paper: —5¢ per 100-pounds

» Newspaper, magazines, phonebooks, envelopes, colored paper (see box on paper making lesson — page 4-6)
» carbon paper
» paper with mailing labels, stickers, or adhesives/glues

4) Cardboard (torn-down boxes) — 5¢ per 100-pounds

PLEASE NOTE: Recycling pricing quoted at the time of writing.

What to expect?

Admittedly, the centers I've seen are not the cleanest, tidiest places in town. They're usually in and around industrial areas. I've always gone with my husband or he goes alone on his way home. Some centers are parts of actual dumps. I'm not saying this to scare you off, just to give you an idea of what to expect.

Some centers have elaborate ramps and conveyer belts to carry the material and weigh it. Some centers use cheap scales and a heap in one area of the yard. They are usually not "safe" areas to let children out to explore. Each one I've seen has had the ground strewn with broken glass, rusted metal sticking up, etc. We have taken our children to the recycling centers as a "field trip," but they stayed in our automobile.

Juice Lids

Recycle the metal lids of concentrated juice cans by turning them into ornaments. After washing them, you can use a hammer and nail and punch in the outline of a holiday shape. For example: using the nail, punch in the outline of a Christmas tree or star. You can then glue lace around the outer edges and glue on a piece of ribbon for the hanger. They have sort of a Pennsylvania Dutch look.

otes:

The paper center we use most often uses large scales, similar to the ones the highway department uses to weigh semi-trucks for road tolls and taxes. They weigh our mini-van full, we unload it in the proper areas, then they weigh our mini-van empty and pay us for the difference per one hundred pounds. Our children were fascinated by this system and it serves as an excellent real-life math lesson.

Wrap-up

Buy items in large quantities and pour the material into smaller containers for everyday use. This way you are re-using the smaller container, reducing the amount of waste in packaging and saving money. With some products you can buy five times the volume that's in the smaller size containers for two or three times the price. (e.g., liquid soaps, ketchup, etc.)

Other ideas and applications are scattered throughout the book. As I write this, The Bonding Place, our company, is involved with the annual "Kids Write" Contest. The 1991 theme was "Our Planet, His Creation." Home-schooled children from across the United States wrote stories, essays, poems, etc., with a stewardship theme. The best work appears in a book we publish.

Stewardship involves wise management from selection to disposal of the waste of any project, be it a meal or a skyscraper. Just slow down and think a minute before you buy another item as to whether you really need it. Or is it just going to go up in the attic in a month or two, and then be given to charity in three or four years? Think before you toss. Could you re-use, recycle, or redistribute the item first?

Your start might be gradual, **congratulations--** it's a start in the right direction.

"Ho, every one that thirsteth, come ye to the waters, and he that hath no money: come ye, buy, and eat; yea, come, buy wine and milk without money and without price. Wherefore do ye spend money for that which is not bread? and your labour for that which satisfieth not? hearken diligently unto me, and eat ye that which is good, and let your soul delight itself in fatness. — Isaiah 55:1-2 (KJV) [comment: true food comes from the Lord, not from recipe books]

CHAPTER FIVE

C.O.R.D.

In my mind, I can still see my brother, Gary, hesitantly walking across the stage to the microphone. He gave the audience filled with proud parents and students' families a big grin as his mind raced with something to say. He had been given maybe all of two minutes notice that he was chosen to give an oral presentation of his science experiment. While his lab partner just trembled, he cleared his throat and with his most authoritative voice, said, "THIS is mold." He showed his experiment, an attempt at reproducing the work of Fleming. He said thank you and exited the stage. The shortest speech in the history of the Union Park Elementary School Science Fair.

I don't know how many times, I've repeated my brother's fifth grade science project — never intentionally, just from sheer negligence of checking out the "Left-overs."

One of my favorite meals while I was growing up was C.O.R.D. My fantastic mother made it fun, sort of like a trip to the finest buffet restaurant. Have you ever eaten C.O.R.D. (pronounced cord)? Doesn't it sound delicious? Perhaps a definition is called for:

C.O.R.D.: <u>C</u>lean <u>O</u>ut <u>R</u>efrigerator <u>D</u>ay

You might have been calling it left-overs for years. It's the food that is still good, but "left over" from previous meals.

Maybe you already have a good attitude about C.O.R.D., or maybe you just need some encouragement. But YOUR attitude is going to set the pace for your entire family.

One of my husband's stories that my children love to hear him tell again and again is about Sydney. While he was growing up, his family had a tiny dachshund which weighed about ten pounds. Once they were visiting friends and were served a delicious prime rib roast. Their hosts didn't "believe" in left-overs. She just threw in the trash the two pounds of roast that wasn't eaten at the meal. The smell of roast beef was more than little Sydney could stand. When the humans went into the living room, Sydney took his chance, knocked over the trash can and had a canine-feast. When it came time for Alan to leave, he went to find his beloved pet. There lay

Sydney, looking at least 20-puppies pregnant. Picture if you will, the short-legged dog with his stomach larger than his legs were long. His feet couldn't even touch the ground. He just rocked back and forth on his engorged belly like a rocking horse. Alan lovingly picked up his dog and carried him home. He said poor Sydney didn't eat again for a week.

This story of the pet is humorous and sad. Every time I hear the poor Sydney story, I think of the waste of two pounds of perfectly good meat. My mind buzzes with ways to fix it: B.B.Q. sandwiches, stir-fry, pot-pies, etc.

I first thought it was an isolated incident. Surely, families that don't "believe" in left-overs are rare. Since then, I have met many families with the same idea. It usually centers around a parent that grew up in an impoverished family and vowed they'd never feed their family left-overs; or from an attitude that eating left-overs is beneath their dignity; or sadly, from a previous case of food poisoning.

I like to think of C.O.R.D., the name my mother coined for left-overs, as my being resourceful and a good steward. While we were living in the Republic of Panama, I was chastened. The Panamanians are very resourceful people. They have to be. It's a matter of survival. Here are two examples of what I mean:

Patsy and the Fish

While living in Panama we had a maid that came in and helped twice a week. Patsy was wonderful. She sang hymns as she cleaned. When she found out that we loved fresh fish, she started bringing some fresh fish from the morning catch to our home to prepare for our dinner. The first time she did this, she was going to teach me an old Bahamian recipe (her family roots were in the Bahamas). I watched her clean the fish basically just as I always had. She chopped off the heads and tails. THEN instead of throwing them in the trash, she cooked them with the good meat from the middle.

Alan came home for lunch, and looked at me with a "what's going on?" look, as Patsy served us a tray loaded with the cooked fish with the heads and tails arranged "beautifully."

Real-life Math Lesson

Tonight it was six-year-old Stuart's turn to clear the table. We had some left-over "Red Square" (going to be my lunch tomorrow). He looked in the bowl at the remaining food and went to the cupboard to hunt for just the right size container. It took him three tries before he found a container that wasn't too small or too large. It dawned on me the value in learning a real-life lesson on the concept of volume. He's learning area and quantity relationships. How much volume is one inch high of food in an eight inch diameter bowl compared to a container only three inches in diameter? Have you ever thought of how much "instant" math you do in your head when you just look at a container and know "instinctively" which bowl to use. That was learned. I like the idea that math isn't just a school subject, but something we use every day.

"How are we going to handle this, without hurting her feelings," Alan asked when Patsy had returned to the kitchen. Try as I might, telling myself that finer restaurants serve fish like this, I couldn't eat with those eyes staring back at me. Then I had an idea, "Patsy, why don't you join us?" And she did. In the conversation, as she carefully avoided eating the heads and tails, I asked her why she didn't eat them. She said that since they were the best part of the fish, she wouldn't dream of eating them — they were for us. Alan and I said that we were already full from eating the other sections, and wouldn't she like to take the left-overs (the heads and tails) home to her family for dinner. She felt honored.

From then on, Patsy would take home our left-overs to feed her family each night. These left-overs I had looked on with the same attitude as Sydney's roast-host had looked on that two-pounds of beef — not worth the trouble. I was a food snob. I had always prided myself on my creativity in rejuvenating left-overs. What I hadn't noticed was the food that never made it to the table in the first place!

Chicha Piña

During our tour in Panama, I often had been served a delicious drink called Chicha Piña, a non-alcoholic drink made from pineapple. Once, when served this fantastic beverage, I asked my hostess, Barbara Bridges, how she made it. She didn't know. Her maid had made it. Since I'm always on the hunt for excellent recipes, I went to the kitchen to get the secret.

Her maid was thrilled that I asked for her recipe. With enthusiasm, she began telling me how to make this tropical drink while I, listening intently, took notes. That is until she started telling about the third day of processing. I realized I probably never would try to make this delicacy. It seems that in their spirit of never wasting anything, they discovered, through a method of boiling, grating, boiling, sifting, boiling, and processing the  pineapple husk, they could extract pineapple milk. Yes, I did say the husk — the part we throw away. And the drink was really delicious.

Options and Opinions

After hearing these stories at opposite ends of the resourcefulness spectrum, maybe we can hit a happy medium. There are foods that you do have to throw away, but even then maybe you can still get some use by composting them. But with good stewardship and Clean Out the Refrigerator Days we'll all have fewer and fewer "mystery foods" in our refrigerators — those foods that we have to guess as to "what they was because they sure enough ain't now." So much depends on your attitude and how you present the concept to your family. For instance, do you

otes:

Left-over Cars

A family in Texas has an interesting ministry. They turn disfunctional cars headed for the dump into working vehicles for families with financial needs. A car that they give away might have an Oldsmobile body, a Chevy engine, and a Chrysler transmission. They have remade more than fifty cars into working vehicles in the past two years. People donate their "wrecks" and this family pours many man-hours into cannibalizing parts from many different cars to make one good car. They do this all as a ministry.

Stale Bread:

Make French toast (try it out of various breads like french bread, dinner rolls, etc.). Use a slice of "hard" bread in your onion soup, top with melted cheese. Make your own croutons or bread crumbs. Or my boys' favorite use of stale bread is feeding the ducks at the park. Think twice before you toss food.

look on it (or does your husband) as "used" food. Instead, why not call it a smorgasbord. There are many approaches you can take in "promoting" left-overs to your family. Be creative.

Even with thorough planning (see Chapter Nine) the best cooks still end up with a little "left-over." Maybe, your family snacked too much between meals, or they're just not hungry or maybe your eyes are bigger than their stomachs. Remember it's better to leave the table a little hungry than stuffed. Teach your children health habits that will leave them trim and healthy for life. Don't take it as a personal offense if they don't eat thirds. So now, what can you do with that half cup of green beans, three slices of meatloaf, and cup of mashed potatoes, or what have you?

Here's some general ideas for all left-overs. Scattered throughout the book are specific ideas for selected C.O.R.D. items. In Chapter Six, we'll cover why cleaning out your refrigerator is not an option.

➡ Home-made "T.V." dinners — make your own frozen dinner from all the dishes from one meal. Wrap it up tightly. Freeze it. It'll be wonderful the next time you need a complete and fast meal. For nutritional value it sure beats the ones in the grocer's freezer.

➡ Sampling or as a taste test — serve a little bit of each left-over to each family member.

➡ C.O.R.D. soup — keep a jar in the refrigerator and drop in all the scraps of vegetables (e.g., those 6 carrots slices that you'd normally toss in the trash) and if you like, meat scraps also. Then once a week, for lunch or dinner, empty your soup jar into a boiling broth, and presto — you have a wonderful, nutritious course, that's "free."

➡ Stir-fry — a healthy method of cooking we've adopted from the Orient. It is a wonderful use of scrap vegetables and meat.

➡ Lunch — why not just warm up last night's extras for a yummy lunch today? It sure beats bologna sandwiches[1].

➡ Baby Food — mush those carrots up for baby's food.

➡ Re-incorporate the scrap food into other main courses (e.g., pot-pie, stews, etc.) Check out the tips in the recipe section.

To offer you another example of resourceful natives of a foreign country, think of the French — world renown for haute cuisine. Just think of all the uses they have created for stale bread: croutons, French toast, sop in French onion soup. Try some of these, or your own ideas.

We average three C.O.R.D. meals a month — a real budget stretcher. Remember, it's really just a matter of attitude. **You** can change it for the positive.

❧ *For if there be first a willing mind, it is accepted according to that a man hath, and not according to that he hath not* — *2 Corinthians 8:12 (KJV)*

❧ *Let your conversation be without covetousness; and be content with such things as ye have: for he hath said, I will never leave thee, nor forsake thee.* — *Hebrews 13:5 (KJV)*

CHAPTER SIX

Equipping the Professional: You

"Oh, how wonderful! I've always thought it would be great to have individual water heaters for each bathroom and the kitchen," I tell my husband as I notice the small 20-gallon water heater next to the washing machine. Alan is showing me our new apartment in downtown Panama City, Panama. It is luxuriously large, an entire floor of the high-rise building in an "old money" neighborhood. Our apartment is located between the U.S. Ambassador's house and the U.S. Embassy. The view from the balcony on this hillside location is what travel posters are made of — the city flowing down to the Pacific Ocean with ships and sailboats off the coast waiting for their turn to travel through the Canal. Alan had hunted for weeks to find this apartment so his infant son and wife could fly down from Florida to this tropical country and join him for his military tour of duty. (We had to live in this apartment for six months until housing on base was available.)

He proudly showed me all the features including the maid's quarters, drying room (a room just for indoor drying of our clothes), and security systems (complete with doormen). Our master bedroom was larger than the entire house we had just left in the States. Chandeliers glistened everywhere, even in the bathrooms. This was a first-class apartment in Panama.

So, I'm naturally thrilled with the hot-water situation, thinking that with medium-sized units in each water area of the apartment, we wouldn't have to wait very long for hot water. He laughs, and says, "This is it. There are no other units." "Are you serious? That's smaller than the one in my parents' motorhome." "As a matter of fact, this was one of the few apartments that even had a water heater at all. This is a supreme luxury in Panama."

I was soon to learn what else was considered a luxury in Panama. The kitchen was a dream — large, 30' x 30' with cabinet space galore. I loved it. That is until I

Sub-small

I thoroughly enjoyed our tour of the U.S.S. Alabama anchored in Mobile Bay. What I didn't enjoy was the tour of the submarine on display nearby. I couldn't wait to get out of the tight quarters.

However, I was convicted when I surveyed the galley — the submarine's kitchen. In this galley the ship's cook prepared meals for dozens of men for months at a time. In those cramped quarters he stored the supplies for months worth of meals. Though sometimes I feel like I'm preparing dinner in a war-zone (four children are quite lively at times) these ship cooks were in a real war zone. That tour torpedoed any grumbling I felt for my tiny "galley" back home.

The Oven

That lovely kitchen I wrote about is back in our house in Fort Worth. As I prepare the third edition of this book, I'm living in a 30-year old house with the original turquoise-colored oven. It matched the exterior of the house back in 1961. It must have come complete with pink flamingos in the front yard. This oven's thermostat doesn't work. So I "average" the baking: turning the oven off and on. It "preheats" to 500° no matter the setting. So by turning it off and on I can average the right temperature. It's a crazy way to bake. Don't worry, all the recipes in this book have been tested and proofed with a properly functioning oven. I mention this to erase any notion that mega-cooking is only for those ladies with model kitchens and state-of-the-art appliances. If I can mega-cook in this kitchen, anyone can mega-cook within her kitchen.

tried to cook. It seemed that electricity was sort of a luxury in Panama also. The kitchen was wired so that in addition to the refrigerator, I could use one other appliance. One! That meant one burner on the stove, not two. The blender OR the oven. The electric skillet OR the toaster. If I accidentally tried to run two appliances at the same time the refrigerator fuse would blow.

It was an adventure in scheduling. I never realized how much I valued cooking supper all at one time before. I usually juggle five or six appliances at once. Then I couldn't even pre-heat the oven while I was using the blender.

And that's when the power was working. There were many times that we'd have no power at all for more than 24 hours. Yet it ran better than the phone did. The phone would go out for weeks at a time. In fact, when I had the good news that I was pregnant and wanted to get word to Alan, who was in the States on TDY (in civilian terms, a business trip) for a few days, I had to send him a telegram!

Through our ten years of marriage, I've cooked in huge kitchens, equipped kitchens, and tiny kitchens. While we were living in seminary housing in Fort Worth, TX, our kitchen appeared to be an afterthought in the corner of the room. While standing in front of the sink, I could reach every inch of the kitchen without moving my feet. I could not open the oven and refrigerator doors at the same time.

Now, fortunately, I do have a lovely kitchen, open, and in the center of the house. (Of course, I could always use more cabinets.)

So, in other words, I know from personal experience that it can be done.

In the Army, many of the military families have plaques that read "Home is where the Army sends us." Military wives are one of our nation's top assets. How some of these ladies have carved a home in every kind of housing across the world is amazing. They make it Home.

I made a wall-hanging for our family: "Home is where the Lord sends us." And I believe it.

Wherever He has placed you, is where you must make it home for your family. No matter how small. No matter how nice. No matter.

Paul wrote to the Philippians, *"I know both how to be abased* [in need], *and I know how to abound: everywhere and in all things I am instructed both to be full and to be hungry, both to abound and to suffer need. I can do all things through Christ which strengtheneth me."* (Philippians 4:12-13 - KJV)

No, many of us don't have large professional kitchens and equipment. Yet we can do much with the equipment the Lord has already provided. Personally, I started using this system when I had very little and have gradually added pots, Tupperware®, and appliances with the savings.

I know you can function quite well in whatever setting the Lord has placed you with whatever equipment and appliances He has provided for you.

At breaks in my workshops, when I'm asked questions about the system, I'm reminded of those ships waiting their turn through the Panama Canal. The ladies wait for their turn to chat with me. And I've heard many "excuses." In this chapter, I'll attempt to answer some of the most common questions I'm asked and hopefully encourage you not to live in the "Only If" world of tomorrow.

Only if I had a big freezer . . .
Only if I had a food processor . . .
Only if I had a husband that would help me . . .

I don't let anyone get away with Only-If statements. God has a plan for you. Read Jeremiah 29:11.

There's an old Irish story that I'll retell to you:

> The town minister, so tired of hearing his congregation complain to him about their troubles and how much easier their neighbors had it, prayed for a special miracle.
>
> So the Lord granted his town a one-time opportunity to swap their troubles for anyone else's in the town.
>
> After the service that week, each family was to bring their troubles and set them in the town square. Then when everyone's troubles were laid out, each family was required to take back home with them as many troubles as they brought. Each could pick and chose, what troubles they wanted to take. If they brought five troubles they had to take five troubles back home with them. After everyone looked at the troubles of his neighbor, each family took back home the exact troubles they brought with them — opting for God's wisdom, after all.[1]

Alan and I might not get along perfectly all the time, but I wouldn't trade him for ANY man in the world. I, quite honestly, get exasperated at my children at times, but I wouldn't trade them for anyone else's. No how, no way.

And when it comes right down to it, I know you wouldn't either. So with no "keeping up with the Jones," "Only if," or "But if you only knew my circumstances . . ." — type thinking let's look at OUR kitchens.

Together, Alan (the engineer) and I will address your most-asked questions, and your options, plus give you some recommendations to serve as goals.

Remember when we discussed Opportunity Costs and I asked if you'd like to buy your grocer a new freezer or your family one? Well, with this system, you can "earn" the money to equip yourself.

So, let's look at some equipment:

Freezers

The "Dinner's in the Freezer!" system does require you to have a freezer. Do you now have a freezer? Is it above, below or beside your refrigerator? Or are you fortunate enough to have a separate unit? You do have a freezer right now, don't you? Think what's in it — frozen foods in their uncooked form. Why not in the same space store them in their cooked form? So, you do have room. Certainly you might not be able to store enough food for six months in it, but you can store several weeks worth.

I worked this system for four years before I had my first separate freezer. And that freezer was given to us. If you want a freezer, pray about it. The Lord has wonderful answers. One lady, Tammy Applegate, who wanted to start this system, prayed for the Lord to provide a freezer for her. She mentioned to her neighbor that she was going to be attending my workshop and that she was wanting a freezer. Her neighbor said, "Oh, I have one out in the garage that I never use. You can have it." So their husbands moved the freezer over to her home that night. The Lord answered another one of my workshop attendees prayers, Kathryn Sleigh, with a huge freezer (larger than mine) for only $25. It had been scratched on the outside, but it worked perfectly. If you're going to keep it out in the garage, what difference does it make if it's scratched? For that matter, it would be fine for the house also.

So give the Lord an opportunity to work, even with such a utilitarian thing as a freezer. Remember, He cares about your family's nutrition (Chapter Seven).

Frost or Frost-free?

Alan: Besides the obvious difference, the two differ in power consumption. Remember that a freezer's job is to pass liquid freon through tubing to coils in the food area, where it absorbs heat and changes phase from a liquid to a gas; then the hot gas is pumped to another set of coils where it gives off heat, then changes back to a liquid and starts over again. Sounds simple, doesn't it? Of course there's more to it, but the point is a regular freezer has the freon-filled coils inside the compartment — usually part of the shelving. A frost-free freezer has the coils hidden in the walls. Both can pull heat out of the compartment, but a frost-free freezer has to pull the heat through the walls. Therefore, it takes more work — either in a larger compressor motor and more freon/coils, or in pumping longer — than a regular freezer.

However, the regular freezer has a basic problem. Each time the door is opened some warm, moist air gets in. Since the cold coils are in the compartment, the moisture freezes on them (and on any food, containers, etc.) The build-up of ice and frost can actually insulate the coils allowing the food to thaw in severe cases. So frost has to be removed. A frost-free freezer may show some light frost against the walls, particularly if frozen food is in contact with the wall, but it doesn't suffer from this drawback.

So what's best? If you are freezing lots of food at once and are concerned with energy costs, go with a regular freezer. The penalties are risks of food thawing and the labor and mess of cleaning out the frost and ice. If you open the door frequently (3 or more times a day) and hate to clean out the freezer, go with a frost-free freezer. The penalties with this type are higher energy consumption, slower freezing (though some units compensate for this with more energy penalties) and usually a higher initial cost for the unit.

Upright or Chest?

Alan: Here again, what's best for you depends on your situation. The comparative advantages of an upright freezer are a small "footprint" (where floor space is a premium) and ease of access to the food. But the chest is not as prone to frost problems. This is because when an upright opens, the coldest air, (at the bottom of the compartment) "falls out." This literally sucks in the warm, moist air into the top that fouls up a regular freezer. Ever wonder why the frost is greatest on the top shelves? Now you know. When you open a chest, the cold air stays at the bottom, so little outside air gets in. Another advantage is the door seal. An upright requires more door seals (distance) thus putting it at more risk for damage and leaks. Plus an upright requires force to close the door while the chest is self-closing. It is a sickening feeling to find your upright door ajar with the coils inside iced over and the food containers dripping wet.

So, choose based on your needs. Also consider the frost-free and frost options in selecting a freezer.

Care and Servicing

Alan: Beyond keeping the coils free from ice build-up, clean the interior, as needed, of food stains to prevent molds from growing. It's also a good idea to clean the hot coils in back of (or underneath) the freezer of dust and dirt so they can give off heat efficiently. If you don't keep these coils clean the system can stop. The biggest service you can do for your freezer is to have a qualified serviceman check the freon level, oil the seals and O-rings in the coolant system and check the compressor motor amperage demand.

Good service is a must, especially if the freezer operates in hot areas. What will wear out first then will be the compressor motor. Replacing one can cost several hundred dollars.

This should give your freezer the best shot at a long service life.

What Do We Have?

Right now, today, we have a 19 cubic foot upright, frost-type in the garage. It was a compromise. I wanted a larger upright that was also frost-free. (I was thinking of convenience and ease of use.) Alan wanted a chest frost model. (He wanted to save money in the initial purchase and in energy costs.) We both "gave in" with his promise of being the one to always defrost the thing. And he has, every time.

No to the Musties

If you need to close your freezer or refrigerator for any length of time, place several charcoal briquets in an old section of panty hose and tie loosely. These pieces of charcoal will absorb odors and moisture. When we moved recently, the packers had us follow this procedure. When we opened our units after more than a month of storage, the charcoal wrapped in hosery was rather rank, yet the interiors of the appliances were tolerable. It worked.

Safety

Recently, on the news, was a tragic story of a missing boy. When the family found him after a massive county-wide search, their hearts broke. He had gone out to their chest freezer, reached in for a popsicle, lost his balance, fell in and the lid closed on him. By the time they found him, he was dead.

Please teach your children freezer safety. Buy a freezer with a lock and only let "qualified" (old enough to know freezer safety) family members use the key. There are usually public safety announcements about empty freezers and that people should take the door off it's hinges. Children do play hide 'n seek. But, also be careful with a fully operating freezer. For this reason, I prefer an upright model over a chest freezer. But I'm still careful with the upright.

The other safety precautions you should take are in the proper temperature and maintenance to keep your food frozen and safe for digestion. See Chapter Twelve.

Old Dog Learns New Trick

Between the different editions I learn from my readers. One new product that I've learned about and am giving the road test to is the Magic Mill DLX 9000 system. I've been testing it for several weeks now and I'm impressed. Very impressed! In my opinion, the engineering of the DLX is superior to the Bosche. (Now Bosche, as I understand it, is using plastic gears.) Since I USE my appliances and need quality machines, I'm recommending the DLX over the Bosche. If you are considering buying quality appliances with all your new found savings from using the Freezer! system and would like the information, please contact the companies listed in the appendix. The Bosche is still an excellent system, head and shoulders above what I was using before, but I now like the DLX more.

Appliances

There's a balance between the good you'll get from purchasing another appliance and the cost of buying and using it. Only you can decide, in your unique situation, if it's worth it. Some of these appliances I have, some I'm saving for, some I feel might be nice — but for our family they just aren't worth the cost.

Food Processor:

You already have one: you and a knife. But I'll admit it was a delight when we bought our first one. It cut down on tears (chopping onions) and time. We first bought one in the medium price range. It worked O.K. for the first year, then it broke so only one speed worked. I gave it to my sister, who feels one speed is better than no speed. I told everyone in my workshops that I'd been saving for a Bosche. It paid off. I received a call from a lady who had a friend that was selling a complete Bosche system for $350. I called immediately. And I love my Bosche. Not only does it mix and knead bread for me, it's a blender, food processor, pasta maker, juicer and mixer. All at a heavy-duty quality. I recommend them highly.

Mixer:

Before my Bosche, I went through 3 hand-held models. They only cost around $15, so when they die, I just donate them for parts to a charity. I still sometimes use a small hand-held to save the clean-up on the big unit. Many recipes can be done just as well with some hard stirring and a strong spoon. My recommendation on a medium-range mixer? My mother's Hamilton Beach is still working after forty-one years. And we used that mixer often. I'm looking at the cordless models for quick uses.

Blender

There are people that have blenders and use them once a year, if even that. I find they're wonderful appliances that serve a purpose that's hard to duplicate by hand.

 A good blender can grate carrots, and other vegetables, for salads and baking (see page 16-27). In the recipe section, I include several recipes that work well in the blender. Soup stock, baby food and frozen drinks are smoother from the blender than done by hand. With a blender you can make your own bread crumbs, confectioner's sugar and grated cheese. Buy a blender at a garage sale or thrift store or from someone that only uses their's once a year. Be sure to clean it each time, taking it completely apart (of course, not the motor unit). Just rinsing it out is not sanitary enough. You have to separate the rubber ring, the blades, etc., from the pitcher and clean all the surfaces.

Crock Pot or Slow Cooker

When I'm mega-cooking, I need all the help I can get. I love my crock pot; it has a high and low setting. So, I can use it like a dutch oven for spaghetti sauce or chili, or whatever. My slow cooker doubles as a crock pot, Dutch oven, and/or an electric skillet. Which introduces a point I want to make. Throughout your home choose multi-function items. The more isolated the use of something the less you're getting your money's worth out of it. Look for appliances and furniture that offer more than one use. Is it functional? What about storage? If you find that you're having to wipe a quarter inch of dust off of something the next time you use it, question yourself if you really need it. Use your appliances or sell them or give them to someone who will use them. We have enough to clean without having to dust old waffle irons.

Can Opener

In this system, I do recommend using the large cans of food. The big #10 can is not a breeze to open. You'll need a heavy-duty can opener. Spring for the $4 model. The 79¢ one just won't cut it (pardon the pun). If your budget allows, an electric can opener is a time saver. I'd only recommend an under-the-counter model though. One, it doesn't take up counter space and two, you have room to open the large cans. The regular table top models aren't high enough to get a "bite" on a large can. Moving it to the counter edge and holding the can over the floor has proven too dangerous for us. These counter-top models just aren't balanced for that kind of use. Our under-the-counter model works very well.

Smoothy-Frothy

One of our our favorite desserts is a Smoothy-Frothy. Basically, place in your blender pitcher: 1 to 2 cups of frozen fruit (e.g., bananas, strawberries, blueberries, etc.); 1 to 2 cups of yogurt, milk, and/or fruit juice. Fill the rest of the blender pitcher with ice. Blend until smooth. Your liquid to fruit ratio will determine if you you'll be eating a "milkshake" or "ice cream." Try different combinations. We haven't found one yet that wasn't tasty.

We keep bananas frozen in our freezer for these low calorie treats. Peel the bananas first and cut them in two- inch sections. Freeze in an air-tight container.

It's a healthful alternative to ice cream.

Multi-functional Units
There is a trade-off: multi-functional units put more wear/tear on mechanicals/electricals. The reliability range should be increased when going multi-functional.

Toaster Oven

Now, along with my precept of finding multi-purpose equipment, I'll choose a toaster oven over just a toaster any day. It might cost a little more initially. In my opinion, it's well worth it. Not only can you toast as well as a toaster could, but you can bake and broil in them. The energy savings of using that little oven for many small casseroles, meatloaves, etc., is significant, not only in the lower amount of electricity the appliance uses, but in shorter pre-heating time. Also, in the summer, the less you heat up your big oven, the cooler you'll be and the less work your air conditioner will have to do. Under-the-counter models are available to leave you counter space.

Pots, Pans, Mixing Bowls, et al

As soon as you can afford one, you'll appreciate a large pot. I use my heavy-duty canner/preserver. It is multi-purpose: for cooking on a range top, for mixing, and, of course, for canning. Here you can be creative. At first, all I had was the sterilizer that I had received as a baby shower gift. It was large and basically a Dutch oven.

A blancher is another pot I use regularly. It is wonderful, of course, for blanching fresh vegetables, but I use it for cooking mountains of pasta. The strainer makes this operation a cinch.

Look at what you already have and think of ways you can utilize them more.

When your budget allows, I recommend you invest in quality cookware. It'll be money well spent. The difference between cooking in inexpensive or low quality, light-weight pots versus in quality pots with good, even heat transfer is noticeable in energy consumed, quality of food, nutritional value of food, and cost of "burnt offerings" (less food ruined).

You'll need a large bowl for mixing all the ingredients together. You'll be surprised at how much the ingredients for eight times a recipe is. We use our canner for this. I also have a lovely set of bowls that range in size from one-cup to 5 gallons. But some other items you can use are (all well cleaned, of course)

- your kitchen sink
- a punch bowl
- the crisper or meat drawer from your refrigerator
- a bucket
- a plastic wash tub (discount store for $5-$10)

You'll need a pair of heavy-duty spoons. These are the only items that you might have to go out and purchase to start this system. All other aspects of this program you can make do with what you have. There's no decent substitute for a set of heavy-duty spoons. But this isn't a major purchase. Top-quality ones from a restaurant supply store sell for $3 to $4. Many grocery stores have the large spoons for sale for about $2, though there is a difference. You'll be mixing a lot of ingredients. You need spoons that don't bend.

Some other equipment you might want to accumulate over time are an extra set of measuring spoons and several measuring cups (1-cup, 2-cup, 4-cup, and 8-cup).

Extra baking pans pay for themselves quickly. My oven will hold eight loaves of bread. So I now have eight pans. Have you tried the new "air" pans. They're wonderful. I would recommend that you wait to purchase pans until you can buy quality ones. I'd rather have one good "air" pan[2] than five plain aluminum ones. Test them yourself. Bake a batch of cookies, some on a regular pan and some on an air pan and note the difference in quality, time, and crispness. I've done many tests with different types of muffin pans. I use the same batter and pour some in one pan and some in the other pan. Bake them side-by-side in oven. With the low quality pan the muffins are black on the bottom and gooey on the top, while the heavier, better-grade pan's muffins are perfect. Also, consider that with inexpensive pans you have to use more "grease" while with quality pans, in many cases, you don't have to "grease" at all. There's an advantage in health and cost.

If you have aluminum pans, I'd personally recommend you get rid of them. The aluminum is porous and your food will get an aluminum taste. Your family could be eating aluminum flakes. It's just not worth it.

Where to shop

The first time I met Ethel Sexton, I knew we were kindred souls. She was charming, funny, and had an eye for a bargain. She's known as "The Guru of Garage Sales." She was addressing our Metochai (seminary wives club) group on the joys of smart shopping. She showed us slides of her gracious home filled with treasures, most bought at garage sales. Her home looked like the cover of a magazine. She has a saying that I want to borrow: "Smart shopping is good stewardship!" She has a daily radio program on our Christian station KCBI in Dallas/Fort Worth. If you ever get a chance to hear her — go.

I agree with her. There are treasures to be found among all the junk at garage sales, thrift stores, and flea markets. Just as someone wants your old waffle iron, you might want their old, big mixing bowl. It's worth keeping your eyes open.

In addition to shopping garage sales (see chapter 10 for more ideas), I enjoy the restaurant supply store. I had never been to one (thinking I'd have to be a card-carrying member of the restaurant association or something) until a friend suggested I go. Her husband works in one. Well, I went. I saw. I conquered. I almost didn't come out. If you have never been to one, check your Yellow Pages®, grab your special-savings wallet and go. Think about it. If your dishes get a workout with

---

Shear Necessity

In my opinion one mandatory piece of equipment every lady needs in her kitchen is a good pair of kitchen scissors. I use my shears more than I use a knife. They make so many jobs quick and easy. See page 16-18 for an example.

If you have a set of electric knives, why not use them? Don't just pull them out on Turkey Day for the "Ceremonial Carving of the Bird." I use mine regularly for slicing home-made breads and butchering meats. It works so quickly when you're cubing ham for recipes. You'll soon see all the jobs it can make easier for you.

your family, how much more so does a restaurant's? These dishes are made for a beating and still come out looking sharp. And they're relatively inexpensive. They have to be or restaurateurs couldn't afford to buy them by the hundreds. And you don't have to buy them by the hundreds. Many of the items you can buy in a dozen or even just one. For instance, I bought a dozen sundae glasses, just like the ones in old-fashioned ice cream parlors — for a dollar a piece! We use them for salads, desserts, yogurt, apple sauce, and even the baby's food. They add such a festive air to even the plainest meals. The restaurant supply store also has quality cookware, real rolling pins, containers in so many sizes, gadgets and what-nots galore. They are there to equip the professional chef. That's us, you and me. My most pleasant surprise was that the chef-quality equipment was very reasonable in price. And so much better than the quality of fare at the local grocery or department store.

Some other questions I am asked about equipment are:

What about Tupperware® verses the brand in the store? (This I'll answer in Chapter Twelve on storage.)

What about the Food Saver (a vacuum sealer)? I have purchased one and am giving it a "test drive." It seems to work very well. This machine vacuum seals items in plastic bags, canning jars, and/or special Food Saver containers. I've been pleased with it so far. I don't feel you must have one to protect your family's food. If you have the money, it is a worthwhile appliance. Try to buy one used or on sale.

What about a flour grinder? (I'm still researching this. I haven't bought one yet; a friend grinds flour for me. There are two brands that I've narrowed it down to. Have you an opinion? I'd love to hear it).

What about a dehydrator? Honestly, I have always bought our dried fruit. This is an option for preserving food that I plan to pursue. I'll print my progress and Bond Test Kitchen results in our newsletter. I'll welcome any comments, suggestions, and opinions.

This chapter is a difficult one to write because the marketplace is changing so rapidly. Companies gobble up each other and then the quality of some items change. These are only my opinions and are for educational use only. If you buy any of these items I've suggested, and have any difficulty, write me and I'll reassess my recommendation. But do not hold me any way financially accountable for the performance of any of these products. Also, if you've had any good experiences with any of these appliances, I'd love to hear from you. The more consumer interaction I can show the manufacturer, the better deals I can negotiate for you in the future.

With the purchase of this book **and** your signed registration (see last page of book), you'll start your subscription to our mini-magazine, "*Bonding Times*." For the companies that we add to our recommendation list after this edition goes to press, we'll print their offer in the magazine. So that way you won't miss out.

So again, if you have a product you can recommend, are thinking of buying, or for which you want me to rethink any of my advice, write me. We'll see if we can't get that company to give all my readers a rebate, coupon, or freebie.

"Mommy, Daddy needs his Allen Wrench," announced Stuart coming in from the garage where he was helping his daddy. "Which one is it?"

"Well, they're all Alan's wrenches. Which one does he want?" I asked.

I head out to the garage with Stuart and ask my husband, who's deep into his latest project fixing the do-hicky on the what-cha-ma-call-it. "Which wrench do you want?"

"Allen wrench," he states, "and hurry!"

"I know they're your wrenches, but which one?" I ask, confused.

He sticks his head out and looks me in the eye. "I guess you didn't hear me, I said the Allen wrench."

"Yes, dear, but which one? The curved one, the ratchety one, or the silver one with the black handle?"

He burst out laughing. Then through guffaws, he takes me over to his workbench hands me a bent over metal stick thing, and says "**THIS** is an Allen wrench, A-L-L-E-N."

"Oh, who's on first?" I meekly say as I leave his realm of thing-a-ma-bobs and do-flangles and go back to my world of sensible equipment. At least we have real names for our stuff. They tell you what they do — a blender blends, a mixer mixes, a food processor processes food.

I hear Stuart who has been enjoying this good natured banter between his parents says, "Daddy, what does baseball have to do with wrenches?"

"Son, it makes sense in your mother's mind. Way back, there were two comedians, Abbot and Costello, and they did a routine. . . ."

Remember Paul's advice to the Philippians and be content with what you have. Plan ahead for the things you need. Be thorough and research what you purchase. Chapter 10 will also give you more ideas on shop-pppiiinnnggg.

Some Basic Measurements

Tomatoes	1 pound	3 medium
Turkey, ready-to-cook	1 pound	2 servings — approximately 1 cup
Spaghetti	1 pound	4-5 cups cooked
Carrots	1 pound	2-1/2 cups diced, approximately
Flour, all-purpose	1 pound	4 cups sifted
Flour, whole-wheat	1 pound	3-1/2 cups sifted
Ground meat	1 pound	About four servings
Onions	1 pound	3 large
Rice	1 pound	2-1/2 cups raw
Rice	1 pound	10 cups cooked (in 5 cups water)
Shortening	1 pound	2-1/3 cups

Space given for you to add your own commonly used amounts.

CHAPTER SEVEN

A Word or Two on Nutrition

After coming home from the book store, I flipped through my five new books on nutrition. Not only did they disagree with each other on certain items, but they at times said the other authors' viewpoints were stupid. I studied the books and compiled options. Each author had studies to back their opinion on food item X, and a plethora of reasons why you should never consume it, or consume it daily, contradicting the other authors. What's a mother to do?

I decided to check the copyrights. Ah, now a trend was developing. The concepts or opinions on such things as drinking cow's milk, avoiding red meat, etc., were almost cyclical.

Back to the "what's a mother to do?" Cook according to the latest study until the next study comes out?

It reminds me of secular books on child-rearing. The opinions and variety of methods expounded on how to raise your child are as consistent as watching T.V. while someone switches the remote control through 40 channels in a minute's time — Just a blur; a foundation that's as firm as the sand (Matthew 7:24-27).

Would the same sources I use for REAL truth on child-rearing help me in feeding my family? Well, I've always said it is The Answer to all of life's problems. But does the Lord give mommies nutritional advice in the Bible?

The search was on, and continues. Have you ever searched the Bible to see what God says about food?

Fascinating! And I'm still searching.

The first passage I thought about was Paul's writing concerning the eating of meat (1 Corinthians 8). Then Peter's vision of a sheet laden with "food" (Acts 10:9-16) came to mind. Then there are all the promises of the land flowing with milk and honey. And every Sunday-school trained child loves the story of Daniel eating his vegetables (Daniel 1:8-21).

Notes:

Bold Prayer:

The daugher of a friend really taught me the true meaning of Bold prayer. Nancy and I were assigned as prayer partners through a discipleship program at our church. To illustrate what I mean about Bold prayer, one week's assignment instructed us to ask each member of our prayer partner's family for their number one prayer request. So I asked Beka what she'd like for me to pray about for her. She didn't even think twice. "More than anything in the world, I want to take dance lessons." Nancy told me later that she had been researching dance lessons, but there was no way they could afford them or have the time to take Beka to lessons because her husband was attending seminary. It seemed a hopeless situation.

God knows how to handle hopeless situations!

I prayed for someone to help them. And I prayed for a miracle. Then I prayed, Lord, if there's anything I can do, I'll do it.

Almost immediately came the answer. He wanted me to be part of His answer.

Through a series of calls and checking, Beka was going to be able to take dance lessons through a special program, well within Nancy's budget. But the classes started an hour before Nancy could leave work to take Beka. So, I drove to the day care center, picked up Beka and drove her to dance lessons. And it was a true joy. She loved her classes.

Bold prayer is asking for the Lord's answer, even if it means **you** have to change, or get involved yourself.

Armed with my parallel Bible and a concordance, I was overwhelmed with the references to food, food products, harvest, produce, meal preparation, and eating. From Genesis and God's provision of the abundant garden, to the Revelation story of the tree bearing 12 different fruits (Revelation 22:2), the Bible makes for delicious reading.

Through my study, I am delighted with the Lord's provision. Who else knows the working of our bodies as well? Who else knows what we need to eat? And He cares! He wants us to live abundant healthy lives.

He has given us important jobs to prepare nutritious foods that our families will eat. He's given us our minds and a wealth of resources to use, plus the Holy Spirit is always with us to give us wisdom and guidance.

First and foremost, depend on Him.

He wants us to be good stewards of the resources He's giving us. The Bible is also replete with verses advising, commanding, and reasoning with us not to waste His blessings to us, but to "invest" them to bring the most to His service. Refresh your motivation with the parable of the wise and slothful servants (Matthew 25).

When you get overwhelmed with the world's advice on what to feed your family . . . from the commercial's cry of "instant gratification," the restaurant's neon allure, and the end-of-the-aisle polished displays . . . rest in His loving, wise arms with a BOLD request for help. "Bold" meaning you'd change your lifestyle, your eating habits, and/or your priorities if He told you to. Bold prayer isn't easy, yet, it's the smartest thing I do each day.

Feasts

The Lord created us, so He knows how enjoyable eating is to us. I heard someone remark the other day that they learned more Bible truths over their mom's kitchen table eating fresh-baked apple pie than they have from a pew.

The Lord knows that meals are joyous occasions and that we are very teachable at that time. He, therefore, commanded the seven feasts for the nation Israel to celebrate. He uses these feasts as a conduit for parents to pass on spiritual truths to their children.

"And thou shalt show thy son in that day, saying, This is done because of that which the Lord did unto me when I came forth out of Egypt." (Exodus 13:8 - KJV)

May I suggest that you study the seven feasts listed in Leviticus 23 during your quiet times soon? Write your notes out on notebook paper and insert among these pages. Here's a suggested outline to follow:

1) Passover
- ✡ To celebrate the Exodus from Egypt
- ❏ 14th of first month, Abib (April)
- ⁊ Exodus 12:1-4; Leviticus 23:6; Numbers 9:5; Joshua 5:10; 2 Kings 23:22; 2 Chronicles 35:1; Matthew 26:17; Luke 2:41; 22:15; Hebrews 11:28

2) Unleavened Bread
- ✡ Celebrating what the Lord did in bringing the Hebrews out of Egypt
- ❏ Starts the day following Passover, 15-22nd day of the first month, Abib, (April)
- ⁊ Exodus 12:15-20; Leviticus 23:6-8

3) First Fruits
- ✡ Celebration of harvest
- ❏ Fifty days before Pentecost
- ⁊ Leviticus 23: 9-11

4) Pentecost (or Feast of Weeks or Shavuot)
- ✡ Celebration of the giving of the law
- ❏ 6th of third month, Sivan (June), at the end of the wheat harvest
- ⁊ Exodus 23:16, 34:22; Leviticus 23:15-22; Numbers 28:26; Deuteronomy 16:10; Acts 2:1

5) Trumpets (modernly called Rosh Hashanah)
- ✡ Celebration of remembrance
- ❏ 1st of the seventh month, Tishri or Ethanim (October)
- ⁊ Leviticus 23:24; Numbers 29:1; Nehemiah 8:2

6) Atonement (also known as Yom Kippur)
- ✡ To cleanse the nation before the Lord of all its sins
- ❏ 10th day of the seventh month, Tishri or Ethanim (October — 9 days after Trumpets)
- ⁊ Exodus 30:10; Leviticus 16:30, 23:27; Numbers 29:7; Hebrews 9:7

7) Tabernacles (Also known by Booths, Ingathering, Shelters, or Succot)
- ✡ Thanksgiving for the harvest
- ❏ 15th-22nd of the seventh month, Tishri or Ethanim (October)
- ⁊ Leviticus 23:34, 39; Numbers 29:12; Deuteronomy 16:13; 2 Chronicles 8:13; Ezra 3:4; Nehemiah 8:14; Zechariah 14:16; John 7:2

Two other feasts that are celebrated are:

1) Dedication
- ✡ Celebrating the reconsecration of the temple after its desecration by the Syrians (corresponds to Hanukkah)
- ❑ 25th of the ninth month, Kislev or Chisleu (December)
   Gives new meaning to Christmas
- ❧ John 10:22

2) Purim
- ✡ Celebrating the deliverance of the Jews from Haman via Esther's calling and obedience in the situation
- ❑ 14th and 15th of the twelfth month, Adar (March)
- ❧ Esther 9:17,22,26

Historical View of Dietary Rules

Searching the Bible to see the development of food laws, restrictions, and allowances is very intriguing and revealing. May I suggest an outline:

1) **The Creation. Read Genesis 1:29-30.**

2) **Sin enters the picture. Read Genesis 3:17.**

3) **After the Flood. Read Genesis 9:3.**

4) **Dietary laws. Read Leviticus 11:44.**

5) **Examples of laws being practiced. Read Daniel 1:8-17.**

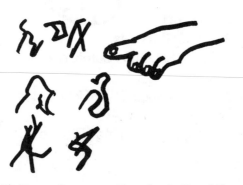

6) **Examples of the Lord's providence in conjunction with meals/eating (blessing and cursing). Read Esther** (from the first banquet that was the end of Queen Vashti, through days of fasting, Esther's banquets for the King, to the beginning of the feast of Purim); also the hand-writing on the wall account — **Read Daniel 5.**

7) **Proverbs concerning food. Read Proverbs 6:8, 13:23, 27:27, 28:3, 30:8, 31:14.**

8) **Fulfillment of the Law in Christ. Read Matthew 6:11, 31, 33; Mark 7:14-23.**

9) **Peter's vision. Read Acts 10:10-14, 28, 34.**

10) Early Church. Read Acts 15:11-29.

11) Paul's pronouncements. Read Romans 14:1-17, 14:5-8,17, 22; I Corinthians 8:8, 13, 10:31-33; I Timothy 4:3)

Specific Items

Topics are listed with the number of references in parentheses from the King James Version of the Holy Bible.

Milk (25 references)

One item that is often debated in nutrition circles is the subject of "non-human" milk. I think it's unanimous that mother's milk is the most advantageous for her infant, but what about the practice of drinking cow's milk and/or goat's milk?

The argument goes something like this: God only made cow's milk for baby cows. So it's harmful to humans. Then you'll see studies that show that children must drink "x" ounces a day. What are we to do?

I love milk. Right up front I want you to know that. I not only love milk, but I snack on cheese, adore ice cream, cottage cheese and yogurt. I really didn't want to know it was harmful. But the evidence was disconcerting, so I questioned my doctor, whom I trust with my life and my whole family's lives.

Given the fact that I'm "allergic" to everything for which I've ever been tested, I've been asthmatic since birth, and I have a niece that rates high (4) on milk allergy tests, my doctor, Sheila Horsley, whose practice is in Fort Worth, TX, and I ran our own test. I went four months without any dairy products whatsoever. It was torture for me. After the four months I was thrilled that there was no difference whatsoever in my condition. I could go back to eating dairy products. Hurray!

But what about the arguments against milk. Some people go so far as to state drinking milk is sin, because it goes against God's plan for cow's milk — cow's milk is only for baby cows.

Test this in your spirit and see if you come to the same conclusion I do: if drinking cow's milk is sin, then using honey is sin, eating fruit is sin, eating eggs is sin, and so on. I don't feel that I have the wherewithal to put limits on what God can and cannot do. My study of scripture reveals that God has made many things with multi-purposes. Eggs for bearing new chickens AND as a food source. Honey for the reproduction and housing of bees AND for a sweetener and treat. Fruit for the continuance of the fruit tree by giving nutrients to the seed AND as a delightful food source.

Admittedly, many people are allergic to milk and have difficulty digesting it. They should stay away from it. But I do not categorically refute everyone's use of it.

If you have mucous retention problems (or you're nursing an infant who does) give yourself a 3 to 4 month dairy product fast and mark your improvement. Also consider that some dairies are giving their cows large amounts of female hormones to increase their milk production. This can have negative impacts, especially on your sons.

Flour (13 references) & Wheat (40 references):

There is so much in the news about "today's" health marvel, oat bran. Whole wheat is sometimes hard to substitute. I'm always encouraged that Jesus ate the whole kernel, right from the stalk (Matt 12:1). If you must, gradually wean your family to whole grain products. Start by substituting half a cup of whole grain flour for white flour. Then the next time substitute a whole cup. And so on, until you're using all whole grain flours.

Honey (31 references)

The Bible is filled with references to honey. A practice that the Hebrew teachers used to teach their lessons was once a child learned a Scriptural passage, the teacher would write it in honey on their slate and the child would literally lick it off. It brings new meaning to *"The fear of the Lord is clean, enduring forever: the judgments of the Lord are true and righteous altogether. More to be desired are they than much fine gold, yea, than much fine gold: sweeter also than honey and the honeycomb."* (Psalm 19:9-10 - KJV)

Fruit/Fruitful (206 references)

Fresh crispy red apples, luscious grapes, sweet bananas, tangy papayas, pungent plums; my mouth is watering already thinking about all the fruits the Lord has created. Fruit is such a fantastic source of healthy, energy-packed sugars, fiber, and sheer taste. Besides, fruit is fun. The Lord even chose to use the allegory of fruit to describe the outgrowth of His indwelling Spirit in us. (Galatians 5:22)

Fat (37 references)

"It shall be a perpetual statute for your generations throughout all your dwellings, that ye eat neither fat nor blood." (Leviticus 3:17 - KJV). Long before modern medicine confirmed the danger in eating fat, the Lord commanded his people, Israel, to refrain from eating it. Our salvation is not at all dependent on our eating habits. Christ covered us on the cross. However, the quality of our life does depend on how we treat our bodies. If you eat meat, buy lean. Cut off all the fat of your meat. Skin your chicken <u>before</u> you cook it. Avoid lard. Use the best cooking oil you can find.

otes:

A friend was alarmed, her 10 year old daughter was evaluated with a cholesterol level of above 200! She was going to have to learn to cook fresh produce, for the first time. Her daughter's health depended on it.

As students we received report cards in school to see how we were doing with our work. One report card that I'm still receiving to evaluate the quality of my present job is my family's lab reports. I'm very careful about getting the saturated fat out of our family's diet and am thrilled to be able to say that Alan's cholesterol level is so low (133) that it's even better than the range for excellent (below 170 is excellent). My level was below 100. A+!

Blood (references with reference to eating, 11 references)

I promise not to become gross here. But be advised to drain as much blood as possible from your meat. Think about it for a minute. Your arteries are carrying fresh blood to your cells, the veins are carrying all the waste products from your cells to be cleared out. Just as you don't want to consume your compost, you don't want to eat the "bad blood."

Pork (Swine, 18 references)

Just as with fat and blood, pork was forbidden of the Israelis to eat. With our freedom in Christ, we can eat as much pork as we want without endangering our spiritual health. Yet, our physical health might suffer. I would never be the least bit upset if you eat pork. We have decided to delete it as much as possible from our diet because of the way the meat and the fat of the swine is intermingled and cannot be completely separated. We try to use turkey meat substitutes for bacon, ham, and sausage.

Closing Thoughts

Eating has played an important part in our relationship with God. From Eve's eating of the forbidden fruit through Christ's last supper with his disciples, to our forthcoming wedding banquet, He always prepares a table before us in the presence of our enemies. (Psalm 23:5) He even describes our fellowship with him in Revelation 3:20 *"Behold, I stand at the door and knock: if any man hear my voice, and open the door, I will come into him, and will sup with him, and he with me."* Eating is so inexplicably identified with life and being "real" that our Lord made definite efforts to eat with His followers after His resurrection (Luke 24:30; John 21:12). Look at the miracles God performed regarding food (Elijah fed by ravens and the widow's never-emptying-flour pot, Elisha feeding the hundred, Joseph and the feeding of Egypt during the famine, Christ feeding 4,000 and 5,000, and Christ's first miracle of the wedding feast).

And there are so many more soul-inspiring verses to study. The Lord does care about our diets.

There is so much more in the Bible about eating, meals, feasts, and our digestive systems. I want to encourage you to study this subject in detail. Throughout the recipe section, I've included tips and hints on ways to move your family's diet toward better nutrition. You might want to re-read the paragraph on page 1-10, if you're feeling weighed down with what other people are doing. Start somewhere, at a pace with which you feel comfortable in your spirit.

For an excellent article on this subject, read "Food & The Bible" in the Summer 1990 Edition of "Home Sweet Home." For a copy of the article, send a LSASE to Home Sweet Home, East 201 Bourgalt Rd, Shelton, WA 98584.

Ellen Lyman of "Right at Home Productions" has written a delightful book, Celebrate With Dorcas. In it she not only explains the Hebrew feasts in detail but gives you recipes, crafts, and family activities to celebrate. So if you're interested in new ways to celebrate and learn about the Biblical feasts, plus Christmas and other traditional celebrations, I recommend Ellen's book. Send a LSASE for a FREE brochure. See Appendix B-3 or the Bonus Page for her address.

"For which of you, intending to build a tower, sitteth not down first, and counteth the cost, whether he have sufficient to finish it?" — Luke 14:28 (KJV)

CHAPTER EIGHT

A Fast-Forward Look at the Program

The ships looked like mechanical robots. The gates seemed to fly open. The locks were instantly filled with sea water. The clouds seem to rush through the sky. We were watching a time-lapse photography film reducing a 12-hour trip through the Panama Canal to a seven-minute movie.

My children love to hold the fast forward button commanding our video cassette player. They laugh as the actors "run" through their movements. I admit it is comical. They especially enjoy running the tape backwards and to watch water flow upwards. As I prepare this chapter, I am putting my finger on the fast-forward button of our "Dinner's in the Freezer!" system, so to speak. We are going to view this program as a "time-lapse photography" format — quickly with brief vignettes.

I'm only going to write this chapter if you promise me not to follow my samples verbatim. My plan is to teach you to customize and write up your own plan, NOT to take this sample plan and fix exactly what my family ate during a particular four-month period.

I have never "mega-cooked" the same menu twice. Each time I'm adding new dishes, and rotating others.

Yet, I know I appreciate samples/examples when I'm learning a new skill. So with that in mind, I'm enclosing a sample menu, shopping list, weekend schedule, tasks list, timing chart, and a recipe. The blank forms are in the rear of the book. You have my permission to copy them for your personal use.

Please don't spend much time examining the samples now. In other chapters we'll go through each form and explain the codes and logic behind the design.

Sample Menu

tested	re-written recipe	shop-ping list	tasks list	Entree/Dish	# of meals	Comments
				Turkey		
✔	✔	✔	✔	Thanksgiving Meal	2	
✔	✔	✔	✔	Aunt Eloise's Casserole	9	
✔	✔	✔	✔	Mandarin Turkey	4	(sar - some assembly required)
				Ground Meat		
✔	✔	✔	✔	Sweet 'n Sour Meatballs	4	
✔		✔	✔	Hamburgers	4	
✔		✔	✔	Meat Loaves	9	
✔		✔	✔	Chili	9	
✔	✔	✔	✔	Mrs. Thomas' Casserole	8	
✔		✔	✔	Spaghetti Sauce	8	
✔	✔	✔	✔	Super Grandma's Casserole	6	
✔		✔	✔	Stroganoff	6	
				"Ham"		**We use turkey ham**
✔		✔	✔	Macaroni and cheese and ham	3	sar
✔		✔	✔	Quiche	3	sar
✔		✔	✔	Baked ham	4	
✔	✔	✔	✔	Lentil soup	4	
✔	✔	✔	✔	Shrimp Jambalaya	5	
				Fish		
✔	✔	✔	✔	Miss Betty's Casserole	9	
✔		✔	✔	Patties	3	
				Others		meals I'll cook another time*
				Stew (or stir-fry)	4	
				Chops/Fresh fish/sausage	4	We use turkey sausage
				Sale items (e.g., for pepper steak)	4	
				Other (e.g., pizza bread)	4	
				C.O.R.D. (see Chapter Five)	9	
				Total	126	

Explanation begins on page 9-2.

Note 1: This sample translates into cooking this way three or four weekends a year! I've been doing even more meals each time we mega-cook — the last four times we cooked, we pre-pared six months worth of entrees each time. That's mega-cooking twice a year!

Note 2: Examples of costs: when we cooked the sample menu, our cash register receipts totaled less than $200! And those dinners lasted four and a half months!

Note 3: You'll still have other groceries to buy, of course (e.g., fresh produce, side dishes, breakfast and lunch food — see Chapter Fourteen for tips on these items).

* Since I like to cook, once a week I cook a meal from scratch like fresh fish, stir-fry, or a meat on sale in a family pack. Even then I double or triple the recipe for later dinners. If you want all your meals to be "in the freezer" then this sample menu would last about three months.

Sample Shopping List

On page 8-4 is a copy of only the first of three pages of a sample shopping list using the menu on page 8-2. This is only re-printed here for you to use as a guide. We'll examine the codes, methods, and procedures in Chapter Nine.

When we go over these forms in detail, you might want flip back to them to refer to or perhaps go ahead now and make several copies of each of the forms to practice with and then use.

All these forms have been developed during years of working this plan. They are the simplest, fastest and most workable forms I've designed. However, once you comprehend the system, you can write your notes on any paper or continue to use these forms.

There is a reason for each of the lay-outs, as you'll understand when you start writing your own forms.

done	Place	Ingredient	1- Thank / 8- strog	2- AEC / 9- ham	3- Man / 10- lentil	4- SSM / 11- jamba	5- Grdmt / 12- mb	6- STC / 13- tuna	7- SGC / 14- other	Total
		turkey as large as possible	5 lbs	5lbs	broth	broth			15 lbs	25 lb bird
	f.m.	bell peppers		10 lrg		3 lrg	5			18 large
	canned	stewed tomatoes		1-#10		1-#10				2-#10
	f.m.	onions		10	1		2	5/1	5 lrg	24 large
	co-op	spaghetti noodles		8 lbs						8 lbs
		English peas		1-#10						1-#10
		Velvetta		5 lbs						5 lbs
		Monterey Jack cheese		2 lbs						2 lbs
		Mandarin oranges			1-lrg					1-lrg
		cream chicken soup			1-lrg			1-lrg		2-lrg or 12-sml
	co-op	rice			4 cups	5 cups				9 cups
		water chestnuts			1-lrg					1-lrg
		ground turkey	10 lbs			10 lbs	30 lbs	10 lbs	5 lbs	65 lbs approx.
		eggs				5	10	5		20 (2 doz)
		pineapple chunks				1-#10				1-#10
		cornstarch				3/4 c				3/4 cup
		juice				1 can				1 can
		vinegar				12 oz				12 oz
		fructose				6 oz				6 oz
	pantry	soy sauce				4 oz				4 oz
		ground beef					12 lbs			12 lbs
		wheat germ					1 box			1 box
		sausage, turkey					3 lbs			3 lbs
	pantry	ketchup					1 bottl			1 bottle
		corn, kernel						1-#10		1-#10
		cream mushroom soup	1 lrg					1-lrg		2 lrg or 12 sml
		sour cream	1 lrg					1 lrg		2 lrg
	co-op	noodles (regular)						1 lrg		1 lrg
		pimento						3-4oz		3-4oz jars
		bacon			1 lb					1 lb
	pantry	brown sugar							8 oz	8 oz
	pantry	BBQ sauce							20 oz	20 oz

Explanation begins on page 9-12.

Sample Weekend

This is a very difficult sample to illustrate. In the workshops, I simply flash through a slide presentation of the steps. Again, don't try to duplicate these steps in this order. This serves only to give you a rough feel, or guide of how with a little foresight you can juggle several tasks at one time. In Chapter Eleven, we'll go through each sample step by step to design your own plan.

Please don't let our pace scare you. Remember we've been cooking like this for eight years and have it down to a science. It might take you years to be able to do all this in one weekend. But please take advantage of all our trials, errors, and goof-ups to speed you on your way. The system in this book can work smoothly.

Jill's jobs	Alan's jobs	Children's jobs (with supervision)
Friday		
Plan menu, make lists.	Check freezer, defrost if necessary.	
Saturday		
Shopping (whole family, Alan might do some on his way home from work Friday afternoon).		
Bake turkey in oven. (We like to start with a Thanksgiving Day-type dinner, and use the leftovers for menus).		
Soak beans on Sunday night.	Debone turkey meat.	
Chop onions and peppers. (Refrigerate some, freeze some.)		
Rest. Prepare for church.		
Monday (of a three day Holiday)		
Start cooking beans.		
Gather ingredients for ground meat mix.	Make mix for hamburgers. Form and package.	
Cook spaghetti noodles (in batches).	Label and freeze hamburgers.	

Sample Weekend, page 2		
Jill's jobs	**Alan's jobs**	**Children's jobs (with supervision)**
Add ingredients to meat mix for meatballs.	Chop turkey. Divide, label, freeze some, keep some out.	
Cook chopped onions in microwave.	Form meatballs.	
Cook chopped peppers in microwave.	Chop, label, and freeze ham. Monitor children's task.	
Add ingredients to meat mix for meatloaves.	Mix and form meat mix into meatloaves.	
Check beans.		
Check spaghetti noodles, start regular noodles.	Label and freeze meatloaves.	
Start browning ground meat (in batches).		
Start chili with first batch of cooked meat. Add beans, flavorings, cook.	Open cans for Aunt Eloise's casserole (AEC). Empty into mixing dish.	
Oversee that all ingredients are correctly put into bowl for mixing.	Mix ingredients, divide, label, freeze AEC.	
Continue browning ground meat. Monitor chili.	Open cans for Super-Grandma Casserole (SGC).	
Mix liquid ingredients for SGC.	Combine liquid and dry ingredients for SGC. Bake, set timer.	
Gather ingredients for tuna patties.	Open cans and jars for spaghetti sauce.	Make tuna patties.
Start spaghetti sauce.	Monitor children's tuna patty making. Help label, freeze.	
Continue browning meat.	Open cans and jars for Miss Betty's Casserole (MBC).	
Oversee that all ingredients are correctly put into bowl for mixing MBC.	Mix ingredients. Divide, label, freeze MBC.	
Monitor cooking pots.	Set SGC to cool some before storage.	
	Open cans and jars for Susan Thomas Casserole (STC).	
Oversee that all ingredients are correctly put into bowl for mixing STC.	Mix ingredients. Divide, label, freeze STC.	
Continue to monitor chili and spaghetti sauce.	Open cans and jars for stroganoff.	

Sample Weekend, page 3	By this time our children need playtime.
Jill's jobs	**Alan's jobs**
Oversee that all ingredients are correctly put into bowl for mixing stroganoff.	Mix ingredients. Divide, label, freeze stroganoff.
Continuously wash dishes, managing progress.	Divide, label, freeze SGC.
Start jambalaya in pot.	Divide, label, freeze chili.
Start lentil soup.	Divide, label, freeze spaghetti sauce.
	Open cans and jars for Sweet 'n Sour Meatballs (SSM).
Start SSM in pot.	

Supper break while three pots are still cooking (now possible because we use crock pots, slow cookers, and the range top. If you don't have these, it will take longer juggling pots and burners.

Clean kitchen, finish any loose ends.	Divide, label, freeze SSM.
	Divide, label, freeze lentil soup.
	Divide, label, freeze Jambalya.

Rest!

Note: This schedule is very fluid and flexible. It is only a guideline. At first it took us much longer to prepare so many meals. Teamwork is a key. The last time we cooked, it took us six hours of actual kitchen work on the second day. Don't expect to be able to match that six hours your first time. Give yourself time and lower the number and variety of meals. Learn a working pace.

There was a time that we spent Sunday afternoons cooking. We've been convicted to spend one day a week at rest. So now we schedule our cooking weekends to coincide with three-day weekends.

Notes:

Update Note:

One time I mega-cooked and our lives were unusually hectic. We had just moved across country and were still waist deep in shipping boxes. I didn't have an extra weekend to mega-cook, so each night I would mega-cook that night's entree (and maybe one or two others). After serving my family their dinner, I would freeze the remaining meals. Within two weeks of cooking in this manner I had my freezer stocked with six months worth of dinners. For example, one night I'd make a hugh pot of spaghetti sauce (enough for 12 meals). We'd dine on one and freeze the other 11 meals worth of sauce.

It was not difficult. It was a very slow pace compared to my usual method.

You might enjoy cooking months worth of meals over the span of days or weeks. Depending on your circumstances, it might be prudent for you to proceed at this one-or-two-entrees-a-day pace.

Tasks to be Done: (for sample recipe only)

✔	Task	Priority	Who?	For Recipe _____	Note
	Bake Turkey	1	Jill	Sample recipe	Saturday
	Chop Turkey		Alan	"	
	Boil eggs		Jill	"	
	Cook rice		Jill	"	
	Chop celery		Alan	"	
	Chop onion		Alan	"	
	Open cans		Kids	"	
	Squeeze lemons		Kids	"	
	Oversee combining		Jill	"	
	Mix ingredients		Alan and kids	"	
	Divide		Alan	"	
	Label		Alan	"	
	Freeze		Alan	"	

Codes and explanation on page 11-4.

Sample Timing Chart

Item:	Start time:	Ap-proximate cooking time:	Check progess at:	Estimated ending time:	Comment/ done
Saturday					
Turkey	3:00pm	4 hours	4,5,6 pm	7:00 pm	✔
Sunday					
Beans, soak	6:00 pm	overnight		next day	✔
Monday					
Cook Beans	3:00 pm	1-1/2 hours	3:45 pm	4:30 pm	

Explanation on page 11 - 5.

Recipe: *Spring Chicken*   From: OWC Fort Campbell Cookbook

Background: This was in the cookbook that the Officers' Wives Club of Fort Campbell, KY published in 1982. For more information see Appendiix D. Used by permission. We've found it more fun to rename recipes so as to encourage our young eaters. Chicken Casserole, the original name was kind of boring and didn't excite the children. So we looked at it — when cooked it has the soft colors of Springtime. So we made a play on the words and call it "Spring Chicken."

x 1	x 3	x 6	Ingredient	x 1	x3	x 6	Measurement
3	6-9	9-18	Cooked, diced chicken (mol)	3	6	9	pounds
4	12	24	Boiled eggs, chopped	1/3	1	2	dozen
2	8	16	Cups cooked rice (cook in chicken broth)	1/2	2	4	cups raw
1	2	3	Cups chopped celery	1/2	1	1-1/2	stalks
1	2	3	Onions, chopped (mol - **see note**)	1	2	3	onions
1	3	6	Cups salad dressing	8	24	64	ounces
1	3	6	Cans mushroom soup (10 oz)	1	3	6	regular-sized cans
1	3	6	Cans water chestnuts	1	3	6	small cans
2	6	12	Tablespoons Lemon juice	1	2	3	lemons
1	3	6	Cups bread crumbs, optional (mol)	1/4	1/2	1	loaves bread

Steps:
Steps that can be done ahead or assembly-lined: (1,2,3,4)

   1) Bake, then chop turkey into bite-sized pieces.
   2) Cook, peel, chop eggs.
   3) Cook rice.
   4) Chop celery, onions.
   5) Open cans, chop water chestnuts.
   6) (Supervise), mix ingredients (except bread crumbs).
   7) Divide, sprinkle each top with 1 cup bread crumbs, label, freeze.
   8) Thaw and bake at 350°, 40 to 45 minutes.
   9) OR bake frozen, Bake at 300°F, 1 1/2 to 2 hours. Check after 1 hour and if it isn't heated through, stir.
   10) OR zap in microwave 20 minutes on medium high, covered. Check after 10 minutes, stir. Adjust this time frame according to your microwave.

Notes/Comments: Sample recipe, details explained in chapter nine.

Side dishes: Home-made bread and fresh fruit cup.

Servings: Each multiple serves six, so x6 will make 36 servings, or for my family six meals.

> **Onions:** The flavor of onions vary so much from type to type. There are some so mild you can eat them raw, while some are so intense one onion is more than enough to flavor an entire mega-batch. My children don't think they like onions, yet unknowingly they enjoy the flavor. I almost puree the onions in some recipes because I want my chilren to eat the food I prepare. I also vary the recipe amounts calling for onions according to the type I'm able to buy at the farmer's market. I usually buy the large white ones that yield 1-2 cups (chopped) per onion.

Explanation begins on page 9-8.

Sample Pricing Chart for Comparison Shopping

Item	Store *Wholesale*			Store *Supermarket*			Store *Co-op*		
	size	price	compare	size	price	compare	size	price	compare
Tuna	6-1/8 oz	$1.04	17¢ oz	6-1/8 oz	$1.46	24¢ oz			
	66.5 oz	$5.98	09¢ oz						
Blueberries				pint	$2.45	$2.45 pt	flat	$6.00	50¢ pint

Explanation on page 10-7.

Pricing Chart (Farmer's Market)

Apple				Okra				
Apricot				Onions - white				
Artichoke				Onions - yellow				
Asparagus				Onions - Green				
Avocado				Onions - purple				
Banana				Orange				
Beans - green				Peach				
Beans - lima				Pear				
Beans - pinto				Peas - field				
Beans - wax				Peas - green				
Bell pepper				Pecans				
Blueberries				Pineapple				
Broccoli				Plum				
Brussel Sprouts				Potatoes - white				
Cabbage				Potatoes - new				
Canteloupe				Potatoes - sweet				
Carrots				Prune				
Cauliflower				Pumpkin				
Celery				Radish				
Cherries				Raisin				
Coconut				Raspberries				
Corn				Rhubarb				
Cranberries				Rutabagas				
Cucumber				Spinach				
Dates				Squash - Fall				
Eggplant				Squash - yellow				
Garlic				Squash-zucchini				
Grapefruit				Strawberries				
Grapes				Tangerines				
Honeydew				Tomatoes - reg				
Lemon				Tomatoes-cherry				
Lettuce				Turnip greens				
Lime				Watermelon				
Mushroom				* Honey				
Nectarines				* Herbs				

Explanation on page 10-5.

❧ *"But seek ye first the kingdom of God, and his righteous-*
ness; and all these things shall be added unto you." —
Matthew 6:33 (KJV)

CHAPTER NINE

Personalizing Your Plan

"Ma'am, these are all sold, but if you will come back in three weeks, I will make one especially for you," the artisan spoke softly to our interpreter who translated for us. I looked at Alan. He nodded. "We'll be back in three weeks," I promised.

I would gladly return to this adorable little village of El Valle. Though we'd have to drive 2-1/2 hours on a so-called highway and then a half hour on a "paved" road that was mostly pot holes to reach this hidden jewel, it would be worth it. Set within the valley among the mountains was this town. It was such a far cry from the big city, that I'd have gladly returned every weekend. Flowers, cool temperatures, mountain streams, homes that were more gingerbread cottages than houses, a large hunting lodge, and the fabulous Sunday market all made our trips a welcome respite. I've seen the Alps, the Rockies, the Smokies, and other mountain ranges, but I'd never seen mountains covered with palm trees. It brought home the fact that we weren't in Europe or the United States, but in the Republic of Panama. Out of these surrounding mountains, basket-weavers, carvers, painters, potters, and many merchants carried their hand-made wares to the market to sell to the tourists. Some walked barefoot for miles, and some led donkeys laden with their wares.

This tourist was back in three weeks. And there the craftsman was with my commissioned work: a hand-sculpted nativity set. He had formed it out of the clay in front of his hut for the latest addition to my collection of creches from around the world. It was more beautiful than the others I had seen him make. Alan paid this bare-footed native as I thought of his God-given talent. Back in America, he'd be well received. I thanked and thanked him as we boxed the fragile pieces. He could not fire the intricately carved figures so they were very brittle. As I sat the Mary figurine in the carton, I noticed how much she looked like the native ladies of the market. Joseph looked remarkably like the artist.

As I look around our home at my collection of nativity sets from different countries, I'm impressed with how personal each one of them is. From the style of each one and the physical characteristics of the figures, anyone can easily figure out the area of the world the set is from.

Our Lord is a very personal God. He internalizes Himself in each of us. Likewise, with His Guidance, we internalize and personalize Scripture. It applies to our everyday lives. He is involved with each of us, wherever we are.

I think of what the Panamanian artisan had said when his able hands cradled the Child figurine, "El Senior." Each of my creches is some artist's attempt to display his love for his personal Lord and, in a way, glorifying Christ's supreme love in becoming a man — Emmanuel.

Reading information is good, but to make it ours, we need to personalize it. We need to own it — make it ours. Taking you from the idea of personalizing Scripture back to the topic of this book is like disembarking an aircraft carrier and being handed a child's toy boat.

Please be merciful with me.

Back to the child's toy boat. For "my" system to work, you must make it yours. That's what we'll begin to do together in this chapter. We'll take the form of my system and put your family's tastes and preferences into it. You have style. You have skill. You have excellent taste. Let's use your abilities.

How does the old adage go? If you fail to plan, you plan to fail. Now let's concentrate on the designing of your system, your plan of attack so to speak.

Isn't it worth taking a few hours to save days worth of work?

Because your family is special, make your plan for them.

Menu

Start off by jotting down a rough draft menu. We'll use this as a launching pad for finalizing your menu:

Think and jot down in the categories:
(Blank form on page 9-4 to write on. **Don't write on your master**)

❶ — Food you like to cook
❷ — Food your family loves to eat
❸ — A special occasion dish
❹ — A dinner-party dish
❺ — Your husband's favorite meals

❻ — Your children's favorite meals
❼ — Food you desire your family to eat
❽ — A new recipe you've been wanting to try
❾ — The entrees you've served last week/month

Note: I sort my entrees by meat. This serves several functions.

- It helps us see if we're balancing out the variety of meats.
- It helps in organizing recipes (most cookbooks are going to sort recipes in this manner).
- It helps us identify our current and future eating patterns, which helps in budgeting (ground meat is cheaper than premium cuts).

But feel free to organize your menu according to other categories: time, style, ethnic origin, etc. Use whatever makes sense to you. You might want to use a pencil.

As we work through these forms, lists, etc., you might want to flip back to the samples for quick reference. (Flagging them with a paper clip, might help.) We'll be referring to them as we progress.

We're going to use this as sort of an artist's palette from which to work. Feel free to add to it.

Now let's calculate how many meals we're aiming toward:

A) How soon do you want to cook again? _____ (in days, months x 30)

B) How often do you figure you'll eat out during this time frame? _____ (Example: several churches we've attended have Wednesday night dinners. Don't forget invitations to others' homes, and those restaurant dinners.)

C) Do you want to supplement with "scratch cooking"? _____ If so, how often? _____ How many times during this time frame? _____ (Note: I usually cook once a week, but then I love to cook.)

D) How many C.O.R.D. meals will you be serving? _____ (See Chapter Five for an explanation.)

E) How many times do you plan on entertaining? _____ (An estimate)

F) How many meals will you want on hand for ministry purposes? _____ (An estimate)

Now plug your numbers into this formula:

(A) _____ - (B) _____ - (C) _____ - (D) _____ + [2 x (E) ____] + (F) _____ = _____ (This is the number of entrees you need to aim toward in selecting recipes and finalizing your menu)

Or in other words, take the number of evenings in your time frame and subtract the evenings you'll be dining away from home, you'll be cooking fresh, and you'll be serving C.O.R.D. Then double the evenings you'll be entertaining (figuring your company will eat as much as your family will, adjust according to the amount of company you're planning on entertaining) and add in meals for ministry.

Fasting

If fasting is part of your lifestyle, you might want to add into the formula an allowance for days of fasting. At this stage of our lives we don't fast as a family and, of our children, only our oldest son has attempted fasting. Or, in otherwords, I still prepare regular meals for the rest of the family, even if one of us is on a fast. You'll want to adjust this for your own family's pattern.

Menu

tested	re-written recipe	shop-ping list	tasks list	Entree/Dish	# of meals	Comments

Choosing Recipes

There are many things you need to look at when choosing recipes. We'll look at the different considerations in detail:

Variety

I see no reason why organization has to be boring. Yes, systems are usually rhythmic, but they need not be mundane. You don't have to repeat the same dish every Monday. If you'll notice, the sample menu only repeats most of the entrees once a month. The most often repeated dishes are served once every two weeks because my family requests them that often. You don't have to plan that every Monday is meatloaf, and every Tuesday is pot roast, etc. Unless, of course, you like it this way. With this system, you can plan your own schedule. But keep in mind that the more often you repeat a meal, the easier it is on mega-cook day. So strive for a balance between variety and repetition.

Your favorites

There might not be another family in America that likes the same foods we do. That's O.K. Isn't your family unique, too? So I encourage you to cook what YOU like. Use YOUR aunt's favorite recipe. Experiment.

I love the story of the woman who invented pudding cake and won thousands of dollars in a baking contest. She was baking a cake and her husband, like husbands are apt to do, came over and started kissing her neck. She got so "unnerved" by his attention, that she forgot what she was doing and dumped the pudding into the cake batter. Voilà! It was a sensation.

My brothers love to go deep sea fishing and were always bringing back new types of fish for my mother to figure out how to prepare. One fish that sounded horrible, turned out to be my favorite: Sheep's Head. You can image the expressions on the faces of our guests when we announced the menu: "Sheep's Head on a bed of rice."

Now your experiments might not always be well received. I remember an incident when I was in high school in Central Florida. Floridians can throw pool parties after high school football games, when much of the country is experiencing sweater-weather. We were having a fun party around our pool. I was fortunate that my parents enjoyed my having the gang over. And I think it kept some of the kids out of trouble. My parents had strict rules about conduct. As a special treat, my brother, Gary, had gone fishing and brought back an interesting fish for us to serve. It was wonderful, the only bone was the backbone and that was very easy to remove. The rest of the meat was a cross between chicken and fish. My adventurous mother prepared it all kinds of ways, cubed and breaded for fondue, in salad for canapes, etc. The 200+ pound football players scarfed down the food as fast as she could bring it out. Our halfback hollered to me in the pool asking what was this delicious meat, "Chicken?" Even though I had seen the movie "Jaws," which had been released that summer, I had no idea the response I was going to get from this tough guy when I answered, "Shark."

Try new foods, even odd ones. Some don't work out. I tried a dish once that our Airedale Terrier won't even eat. But I'd guess that 95% of the time we have a winner (or at least "next time leave out the _____" successes).

Also, be creative in substituting ingredients. Some ideas for this are scattered throughout the recipe section.

Freezability

For this program, checking for the freezability of the entree is a **must**. Please test the recipe once before you cook multiples of it. I'd recommend that you cook the recipe first just as prescribed. Before you take it to the table, dish up one serving. Put this serving in an airtight container, label it with the date, and freeze it. Wait several days, and thaw and warm it up. You be the judge, or give your family a taste. See if it meets your tastes. If it does, you have an excellent candidate for "Dinner's in the Freezer!"

Please don't ruin a mega-batch. Preparing eight times a recipe is not the time to taste it for the first time. It's too costly.

Here are some things that are red flags in a recipe to tell you they **won't** work as freezer meals:

- grease (just gets grosser in the freezer)
- celery (gets soupy; either cut down the volume and/or leave it almost raw; it is OK for soups)
- mayonnaise (use salad dressing instead — mayo separates)

Tastes are relative. We all are food snobs to some extent. But we call it being a connoisseur. There are going to be foods, even in this book, that just aren't going to be satisfying enough for your refined tastes. Granted. That's why I highly recommend that you customize this system. I'll be the first to admit that food is better fresh — pulled out of an organic garden, washed and eaten immediately. This system is a compromise between your gourmet tastes and budget, time, and energy constraints.

The check-out lady at the grocery store asked, "Are these the large oranges or the small?" as she weighed them. I smiled and jokingly said, "I grew up in the midst of orange trees in Florida and by comparison these are tiny." She asked the produce manager and he said they were large. I guess I'm a citrus snob. I've seen fish served that I wouldn't even consider a "keeper." I'm sure my readers from Idaho might be appalled at some of these potato recipes. Ranchers might cringe at the thought of freezing grilled steaks. But if you can deal with good and not best, you'll really benefit from this program. And, in most cases, by freezing within hours of your purchase, the food is healthier than if you just let it sit in the refrigerator for a week. Either way, weigh what's important to you. It's up to your set of priorities.

Escargot is an acquired taste.

Raw Oysters is an acquired taste.

Oatmeal is an acquired taste.

Everything you enjoy is an acquired taste. We are taught from infancy our tastes in food. Chuck Swindoll, pastor, author, and speaker on the "Insight for Living" syndicated radio program, wrote about this in his book, "You and Your Child":

> "The term [train up in Proverbs 22:6] was also used in the days of Solomon to describe the action of a midwife who, soon after helping deliver a child, would dig her finger into the juice of chewed or crushed dates, reach into the mouth of the infant, and massage the gums and the palate within the mouth so as to create a sensation of sucking, a sense of taste. The juice was also believed to be a cleansing agent in the newborn's mouth. Then she would place the child in its mother's arms to begin feeding from the mother's breast. So it is the word used to describe 'develop a thirst.'"[1]

Think about this in your own life. Do the thoughts of some foods bring back happy memories? Of course, they do. And I wouldn't wonder but that they are some of your favorites.

Whenever I read about John the Baptist eating locusts my "civilized" tummy flops over . . . (I mean really? Eating insects — and enjoying it?) That's a taste I don't ever care to acquire.

I've learned this in my own children. Reed had never said the word "yucky" or had turned down any food until he went to "play-group" and learned that finicky-ness had its own rewards with his new friends. Eating food that was good for him, but that the other kids called "yucky," had negative social implications. He adopted the "food snob" mentality. We withdrew him from that peer group situation and it still took about three months until I had him eating anything out of my hand again. Trent, our third son, on the other hand, is our best eater. He will run to the table, sit down and say "Eat, eat!" whenever he's called. He has yet to find a food that is "yucky."

Be careful what you're teaching your children about tastes. Elitism is a by-product of our wealthy society. Remember your mother telling you, "Eat your beets? Remember all the starving Armenians." It was just one of those things parents say, right?

Our demand, our tolerance for food quality is definitely dependent on the supply. We're not hungry. We're hungry for something specific. We're not thirsty. We're thirsty for a certain beverage. Oatmeal and water will satisfy hunger and thirst. But we want filet mignon and soda-pop. You see, we have refined tastes.

It's just a suggestion, but you might want to re-calibrate your finely-tuned palette. Health and living within your budget might need to take a higher priority than your taste buds.

When you're choosing foods to include in your program, consider if you will be pre-cooking the food or freezing it raw. To illustrate this point meatloaf can be handled either way. Depending on your lifestyle, you'll want to adjust accordingly. If you rush in the door and need a meal on the table in fifteen minutes, then you'll want to pre-cook them altogether on your mega-cook day, and just finish baking or microwaving them on the day you serve them. However, if you'll serve it on a day when you'll be home, you can set it in the oven, and go on to something else an hour before dinner time.

Flexibility

One thing I really enjoy about this system is how flexible it is. You can incorporate your recipes with some of mine in this book, or use all your own recipes. You know your own pace. The basic system can be varied to your level of participation (see page 11-1 for details). You don't have to cook twice a year like I do on your first attempt.

Now that you know what to look for in recipes, have fun. Thumb through the ones in this book and your collection at home. Keep in mind the things to look for. You know that if it states "freezes well" or "refrigerate overnight" the chances are good it'll work. Select some of your "possibles," test them, and start to re-write them into a more workable format.

Re-writing Recipes

Re-write your recipes in a format that will make batch-cooking easier. One of the keys to this program is working out the re-writing of the recipes. Once you learn the pattern, you won't have to literally re-write the recipe on the form, but can jot down notes in the cookbook or card on which the recipe is already printed.

Note: If they are your books, write in them. My cookbooks are loaded with notes, calculations for multiples and big "X's" through recipes that bombed.

At first, though, I'd recommend that you work a few out on the forms I've provided. Make as many copies as you need for your personal use. Or design your own form. Or use it as a style sheet and write down your revision on blank paper.

- Don't be ashamed to get out the calculator
- Get your kids involved — this makes a great math lesson
- Don't be a slave to precision
- Use the Equivalent Amounts Chart on page 11-8.

When re-writing a recipe, you can make it as detailed as you like. You know your level of expertise, so you can skip steps, or spell out each possible step. This is a

Estimates:
We had been notified by the electric company that there was going to be a rate increase. Little did we know what that meant. Back in 1970, I handed my mother the mail and she opened the electric bill. Her expression caused me to read over her shoulder. Amount due: $2,158.45. Of course, it was a mistake. But it took my mother nine phone calls and two trips to the electric company to get it straighted out. (To joggle your memory electric bills way back then usually ran $21-$23 a month). One account representative told Mom to send in the amount and if it was over, they'd credit her the amount on the next month's bill. Right! Her supervisor in a very sarcastic tone said, "Well, I don't see what the problem is. Doesn't the bill state that this is just an estimate?"

great exercise in logic to teach the children process, order, and follow-through. Use your own methods instead of verbatim from the recipe. For instance, many recipes for the conventional oven can be easily adapted to the microwave. I'm a big proponent of leaving out the fat or butter altogether when "sauteeing" vegetables and meats. Look for additional hints and tips in the recipe section.

When converting a standard recipe to multiple servings, keep in mind:

- Use the most expensive ingredient as the multiple (e.g. large can of Tuna). If a large can of tuna will make five multiples, use that figure for all your other calculations. This is just using the "economies of scale" principle to your advantage. Manufacturers have known for years that bulk buying brings the per-unit price down. Businessmen have elaborate charts and calculations to figure out the optimal production level to maximize raw materials with the costs. We, as professional mommies, have been doing this in our heads for years. Use some of that savvy now.

- Try adding more moist ingredients (larger ratios) for freezing casseroles. It is less dry when served. For instance, on most creamy casseroles I throw in a large carton of sour cream. It really freezes well and acts as a bonding agent for the other sauces.

- Don't feel locked into exact mathematical portions for casseroles and meat dishes. Round the amounts to the nearest standard can/carton/crate/bushel size. In most recipes when you're cooking eight times the recipe, it is not going to make any difference if you have a cup too much or too short of kernel corn. Check the standard size chart on page 15-14. This is your book, customize the chart for your area, your brand selections, your part of the country.

- Use the recipe as a tool. You're the boss. Be bold. Leave out the pimentos if your daughter thinks they taste bad. Add nuts if your husband loves them.

- **Note:** This varying ratios/portions works well in casserole (meat and vegetable dishes). I'd advise you not to play around with ratios when baking cakes, breads, etc. Those need to be exact. The only thing I do is cut down on the sugar (usually substituting fructose for the sugar and still using only about half the required amount) and salt.

- Do keep in mind your equipment. Don't decide to make 12 times a recipe and then not have anything large enough in which to mix it. For information on equipment see Chapter Six. Especially, don't make more food than you can freeze. That would be a horrible waste of money, time, and food.

Now with all those precautions, keys and suggestions in mind, let's walk together through a recipe.

Recipe Book

Is your time precious? Mine is, too. One thing I have learned is to not copy over every recipe. I keep a loose-leaf notebook filled with clear paper protectors. When I find a recipe (in a magazine, on a box or given to me by a friend), rather than take the time to copy it over onto a recipe card, I simply insert it into one of the paper protectors. It takes seconds, but then I have it readily available, plus it is easy to read. You can put in standard page dividers for frequently used categories (e.g desserts.) For those dishes that you find freeze well, you can convert the recipes — rewrite them and start a "Dinner's in the Freezer!" notebook — a notebook where you keep all your filled out forms and new recipes. Also, I'd like to try your favorites. If you find one that is good, please send it to me. It might appear in our newsletter or in an update supplement to this book.

This is exactly how a recipe appears in one of my cookbooks, (permission granted to reprint):

Chicken Casserole

3 cups cooked, diced chicken
4 hard boiled eggs, chopped
2 cups cooked rice (cooked in chicken broth)
1 1/2 cups chopped celery
1 small onion, chopped
1 cup bread crumbs
2 Tbs. butter

1 cup mayonnaise
1 10 3/4-oz. cans undiluted mushroom soup
1 3-oz. pkg. slivered almonds or water chestnuts
1 tsp. salt
2 Tbs. lemon juice

Mix all ingredients, except bread crumbs and butter, and place in a buttered 9 x 12-inch casserole. Brown bread crumbs lightly in butter. Sprinkle over casserole and refrigerate overnight. Remove from refrigerator one hour before cooking. Bake 40 to 45 minutes at 350°. NOTE: One large fryer (3 1/4 lbs.) per casserole should do it.

Yield: 8 to 10 servings

Refer to the chart on page 6-12 for basic conversions.

1) Read through a candidate recipe looking for ease of preparation, any red flags, and any pluses.
   - Red flag: celery and mayonnaise.
   - Pluses: "refrigerate overnight." This means there's a good chance it will freeze well.

2) Start to re-write. Make a copy of the master recipe form for practice. Do not write on the master itself. Save the master form to make more copies.

   Take the first item, 3 cups cooked diced chicken. In the first "x1" column write "3," then in the multiples (for example, lets use 3 and 6) write "9" and "18". Note: since I reduce the amount of meat in recipes, I use 6-9 cups, and 9-18 cups. In the "ingredient" column write "cups cooked/diced chicken or turkey." In the next three columns ("x1" and the two "x___"), write the multiples of shopping/measurements. Then write the type in the "measurements" column. You won't find chicken sold in cups, so, for this recipe, you'll have to convert to pounds. Refer to the chart on page 6-12 for basic conversions. They are not precise, but are averages. So here you'll write "3," "6-9," "9-18" and "pounds" respectively since poultry is usually a cup per pound. This will definitely aid you in writing your shopping list.

   Look through the recipe section for more examples. This recipe is repeated in the recipe section with the personalizing columns blank for you to customize it.

3) I like to jot down notes on the steps with each ingredient. For example, after writing down turkey(chicken) on the list, I'd write on step 1, Cook and dice turkey. You might even want to write this out as two separate steps. This information will be very useful later when we organize all the steps from the different recipes.

Turkey — Our Family's Favorite Fowl

We substitute turkey meat for other meats in most recipes. Usually it is less expensive. We appreciate that it is a lean meat.

Try this experiment with your children: cook 1 pound of ground beef and then cook one pound of ground turkey. Show your children the fat that comes from both. Allow them to compare it. Refrigerate the fat and let them come to their own conclusions about the glob of fat they see.

Turkeys can freeze for up to nine months according to a national turkey hotline. This year I found turkeys on sale for 19¢ a pound right before Thanksgiving. If you have the freezer space, I'd suggest you buy as many turkeys as you will need for mega-cooking for a whole year when they go on sale around the Holidays. If you time it right, you'll have good, inexpensive meat for all your "chicken" recipes for the year.

I usually cook a bird over 20 pounds. De-boning turkey meat is easy. It takes so little time as compared to de-boning chickens for the same amount of meat.

4) Go through each item, converting and multiplying out the amounts needed and jotting down the required steps to get to that point.
Examples:
» Item #2 is 4 hard-boiled eggs, chopped. In the steps, jot down "Hard boil eggs. Chop eggs."
» Item # 3,..."Cook rice" (note: 1/2 cup raw rice equals 2 cups cooked rice).
» Item #4, since celery doesn't freeze well, you can either keep the volume down (instead of full multiples, cut the amount in half), you can add it in raw or delete it all together.
» Item # 8, substitute salad dressing for the mayonnaise.

5) Now that you have all the ingredients figured out, check your work against the sample recipe on page 8-10. Once you get the hang of this process, you'll be re-writing recipes quickly and easily.

6) The next step is to finish the "Steps:" Now go through the methods of the recipe — the instructions. Here's where experience comes in handy (all those years you've already spent cooking). This can be a fun game of learning sequencing for the children. I'm all for getting your children involved. The more you can apply education to real life, the more it'll benefit them in years to come.

The recipe states, "Mix all ingredients, except bread crumbs and butter, and place in a buttered 9 x 12-inch casserole dish." You'll need to re-write this into steps that you can combine with steps in other recipes. That's the beauty of this system. You chop onions all at once in a few minutes while the food processor is ready, rather than chopping onions and washing the processor every night. Just let it run a few minutes longer and chop enough onions for months worth of meals.

Ask yourself some questions about what steps you'll need to accomplish before you can mix all the ingredients together. Are there any cans to open? Any food to pre-cook? Any ingredients to chop? Check to see that you wrote down all the pre-preparing you need to do with each ingredient when you jotted them down.

Then proceed through the recipe's instructions. Re-write the instructions into their most generic form. (e.g., open cans). This simplicity will help you in combining tasks. Re-read the paragraph on page 9-8 to decide if you want to freeze this casserole "raw" (after ingredients have been mixed, but before baking) or "cooked" (after baking). Then add the line about dividing, labeling, and freezing as appropriate. Your last line should be about thawing, baking and serving. [See page 13-5 for options on thawing, etc.]

Again, the first time through these recipes, you might want to jot everything down in pencil.

7) Next, cook the recipe regularly once. Freeze a portion. Have a taste test. THEN, if you like the result, mega-cook!

I can't stress enough the importance of testing a sample first. Please, learn from my boo-boos. Someone had recommended a sugar substitute to me and

otes:

Rename Your Recipes

Make recipes your own, make them special by renaming them to some title that means something to your family. We name some after the person who gave us the recipe, or a fun name, or we let the children name it. We really emphasize family and friends, so naming these meals after the person who gave them to us helps reinforce the priority system we want our children to learn: people are important. However, the people that we've named our dishes after aren't special people to your family, so feel free to rename them. Make up fun names like Pioneer's Delight, Chuckwagon Casserole, Peasant's Feast, or Tummy Pleaser. I want to come up with a recipe called "Frozen in Thyme." Be creative. Let your children name it. You'll get more ideas as you read the background sections of the recipes.

Supervise

In the sample recipe, step 6, I wrote "supervise" just to offer this suggestion to you. I don't write it on any other recipe because I know to do it automatically. I use it here to show you that you can make the steps as detailed as you desire. Also, if you have older children you might want to assign them the job of supervising a particular recipe from start to finish.

otes:

applauded it highly saying it behaved just like real sugar in baking. So, I had purchased a bushel of zucchini and decided to bake volumes of zucchini bread, one of my family's favorites. This was in the days before I had a food processor, so I grated and grated AND grated zucchini. I mixed batter and poured up eight loaves. As they baked, the whole house smelt wonderful. I was ready to slice into a loaf for our snacktime. When the buzzer sounded, I reached in and was horrified to see eight loaf pans filled with 1/2" high rocks. The artificial sweetener didn't react with the baking powder and so the batter didn't rise. It fell. They were so horrible, my husband joked about using them with mortar around our flowerbeds to match our brick work. I was sick, all that grating and work. So please, remember my zucchini bricks and test a small amount first, even if someone you trust recommends it.

Master Lists

The next step is making your master lists. And even these aren't set in concrete.

Final Menu

Now that you have re-written and tested your recipes, you're ready to finalize your menu. Use the form or a scrap paper and write down the recipes you've selected. Using the form style you see quickly if you're balancing styles, textures, and main ingredients. You'll appreciate this list many times.

Shopping List

Please refer back to the sample list (Page 8-4). Before we walk through it step-by-step, I want to encourage you to take the time now to write out lists. Save time now and do as much as possible at home. When you're tired from all day shopping, you aren't going to be in the best state of mind to remember all the ingredients in a recipe.

Notes:

Each step in this form has a purpose. I don't like to waste time. With that in mind, I took out all the frills and any "busy work" in designing this form. Believe me there are quite a few things you could write down in addition to what I'm suggesting. But I want to make this simple and easy to follow.

1) Write down the date, and page 1.

2) Take the first item on your menu, and write its abbreviation next to the number 1. Do the same for all the items on your menu. Go to a page 2 if you have more than 14 items. Many items you can group together, like meat mixed entrees (hamburgers, meatloaf, meatballs, etc.).

3) Take your first recipe and write down the first item. Then under column 1, write down the amount you need of this item. Use the store equivalent figures. You aren't going to find rice packages labeled in cooked cups. Next, write down the second ingredient and the amount in the first column. Proceed through all the ingredients.

> **Bonus Form**
>
> We've added a new form to this edition to benefit ladies who use more entrees in their plan. It's basically the same form, but laid out sideways as to give more room for more entrees. Note, it will take more pages to list the ingredients. Use whichever version suits you best.

4) Take your second recipe and write down each ingredient, but this time write the amount needed in the second column. Note: If any of the ingredients are repeated, all you have to do is jot down the amount in the proper column. Continue through all your recipes, writing down ingredients and amounts.

Why separate columns? So that you can track what's in each recipe (this helps immensely if you have to substitute items or scratch an entire entree), plus it helps in adding up totals. With most lists, once in the store you don't know what all you needed green pepper for. Now you can easily see (in case you have to make a choice about quality/price, color, number, etc). This also helps later when you're cooking and you're trying to divide up the chopped onion into which recipes it should go. One glance and you know the onions go in 2,3,5,6,7, & 13.

5) When you get to the second row of numbers (#8-#14) and if any of the items are repeated, I usually differentiate them with a "/" or with colored highlighters.

6) Total up the rows. Just go straight across and add the amounts to come up with the total you need of an item. Go down the pages and fill in the total column. You might have to adjust some figures by rounding up or down for standard sizes. Having the items listed by entrees helps when you have to consider if it is worth buying another bottle of vinegar just for 1 oz. The bottle comes in 11 oz and you need 12 oz. You see it's Sweet 'n Sour meatballs and realize that one ounce isn't going to be critical. So you opt for only one bottle. With another recipe you may not have that flexibility.

7) Carry this list to your pantry and look to see what you already have on hand. In the "place" column, note "pantry" (or whatever) to signal that you already have enough on hand.

Why put on a shopping list items you already have at home? Because you may have mustard at home (for example), but do you have 4 ounces? Between the time you make the list and you cook, will little hands squeeze out that mustard you thought you had? And again, you'll be referring to these lists when you are cooking to help in deriving the total amounts needed.

Use whatever codes you like to give you a clue as to where you'll be procuring these items. For instance, I canned my own tomatoes and so I didn't need to buy any from the stores ["f.m." means farmer's market].

8) Next to the ingredient, you might want to jot down substitute items. For instance, if you can't get mushroom soup, use golden mushroom. For many recipes, almonds and water chestnuts can be used interchangeably. Or for other recipes calling for nuts use sliced raw carrots for that crunch, added color and a much reduced cost. Use sour cream or plain yogurt, etc.

We'll cover more of where to shop for the ingredients in Chapter ten.

While you're planning, you can now make out tasks sheets (see page 8-8 for sample, page 11-4 for explanation) or fill them out at another time. We'll explain these in Chapter Eleven. Armed with your plan (menu, shopping list, and recipes) let's look at the mega-trip; shop-pppiiinnnggg. . . .

❦ *"Who can find a virtuous woman? for her price is far above rubies. The heart of her husband doth safely trust in her, so that he shall have no need of spoil. She will do him good and not evil all the days of her life. She seeketh wool, and flax, and worketh willingly with her hands. She is like a merchants' ships; she bringeth her food from afar. She riseth also while it is yet night, and giveth meat to her household, and a portion to her maidens."* — *Proverbs 31: 10-15 (KJV)*

CHAPTER TEN

The Mega-trip: Shop-pppiiinnnggg

Some women love it. Some don't. Some men refuse to help. Some men enjoy the hunt. Shopping.

Shopping for this system might not be like anything you've done before. It's like shopping for a family of 50.

Have you ever had to shop for your church's kitchen, been to a military commissary, or pushed/pulled/tugged more than one cart in a store? Then you'll feel right at home.

Notice that the virtuous woman described in Proverbs 31 shops wisely. She seeks out her wool and flax. That's not being haphazard. She gathers her food from afar. She doesn't just buy the first thing she sees at the easiest outlet. She's a thrifty, wise shopper.

Before you load everyone in the car, let's look at your alternatives to driving one mile to the state-of-the-art supermarket. Let's look at some options. I'll address them in the order I use them.

Your Own Garden

First and foremost, the best place to get your food is from your own garden. You control what toxins you want in your food. You can go all organic if you want. You can pick the food and freeze it the same day. It seems so obvious to me that your garden is the best source of food for your family that I don't want to take up paragraphs about it. But I do realize that gardening is not an option for some people, and that gardening is seasonal (that's why the freezer is so valuable). One thing you might want to try planting is an edible landscape. If you're going to plant a tree in your yard, plant a fruit tree. We have strawberries growing in our front flower bed and they're beautiful. My mother-in-law, Virginia Bandy, even planted gardens among the elaborate landscaping of her apartment complex. She first obtained the groundskeeper's and the management's permission, then she planted her tomato plants and other vegetables, and grew enough to feed herself and her husband.

County Agents and the USDA

Give your county agent a call. Their office, along with the county extension department, is a wonderful resource. Some departments even have radio and/or T.V. programs that will announce the best buy of the week. They are a welcome source for information about nutrition, horticulture, agriculture, canning, food safety, home cleaning, budget management, etc. Some departments have extension agents that will give informative talks to your groups, clubs, etc. They should be listed in your phone book. I have never been charged any fee for any of the research and information they've given me. It's your tax dollars at work.

Co-ops

If your garden is not producing enough for your family, then co-oping is well worth your consideration. I managed a produce co-op for more than a year and have been a member of different ones for years. There are good ones and not-so-great ones. Shop around for one that fits your needs. Look up "Co-op" in the phone book, check with your county agent, extension agent, or use your friend network. Many metropolitan areas have co-ops, as do smaller communities.

Basically, a co-op is a group of members that have combined their buying power to obtain quantity discounts. Groups can reach volume levels that sometimes individuals can't. There are produce co-ops, dairy co-ops, bread co-ops, spice co-ops, etc., and any combination therein.

Some require a small membership fee. Some require that you work a specified number of hours either shopping, delivering, sorting, playing cashier, handling paperwork, serving as the contact person, etc. Some co-ops are so large they have full-time paid staff. Time frames and minimum orders vary.

Some definite advantages of co-oping are:
- Shopping at home. (You usually call in, or send in your written order in advance. This saves wear and tear on you, the kids and the car.)
- Great Prices. (The savings are significant even on small quantities.)
- No impulse buying. (Since you are pre-ordering you aren't tempted to put extras in your cart like at the grocer's.)

➡ Healthier food. (Usually the food is of a higher quality. You can join health food co-ops and purchase organic, salt-free, and sugar-free food. Sometimes the produce is fresh from the farmer. You are also getting it quicker, the food hasn't been going through several middlemen.)

➡ Depending on the co-op, you can buy in large quantities (with substantial savings).

➡ Their timing—this can be an advantage, as it forces you to plan and be organized. You can't walk down the aisle and buy what strikes you. You learn to plan ahead, sometimes weeks ahead (depending on the time factor of ordering). This can really help if you have a tendency to be disorganized and haphazard in planning your meals.

Co-oping has its disadvantages also

➡ Quantity (both pro and con). You might not need 50 pounds of rice. In this case, share it. I've found that considering the prices, sometimes as much as 50% of the food is free (compared to what I would have had to pay elsewhere). So, if it's more than you need, donate it to a food closet or put it in your church kitchen, or store it for next time.

➡ Their timing (both pro and con), this can be frustrating at times, especially if you miscalculated your last order and ran out of something and have to wait weeks for the next shipment. For those unforeseen needs, just shop locally.

➡ The biggest drawback I found was not getting exactly what I ordered. When you're with a local group, and you are depending on a group order, it's always interesting to see what didn't get enough demand to qualify for the order. If you're in a co-op where different members shop each week, you're left to their tastes. This is great if your tastes are similar.

> For instance, we were in a co-op where the shoppers had to come back with three fruits, three salad vegetables, and three cooking vegetables. They were given the pooled money (then $84) to shop at the farmer's market. I'd guess that 90% of the time we were pleased. But there was one member that loved greens (collard, mustard, etc.) and we don't. Whenever she shopped she'd buy all greens, so we just gave them to a neighbor that loved greens, also.

You can work with some major co-ops directly. Sometimes there's a minimum order amount of $300-$500 (which isn't bad, if you only order once a year). Then you're assured to get what you order. Or, team up with some friends to meet the minimum order requirement.

Market Tips

Some farmer's markets have huge walk-in refrigerators as part of their facility. The one in Tampa, Florida is designed this way. And it is cold! I recommend as a precaution, carry a sweater or jacket with you to your outlet so you can shop in comfort.

Some markets have "samples" on display. You place your order then a clerk goes and pulls a box from a storage area. Be careful and double check the quality before you accept it.

Our family is usually such an oddity among all the dock hands, restauranteurs, and grocery store purchasing agents that the vendors are wonderful to us. They hunt for the best crate for us. In some instances the vendor gave me the picture perfect display bushel at the same price. Or perhaps since you are the ultimate consumer, you can get some produce at reduced cost because the crate is damaged. For instance we bought a damaged crate of seedless white grapes. The grapes were perfect. Just the crate was damaged. The grapes cost $6. The same amount of grapes at our local grocery store would have cost over $30.

I'm always honest with the vendors and briefly tell them what we're doing. You'll be suprised at how helpful and interested the clerks will be.

I feel I must warn you that some of your polished sensibilites might be tested. The atmosphere is rough. No one has used foul language around us, yet we were ready to explain some things to our children — like what a tattoo was.

Catalogue Shopping

Did you know you can mail-order food — not just the gift-wrapped boxes of oranges at Christmas, but cans of soup, cheese, and meat? Especially in the health-food arena, there are wonderful options available for toxin-free food, hard-to-find substitutes, and organically grown vegetables. Many of the pros and cons for co-oping are applicable here as well.

In some cases the food mail-order houses can beat the local health food store prices. They are a good source for "specialty" foods — canned and processed foods similar to the quality of foods that you'd can yourself if you had the time.

My warning here would be to watch out. The New Age movement has infiltrated the health food marketplace, with their crystals, holistic perspectives, and "enlightened" nutrients. Be wise. Be discerning.

If you know of any trustworthy mail-order food stores, send me their address with your recommendation.

Farmer's Market

I enjoy the farmers market. It's a true adventure. The Dallas market is quite large and well stocked. The farmers pull their trucks right up to the stand and start selling. Through my many trips to the market and training others there, I've learned a few tricks. My top advice to you is — ask questions. It's better to ask than come home with a peck when you needed a bushel. In all my dealings with the farmers, I've only met one rude person, and I found out later that she's known as the not-so-nice woman of the market. In fact, most of the workers like to answer questions, they're proud of their work.

Start out as early in the morning as you can. The large grocery chains are shopping, too, and they might buy an entire truck-load. Also, the heat of the day isn't beneficial to the produce. Then again, later in the day, though the selection isn't as good, the prices are sometimes better. Their products are deteriorating and they need to sell them.

If it is a rather long drive for you, you might want to use a cooler to keep your produce fresh until you arrive home.

Take a clipboard with you for notes. I've enclosed the form I use to jot down notes. Sellers take you more seriously if you have a clipboard. They know you're comparing prices. Therefore they will usually come down in price.

Prices vary. Amazingly so. From one seller to the next, prices can double. Almost all the prices are negotiable. Their product has a short life-span so any money is better than throwing the food away.

If you have the time, don't buy anything your first time through. Just make notes. Note the booth/stall number, the amount and the price. After hundreds of stalls, they all look alike, so I also make a notation about quality.

After you've priced all the items you need, sit down, pull out your calculator and shop on the paper.

Then go and pick up the items and pay for them. Sometimes, they will be sold out by the time you return to them. Simply go to your second choice.

Often you'll have to make a choice between quality and price. That's when your shopping list helps. You'll know the quality you have to have depending on how much the food will be processed in the recipe. (E.g., do you need it whole and perfect looking, or will it be grated?)

Remember, freezing bad food doesn't make it good. You just have frozen bad food. The fresher the food the more nutrients you'll keep for digestion.

Often, the farmer was up during the night picking by flashlight to bring it to market. That's fresher than you'll find in the stores. Ask him how he grew it. Many of the small farmers grow organically and don't charge extra for it.

If you are used to the produce section in your supermarket where the fruit looks like a choreographed mural, then you're in for a surprise. The food might not look as good, when in reality it's hundreds of times better. The produce hasn't been waxed, or dusted for that "artificial" look.

Slogan

In Albuquerque NM, a local Farmer's Market logo is "A Fast Nickel is Better than a Slow Dime."
— Kathryn Sleigh, TX

Market Form
In the back of the book, I've designed a form that can help you as you shop a farmer's market or any produce outlet. Listed are many vegetables and fruits. The boxes are for you to make notations of price, quantity, quality, and location of vendor.

Pick-your-own center

This is a prime option also. We have friends that have a pick-your-own peach orchard. Not only do we choose our own fruit fresh off the tree, but we receive an education on peach growing. It's a field trip of sorts.

My father had a pick-your-own citrus grove and he found that tourists loved to climb the ladders and pick their own oranges. A standing joke is the big brother, trying to sound smart to his little sister, pointing to the large water reservoir painted orange, saying, "See. That's where they store the orange juice, and the yellow one is for lemonade." The little sister pointing to the water-irrigation lines coming from the orange painted tanks says, "Then how come that man is watering his grove with 'orange juice?'" Thinking quickly, the boy says, "To get juicier oranges, of course."

However, some do-it-yourself places just aren't worth the trouble.

Years before I was born, when my parents moved from coast to coast — Tampa, FL to Cape Canaveral, FL — some friends asked my parents to join them on a shrimp catch. The idea was simple, the men would go into deep water and with flood lights flush the shrimp to shore, where the ladies would scoop them up. Mom stood in knee deep water, watching her son, Mark, then age 4, (he'll be forty soon) playing in the shallow water. He was thoroughly enjoying this special outing late at night. Mom saw the men working the flood lights as they shouted to their wives to get ready. Then she felt something tickling her legs. She looked down and the warm water was alive with wiggling shrimp. Their translucent bodies squirmed around her legs. But it was those eyes, those fluorescent antenna eyes dangling on stems off their slimy bodies, that unnerved her. Certainly, they returned home with a bucket load of shrimp. But from then on, the men had to go by themselves. None of the wives were willing to be inundated with creepy-swimmies again.

Sometimes it is worth it to pay someone else to do the hard work. You have to figure out what your time is worth and if any amount of money is worth being frightened or hurting yourself. Recently, my mother and sister, Kay, drove over to Plant City, Florida, "The Strawberry Capital of the World," and picked a trunk-load of strawberries for an unbelievably low price. That is in dollars. It was more than a week before their backs stopped hurting from that day of leaning over and picking berries a few inches above ground. Both of them heartily agree, the price they pay for picked strawberries is worth every cent. You decide. In all my experiences, it's been well worth the effort, yet. . . .

Health Food Stores

I'm not an expert in health food stores. The sticker shock I get from their prices leaves me reeling — back to my co-ops and mail-order houses. If I'm in a hurry (from my own poor planning), I will break down and buy from a health food store. I do hear stories of reasonable centers. That's great if you have a good center in your area. Be advised that just because it's in a health food store, doesn't mean it's health food. On the news the other night, the reporter covered a story about a chain of "health food" stores that were carrying beer. Be wise.

Wholesale Store

If you can join or shop a wholesale store, you'll appreciate the savings. Some stores are really clubs that restrict membership. One that we're members of we could have our membership through Alan's work or as being business owners. It also allows group memberships such as military, union members, charities, etc.

The club we use regularly is a cross between a supermarket and a warehouse. We can buy in mass-quantities at substantial savings.[1]

My one caution to you is to compare prices. Sometimes the generic product at a regular supermarket can beat the name-brand price at the club.

We are also members of a club that pools individual household's buying power to enable us to buy major household purchases (furniture, appliances, electronics, etc.) at wholesale prices.[2]

We have a motto, "Never Pay Retail" that we try to follow. We don't need the glitz and glimmer of elaborate show rooms. Because, after you spend a few minutes in a store, you leave with the product. The product that you'll have for years is what you should pay for, not the memory of an upholstered waiting area, voluminous dressing rooms, and elegant staff. (Isaiah 55:2 is an encouraging verse.)

I can now admit to it. While I was in college, I was a store snob and only shopped at the finer stores on Park Avenue (Winter Park, Florida) where some sales staff members would greet me with an iced soft drink at the door, and treat me as royalty. I learned my lesson though when I found an exact duplicate (same label) of my fine $100 wool skirt in another store that didn't even have carpeting for $25. I figure that soft drink and lesson cost me $75.

While growing up, my sister **had** to have a John Romaine purse and Aigner sandals. All her friends had received them for their 13th birthday, and now it was

Postpurchase Dissonance

This is a term market analysts use to describe that sick feeling you get after you buy something and are disappointed after the sale, usually from finding the same item cheaper someplace else.

One way to avoid this is by buying items at wholesale. I've been delighted that with some companies you can become the "middleman" or a dealer for very little investment. In some cases the savings from your first order would pay any dealer registration fees. For example, I'm a registered dealer for a health food supplement company and can order at the wholesale level. It only cost me $30 to register and I more than paid for that with my first order. It is definitely worth you checking into. **Note: Be sure to check for requirements and minimal sales quotas.**

Comparison Shopping

There's a form for your use to jot down prices at different stores. Page 8-11 gives you a sample. Write in the different stores you shop. Take each item and write in the prices from your different stores. Use the "compare" column for the per unit price, so you can compare ounces with ounces and pounds with pounds.

her turn. But the deal was that they had to be bought at a particular store where we'd luncheon on cucumber sandwiches and shop while models paraded their dresses for us, though my mother could find these admittedly quality wares for 75% the price in a less posh establishment. The value that was put on a plastic bag with this elite store's name seemed natural to a teenager. Now, I'm happy to say, Sister gets deals at garage sales. It's amazing how, when it's your money and not someone else's, your priorities get in better line. I say all that to say this: What are you teaching you children about name brands, designer labels, and the "finer stores?" Is it glorifying to the Lord?

Along with that question, let's take a few paragraphs here to discuss quality. "Never paying retail" is not the same as buying cheap goods. Not worshiping materialism is not the same as avoiding good names. Some companies have rightly earned their reputation.

Perhaps this example will help clarify what I'm saying. With each pregnancy, my feet grew a half size — an expensive little habit. After Trent was born, I went shoe shopping and tried a bargain basement house. I came home with seven new pairs of shoes for less than $50. I was thrilled with my adventure into bargain footwear. I wasn't so thrilled in three - four months when the shoes were all junk. They were cheaply made with lousy materials. Always before I had purchased quality leather shoes. Some of those shoes, while expensive, are still in excellent shape, even 10 years later. Leather stretches. Plastic wears out. We're back to buying quality leather shoes and regret ever going the bargain basement route. Yet, we still look for the best price for quality.

Buy quality for quality's sake — not for "keeping up with the Jones," media hype, advertising gimmicks, peer pressure, or snob appeal. But get quality for the best price.

Wait until you can buy what you really want. Few purchases are such an emergency that you can't wait until you can shop around and get a better price. If you're given a "this price is good for tonight only" ultimatum, I'd advise you to refuse this offer, regardless if they'll take hundreds of dollars off the price. We have a policy that we tell all salesmen: "If we can't go home and pray about this overnight, we aren't interested."

Day-Old Bread Store

Yes. Of course, it's healthier to bake your bread fresh each day. The next best thing is to bake your own bread one day and freeze enough loaves for your family to last until you can bake again. But, for those of you who can't bake your own bread for all your family's needs (for whatever reasons), one option worth your consideration is the Day-Old Bread Store or Bakery Outlet Store.

By the time you buy a loaf in the store and bring it home and eat it, it's probably a day old anyway. So why not take advantage of big savings (for example four loaves for a dollar) and freeze the loaves. Just pull out what you need as you need it. The bread outlets usually carry a variety of breads and baked goods that can help to supplement your own baking. Certainly, I forewarn you to check the labels for added sugars, chemicals, and preservatives. The bakery outlet store we use has bread baked within 24 hours, and if we freeze it immediately, it is a bargain and still quite tasty and "fresh" when we pull it from the freezer.

Local Grocer

Admittedly, I consider much of the standard food at the local grocer as unfit for human consumption. Some foods have shelf lives of years and years. This sends up a red flag in my mind. Could any nutritional value be left?

However, many grocers are becoming attuned to their customers' needs of better foods. For instance, our grocer has a fresh fish section that we appreciate. They even carry non-sugared food, albeit in the Diabetics section of the store and at very high prices.

One aspect of the local grocer that really merits you adding them to your marketing list is that they carry generics. I'm an aficionado of store-brands and plain-labeled goods.

Recently, one lady attending one of my workshops told me she used to work for a major pharmaceutical company. She told me of how they'd just switch a button on the conveyor belt and the exact same bottles would be labeled with a generic label instead of the name brand label. The exact same bottle, the exact same ingredient. The only difference was the label. Oh, and about twice the price.

Why is there such a difference in the price between the generic and the brand-name product? The answer boils down to advertising. Personally, I love the idea that when I buy a generic product, I'm NOT buying part of a 30-second spot on a television show of which I don't approve. I honestly try to support boycotts against advertisers that support filth on the air. I carry my products list, and check to see that I don't let one of their products into my cart. I avoid stores that sell pornography or own other companies that do sell it. For instance, there is a store near me that I previously used for household items. I haven't shopped in it for more than two years since I found out that they support the murder of children through contributions to a leading abortion supplier.

Purchasing generic foods, I can feel more confident that I'm not financing anti-Christian television shows. Besides, I'm saving my family money by getting quality products. In many cases, the plain-label product is healthier for us and for our environment (not as many artificial colors to make it more "attractive").

27 years

Recently in a television interview a Christian healthy-living author stated that the shelf life of America's favorite snack cake is **27 years!** That means that the one sitting on the shelf could have been made when I was 6 years old. That isn't food. The shelf life is the allowable time an item can be stored or shelved before discarding.

If you've been hesitant about buying generics, wondering about the quality, please try them. Remember, in many cases it is exactly the same ingredients, just a different package. Ask yourself if the picture on the box is worth an extra 79¢.

Convenience Stores

My absolute last resort for shopping is the convenience store. In fact, the only thing I can think we've bought in a convenience store in the last few years, is bottled water on a quick trip when I forgot my thermos and was too thirsty to wait until our return home. (See hint on page 16-28.)

Many of you are already aware of the high markup these stores charge for their convenience. The reason I mention it is that I'm surprised at how often it is considered by some ladies when they realize that they need a can of something to finish the recipe for that night's dinner, sending hubby off in the car to get it. He goes to the closest place and brings back a $3.00 can of black olives.

By using the "Dinner's in the Freezer!" system, you shouldn't need to buy a missing ingredient, thus avoiding the convenience store trap.

Blinders

Now that you have an idea of where you'll be shopping, lets discuss the actual aisle assault.

Memorize this verse and use it whenever you are tempted by that beautiful display at the end of the aisle:

> *"There hath no temptation taken you but such as is common to man: but God is faithful, who will not suffer you to be tempted above that ye are able; but will with the temptation also make a way to escape, that ye may be able to bear it."*
> (1 Corinthians 10:13 - KJV)

Just as blinders are used on a horse to keep it from straying off it's own path, use this verse and your shopping strategy (lists) to keep you on your mission.

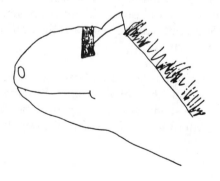

Think of shopping as "YOU against Madison Avenue." Arm yourself with resolve. Remember that "your" money is not really yours, it's provided to you by the Lord for your needs.

When I was in high school I helped my home economics teacher with her shopping. We had to calculate exactly what the students would need for the "lab cooking" the next day, for all five of her classes. We worked through the list and presented a purchase order to the school office. They approved the list. Once in the store we could only buy exactly what was on the purchase order. If we remembered something once we were in the store or needed an alternative, we would have to return to the school and get a new purchase order. We were shopping with someone else's money.

I don't suggest you adopt this legalistic style, but do prepare yourself before you go and do look at your shopping as stewardship.

Stick to your list, but don't shoot yourself in the wallet. Alan, my husband, is a tough cookie. If it's not on the list, I have to negotiate with him to buy anything else. I have to really prove my case that it's not impulse buying, but a true "find." I had to convince him beyond a shadow of a doubt that we hadn't detoured too far from our plan when we found chicken for 39¢ a pound.

Some of those specials are really special, but there are very few. Once a month, while growing up, I had the distinct privilege of paying our family's mortgage. This was my favorite chore. Mrs. More had sold us a corner of her family estate to build our home, and each month I would walk through our gardens to her home and hand deliver the check. Her home was fascinating. When she'd open her door, it was like stepping back in time. Her couches were decorated with wooden accents of carved roses. Now days there's a Victorian revival in decorating. Her home wasn't a revival; it was the real thing. It even smelt of roses and lilacs. I could spend hours enjoying her furnishings. But, even more so, was this elegant lady in her high lace collar. Her father had been one of the first settlers of the town. I would curl up in her soft chairs, sip spiced tea, and munch on home-made cookies as she'd tell me stories by the hours. Looking back, I wish I had had the wherewithal to write them down, or to tape her melodious voice. Florida was settled, too. It was quite different than the life in the Little House on the Prairie. One story I do remember was her favorite. She re-told it every time I'd visit her.

Her father had the general store in town. One day, a can of kerosene fell over and spilled into a crate of sugar. One settler came in and asked about the sugar. Her father said, "I can't sell you that, kerosene fell in it." The farmer replied, I'll give you a dime for the whole crate." The store-keeper replied, "Didn't you hear me? I said that there's kerosene in it!" "Sure, sure, but it'll ever-pour-ate" Mrs. More, the proper lady, would just giggle as she remembered the way the settler had pronounced evaporate.

Notes:

Portraits

I felt betrayed, cheated, swindled, but I did have pictures of my precious first born at just a few months old. I had "fallen prey" to a gimmick coupon ad for a portrait packet.

The MAJOR department store had advertised a special packet that included the sitting and a stated number of pictures. It sounded great and within our budget. So, Alan, baby Reed and I posed for a number of shots. We waited a couple of weeks and then I went to pick up my pictures.

At last my number was called and the clerk, spread out the stated number of pictures. "This is what you paid for in your packet," she mocked. I was horrified. In one pose Reed's eyes were closed, in the other his tongue was out. They were horrible. Upon seeing the look of disappointment on my face, she said pulling out another batch of portraits, now **these** weren't in your packet but you might want to buy them for an extra charge." These new pictures were super — everything I had hoped for. I asked for those for my package instead of the bad ones. She gave a sickly little smile and said, "You coupon clearly stated that the poses were OUR choice. We choose those." She had me and she knew it. I was visibly upset and she said, "Well, how do you think we make our money?"

I was trapped. We had planned on those pictures being our Christmas presents that year. I bought the entire lot for an overall amount that was five times the coupon price.

But, I will never set foot in that national department store's photo section again.

*Note: Since then I've used a **different** chain store with complete satisfaction: Walmart.*

Surely, ten cents for a whole crate of sugar was a special price. But it wasn't a good buy. How many times have you heard the joke about the lady who proudly shows her husband her latest purchase? He asks her, "What is it?" but all she can answer is, "I haven't any idea, but I saved ten dollars off the regular price!"

Don't fall for the fancy end-of-aisle display. Junk food is junk food at any price. Two-for-one of something you don't need just gives you twice as much of nothing.

My safety net is taking my husband with me. As I stated earlier, he's like a hard judge that I have to defend my case before. I like this trait in him. It keeps me straight. Yet, I've heard hilarious stories of women whose husbands go wild in stores and come home with carts of cookies and doughnuts and snacks. You know your husband. Consider asking him for his help with the shopping. Personally, I don't know how I'd physically handle some of the large quantities we buy without Alan's brute strength (e.g. to lift a 50-pound bag of brown rice).

Or, let hubby do the shopping. Alan will only buy what's on the list. When he shops on the way home from work, I'm sure we won't extend beyond our budget.

Don't let your children ruin your resolve. If it's advertised on Saturday morning cartoons, it probably isn't good for them. Fortunately, my children don't watch T.V. on Saturday. We all love the children's radio programs our station airs, including Focus on the Family's "Adventures in Odyssey."[3] I mention this because I very often see whiny children in the stores begging for things advertised on T.V. What priorities is this instilling in the children?[4]

I've already mentioned that Alan was in the military. They dealt with missions. They would be thorough in following their mission. It was their task, their orders. If it helps you, look at your marketing as your mission. Choose to accept it. It's not impossible.

With all the planning you've done, don't blow it now. It's in the store that you can dissolve all your savings.

Don't shop tired. When I'm tired, I'm stupid. I don't think clearly and just stick things in the cart to get it done and get home. Once rested, I have to cope with my bad choices both in cooking and in budgeting.

If you only remember one bit advice from this chapter, please remember this:

DON'T SHOP HUNGRY

If there's one thing that will attack you while you're shopping, it's your own stomach. I don't know of anything else that will destroy your shopping strategy to just get what you need than a growling stomach, a headache, or that dizzy/weak feeling you get when you're hungry. Don't shop hungry. Eat before you shop. Not while you shop. If you're shopping with your family, don't let them go hungry. Feed them well before you go. There are all kinds of surveys that prove that people will buy more when they shop hungry.

Less is Better

Have you ever run in the store for one gallon of milk and come out with a sack of groceries? Why do you think stores advertise big savings on special items? To get you in the store to buy non-specially-priced items, also. Why do you think the milk is in the back of the store? For the convenience of customers they should stock it right up front near the registers. But no — it's in the rear so you must parade past all the other items and temptations. Some research shows that people spend an average of more than ten dollars each time they run in for only one item (e.g. milk, eggs, loaf of bread). So the fewer times you shop the better off your budget will be. Try not to have to "just pick up a few things." If you do have to run in for a gallon of milk, leave your purse in the car and only take in the two dollars. You then won't be able to buy all the wonderful things saying "buy me" from the shelves. You just won't have the money (or a checkbook) with you.

Reading Labels

"I didn't understand what was happening. I felt like I was choking to death," I begin telling the doctor. He interrupts me and describes the rest of my symptoms as if he'd been in the restaurant with us. "You were suffering from Chinese Restaurant Syndrome. It's a good thing you proceeded as you did because it can be fatal."

"It couldn't be that, doctor, I've been eating in Chinese Restaurants for years. It's always my first choice for a restaurant. Alan and I have eaten in similar restaurants all over the States" I inform him.

"That's it. In the States. Here in Panama we don't have an FDA (Food and Drug Administration) and health inspectors. No one monitors the amount of monosodium glutamate (MSG) chefs are allowed to put in food. I suggest that as long as you're in Panama don't order any Chinese food. It could prove fatal," he advises.

I felt numb. I had never appreciated our country's strict rules and regulations.

Yet, we still have to be careful with labels.

"No additional sugar" doesn't mean the same thing as "no sugar."

Since I was diagnosed as hypoglycemic, I've been amazed at the products that contain sugar. Items that I'd never think would have sugar sometimes do. Often "sugar" is disguised as dextrose or sucrose, but it's still sugar.

While we were living in Seminary housing apartments, one night we had a dinner party for our building neighbors. We furnished the grilled steaks and asked each family to bring a side dish. One couple brought the tastiest green beans I've ever had. I ate thirds. After the last guest left that evening and I was starting to clean up, I blacked out. We found out later that the husband had fixed the beans. When he was reaching for the spices, he accidentally knocked over a full bowl of sugar into the beans. Being hypoglycemic, I had known not to eat anyone's dessert, but it had never occurred to me to question the vegetables. Now I question everything.

Did you know that the ingredients list is written so that the main ingredient is listed first down to the least ingredient mentioned last. There are certain ingredients that don't have to be mentioned at all. Our public library has volumes of the FDA's regulations on labeling. Not what I'd call interesting reading, though I have spent hours pouring over the books. The regulations on dyes, preservatives, and chemicals is mammoth, but still, in my opinion lenient. There were so many exceptions to what had to be included in the labeling. I had planned to give you a listing of such allowances, but once I started the research I realized that is why the information is in

Sugar by any other name will taste as sweet

"Sugar" is synonymous with sweetner. Some sugars are sweeter than others — sucrose and fructose, for example. But each sugar is broken down in the body for its quick energy, though each has different by-products the body has to deal with. The different sugars are sucrose (cane sugar), fructose (fruit sugar, also called levulose), lactose (milk sugar, made from the whey), maltose (malt sugar), glucose (corn sugar), dextrose (cane or beets), molasses (is 36-50 percent sugar and is a by-product of cane and beet sugar).

volumes. It's far too much for me to present here. If you're interested in a particular ingredient or chemical, ask your reference librarian to guide you to the Federal Regulation Publications. Then you can read the pages and pages dealing with your particular interest.

One thing that I did find interesting in my research is that an item stating "no cholesterol" can be very truthful in that it, in itself, doesn't contain cholesterol. The catch is, once in your system it can cause your body to produce cholesterol, as in the case of saturated fats. Very misleading.

Adapting

"Sometimes the best laid plans of wife and. . . ."

Even with your thorough planning, there are going to be times when you can't find everything you need for your recipes. This is when the work you spent at home really pays off. Collect yourself, don't panic. Just look down your list and either substitute, strike an entire recipe, or check your priority list. You may have to go to other stores. If you didn't include flexibility in your plan this time, you'll definitely be motivated to allot some next time.

Employ your sixth sense: HUMOR.

Here in the United States we have such a wealth and availability of goods. We're spoiled. If this store doesn't have pitted prunes, the next one will.

I'm reminded of the situation military families who are living overseas are in. Our commissary in Panama would receive shipments of items once a year. It became humorous. We wives had a network and would call each other when an item would come in. "Elizabeth, the commissary just received sour cream. Better stock now for Christmas baking." Never mind that it was February. This was the only shipment expected until next February. Have you ever walked down an aisle with thousands of cans of soup? All one kind? Twenty-feet long, five shelves high of chicken noodle soup? We'd have to buy then because the next week there'd be a different kind. We had to adopt interesting shopping strategies out of necessity. On a trip back to the States, I really embarrassed my mother. I was like a little child, walking around pointing at things, all excited and saying silly things like "Look! Look!" No, I wasn't at Walt Disney World, but in the local grocery store amazed at the selection. "You have more than one brand of soup!"

Enjoy your shopping, we use it as an economical field trip. Let your children hunt for items, count apples, and calculate totals. Have fun.

We'll cook next.

Old Military Wives Tale

I was advised by my friends to store sour cream, cottage cheese, etc. upside down in the refrigerator. Of course, make sure the lid is secure first. I was told that this trick will make the cream last longer. I don't know why it works (maybe something to do with air flow) but I experimented with one upside down and one rightside up. The upside down one lasted for months, while the rightside up one only lasted for a few weeks. Note: if you're going to freeze it in a recipe, you can store it in the freezer for later use. It won't be of high enough quality for direct serving as in topping for baked potatoes.

CHAPTER ELEVEN

The Mega-cook

I have no idea what I was thinking. Looking back, I like to think I was helping — that I had a real spirit of helpfulness. I was three years old and "Mommy's big helper." She was preparing for a baby shower for a young friend, pregnant with her first child. While Mother talked with the soon-to-be-mother, I "prepared" the food for the occasion. I spread out an entire loaf of bread on the table and salt and peppered each slice. Then I thought about decorations and with my favorite colored crayon I stretched as high as I could reach and as low as I could kneel and colored a wave pattern down the hall from the living room, past each bedroom, by the bathroom and back to the living room.[1] Then I thought about entertainment for the party and went to Daddy's drawer. I pulled out the rolls of home movies of our trip through Europe, and with my trusty scissors, I cut an entire hour's worth of film into inch long strips so the ladies could see them without Mommy having to set up the projector. They'd be just like slides was the "logic" of a three year old. I can remember my mother trying to calm the young lady, assuring her that all days weren't like this — that children really were a blessing.

Children do want to help. Sometimes they don't know how, but with the slightest bit of encouragement, they will work for you. That's one aspect of the "Dinner's in the Freezer!" system that I want to encourage you about — involving your family. But what else do you need to think about?

Ah, here we are. You have all the ingredients. What's next?

You can proceed several different ways:

- All in one afternoon — this is how we like to cook. We team-up and get it all done quickly.
- Little bit all week — I've used this schedule also, especially when I knew I'd be preparing the food all myself due to Alan's work schedule. One

day you prepare the ground meat recipes. The next day you fix the poultry recipes. Etc.

- Partial — This is the way I started. Whenever I prepared a meal, I'd triple the recipe. Any pre-cooked meals can save you calls for delivery-type dinners. Pick a favorite casserole and freeze several meals worth for those busy days.
- Team cook with a friend — Do you have a friend that wants to try this system, too? Work together and split the meals, the work and the finances.

Next we'll cover a basic plan that you can customize to whatever speed you want to work this system.

Recruiting

First you need to recruit help. You know your own patience level. Keep this in mind when you're recruiting help. Consider your family's skill level. Help them stretch into new skills. This cooking session has many teachable moments. Try to make it fun. Your attitude is paramount in setting the overall atmosphere of this working time. I call it recruiting rather than drafting. You can order your children to work. Certainly that is an option. I like to recruit my children into helping. It raises their self-esteem to feel like a part of the endeavor. There's nothing like being in charge of something to teach a child responsibility — even if its just the tomato cans.

Teamwork

We like each other. That is what families are about. Of course, we love each other, but we also like each other. We like to do things together, we don't view home as just a hotel, but as the place where we can develop into what God would have us become.

You have the best team in the world. I think of a little league coach who has to encourage sometimes total strangers into a team. This must be hard, the kids don't know how each other plays, thinks, or will react. That's one reason little league games are so funny sometimes. There are nine individuals out there all paying more attention to what their dad told them to do than what the coach said. Wearing the same color T-shirt doesn't make strangers a team.

Yet, you already have a fully functioning team. You all love each other, and know how to work together. You have a goal that benefits your whole family. You don't have two coaches advising different plays. And most of all, you're not competing against anyone else. No one is keeping score of your errors or successes. You can work at whatever pace you best function.

How many sermons have you heard about how important it is to feel useful? The Lord has balanced your family well. I believe that. Just as He's given the perfect balance of gifts to the Church, so has He endowed your family with talents, abilities, and gifts.

Each of your children is different. I have a dear friend that remarks at how different my sons are from each other. One night, as J.J. and I talked, my two oldest sons came out for their night-time kisses. Reed was dressed in full pajamas, robe and slippers. Stuart barely had a T-shirt on over his underwear. She laughed that even in the way they dress, their different personalities come through.

I remember when we were growing up my brothers would handle the same situation in opposite styles. Coming home to an empty house (my mother might have been at a Ladies Bible Study), and hungry, Mark would just turn around and go out to eat. He wouldn't even attempt to fix himself anything. Gary, on the other hand, would thaw out a steak and fix himself a feast. Same parents, two different personalities. These differences aren't to be complained about, but to be rejoiced over. Paul wrote a most beautiful example of this Divine truth in his allegory to the human body. We all can't be eyes. See 1 Corinthians 12:12-31.

It's important that each member of your family feel like part of the team. There are jobs for everyone. Toddlers can roll cans and shake bottles. Pre-schoolers can "goush" meatloaf mix. Babies have the all-important job of encouragement and adding sunshine. Small children can open cans and measure ingredients. Older children can run appliances, serve as the official timer, and guide younger children. Teenagers can do just about anything with which you need help.

This method does allow for a certain closeness between you all. You'll be working together in close quarters. I think this is a plus.

Please keep in mind that you're family, not paid help. There is a difference between a servant you pay to work and your own family. There's a difference between being a boss and being a parent. It has to do with love.

Maximizing the equipment

Let your plan do the work. For instance, do all the onions at one time. Use your equipment. It's your home, set up a card table in the living room if you need more counter space. It's only for one weekend so take up all the room you need. Use what you have, be creative. As mentioned in Chapter Six, you might use your clean kitchen sink now for mixing ingredients together with the goal of getting a large bowl soon. You might make do with a knife and a cutting board now and later get your own processor.

You'll be amazed at what you already have in your cabinets to use. Let them do your work.

PERT and CPM

Program Evaluation and Review Techniques (PERT) and Critical Path Method (CPM) are management tools used for scheduling. They can be elaborate designs spanning years of development, as in the U.S. Navy's Polaris weapon system.

Though we don't need these charts, we almost automatically use the same techniques in preparing an average dinner. Though all the dishes take varying amounts of time to prepare, we manage to have dinner on the table all at one time.

Maybe you haven't appreciated the mental gymnastics you have been performing for years. Yet, you have accomplished scheduling techniques that are on the par of industry — masterminding a multiplicity of tasks with varying degrees of difficulty, time constraints, equipment requirements, resource needs, and time table preconditions.

And you thought you were just getting dinner on the table.

With this system you are just taking the skills you have in scheduling one dinner and applying it to mega-cooking.

Your mind is an amazing thing.

Organizing the Effort

I'm developing this now for continuity in the book, but be sure to have this planning done before you start cooking. I'd recommend you prepare this list when you write up your shopping list. Refer to your tasks work sheet (page 8-8). Let's work through this list now.

- Look at your recipes.

- Take the first one and write down on the tasks work sheet the first step under the column heading "Task." In our sample recipe, page 8 -8, this would be "Bake turkey."

- Next give it a priority rating. Since the first thing I have to do is bake the turkey before anything else, this has a #1. This is just a guide. Once you begin working, you might want to revise these.

- Next assign the task to someone. In this case, baking the turkey is my responsibility.

- Next I jot down the recipes this step is for.

- In the note column, I jot down clues, hints, and ideas that I want to remember. Sometimes this is my estimate of when we'll be doing this task.

- Go through all your recipes this way. For all repeating tasks, just make the appropriate notation on the first entry.

As you learn this program, you might not even need to write down a tasks list. I find that I don't. But I do run through the recipes and make a mental list. Sometimes I'll jot down anything I might forget, especially when I'm using a new recipe. We've done this so many times, that we can just work without calculating each step. But that synergism takes time to develop.

It's this combining of tasks that makes this system easier and so efficient. Now's a great time to discuss assembly-line production with your children. Basically, this is what you're doing. You're washing and chopping carrots all at one time then moving to the next step.

Use your mind first, then your elbows. Look for any and all tasks that you can combine. Group similar tasks together. It's more efficient with energy use — yours, theirs, and the electric company's.

Operation: COOK

The morning that you're going to cook, read all your recipes again. That way nothing will sneak up on you as you cook. You'll be prepared. To keep track of where you are, simply check off the ingredients as you use them and the tasks as you complete them. Highlighting pens are helpful.

Don't leave out any small steps. Combine and do together as many as possible. That 's the beauty of this method. Don't retrack any steps.

Prioritize your tasks. Figure out when in a recipe you'll need to have each task accomplished. Keep in mind what appliance you'll be using. You'll have to stagger your use of that one pot. Think through if there are any prerequisite steps that you'll need to already have done before you can do another task. For instance: "brown meatballs" — you'll have to form the balls first. What other tasks are dependent on this task being done? Or what comes next?

Delegate tasks. You'll be surprised at how capable your family is.

Assign work stations. That helps keep down bumped elbows and spills. It also gives your child his own "command center" and helps make him more responsible.

Pull out groceries as you need them. This helps managing space. One advantage of shopping and cooking all in one weekend, you don't have to store cans, boxes, etc. for long. When we lived in Seminary housing, we stashed them under the bed until we needed them. Retrieving the right package is a challenge to a young child. Try describing the label to a non-reader, or for a reader give him the brand and contents and let him bring you the groceries as you need them.

I recommend you clean as you go. We have to. I don't have enough pans and pots to continue cooking without washing as we proceed. I might use the same pot ten different times in the day. To save water, keep your sink filled with soapy water, ready to wash.

Don't be a slave driver. Stop when you're tired. You can continue the next day. When Reed was a baby he'd take mini-naps. He'd stop mid-crawl and snooze for five to ten minutes and then wake up and continue in the same direction. It was like he was on "pause." Some people need pauses. Take them. Take breaks. What good is this program if you all get grouchy at each other?

No one is grading you. Go at a pace that works for you. It took us eight years of work to get to the speed we're at now.

Can Lids

For the health of it, be certain to wipe your can lids before you open them. Take a look at the tops of cans. They're covered with dust, grime and who-knows-what. If you aren't in the habit of washing off the tops of your cans, that dust and yuck is going into your food whenever you open the can. The opener actually forces the dirt on the edge into the open can. Think about it and, for the health of it, wipe off your can tops .

Timing Chart

I only have one timer. Since at times I might have five different dishes cooking at one time, it is easy for me to lose track of a dish.

The timing chart (sample on page 8-9 and blue master in the back of the book) is provided to help you keep track of all the pots, pans, and appliances you will be operating at one time.

Write down the dish or item you are timing. Then write down the starting time. How long does it need to cook? Is it a recipe you need to check while it is cooking? Jot down these times. Approximate the ending time. Check off the dishes that are finished.

With normal cooking it is easy to remember the time to check your baking, but when you are juggling several it is all too easy to forget when you put something on to cook.

Use this chart or scrap paper to keep track of your progress.

Six-month-old Stuart was screaming at the top of his lungs. Cars were darting all around me. I was in an area of town I had never been in before. I couldn't read any of the signs. They were all in Spanish.

Patsy, our maid, had worked late that day and missed the bus. So, I offered to take her home and loaded my baby and toddler into our car. She said it wasn't far.

Her idea of not far and mine are quite different. She directed us down one-way streets, around corners and up hills, through areas of Panama City that had such poverty as I've never seen in the worst parts of the United States. I was thoroughly lost. I let her out near her apartment and she gave me directions to get back home.

We hit the traffic at RUSH hour. The drivers in Panama think a yellow light means floor it, a red light means a fight, and a green light has no meaning whatsoever. By this time Stuart was starving and telling all of Central America about it with ear-piercing screaming. I didn't even have a juice bottle to comfort him. Taxi drivers hollered, passengers yelled back. Ostentatious, ornately-painted, circus-type muraled buses zipped around me. I was white-knuckle driving. Stuart was hysterical. I was definitely lost. This situation was stressful.

Then silence. Stuart stopped crying. I looked back and 2-year-old Reed had reached for his brother's hand and was praying, "Help us, Jesus. Mommy needs you."

Suddenly, I looked forward and a driver was letting me into the traffic stream. I recognized a road and knew my way from there. Stuart didn't cry again during the 30-minute ride home.

Don't do as I had done. Don't forget your Source. He's waiting for you to ask Him for guidance. When things get stressful, rest in Him. No situation is too tough for Him to handle.

Thinking about an incident 28 years ago, I wonder if my brother's friend ever tried to water ski again. Gary had offered to teach this cute girl to ski. It was easy. Even his five-year-old sister could water ski. So, the plan was for me to ski one turn around the lake then drop-off and go on home and he'd teach his girlfriend to ski. The plan went haywire when, through a misunderstanding on my part, I skied full force into the floating dock. My screams sent my mother racing to the dock. They rescued me and rushed me to the emergency room. There was no permanent damage to my leg and as soon as the doctors allowed, I wanted to ski again. I knew skiing was fun and worthwhile. But I wonder about that girl. She had no history of skiing to convince her that it was safe. All she knew was the terror that my accident had caused.

If you've tried multi-meal cooking and had a disaster, try it again. If your first time doesn't go smoothly, try again. I have a history of knowing the successes you can have. If you doubt the merit and benefits of this system, re-read Chapters One through Seven. It really isn't as complicated as you'd think. Just take it one step at a time.

As you finish with each entree, your next concern is its storage. The next chapter will give you options and ideas to consider.

Equivalent Amounts

1 Tablespoon	=	3 teaspoons
1 Tablespoon	=	1/2 ounce
4 Tablespoons	=	1/4 cup
5-1/3 Tablespoons	=	1/3 cup
8 Tablespoons	=	1/2 cup
12 Tablespoons	=	3/4 cup
16 Tablespoons	=	1 cup
1 fluid ounce	=	2 Tablespoons
1 cup	=	1/2 pint (liquid)
2 cups	=	1 pint
2 pints (4 cups)	=	1 quart
4 quarts	=	1 gallon
8 quarts	=	1 peck (dry)
4 pecks	=	1 bushel
16 ounces	=	1 pound

Space given for you to add your own commonly used conversion
amounts.

CHAPTER TWELVE

Storing It All Away

Drip. Drip. The I.V. fluid was dripping from the elevated bag down a tube and into my right arm. The device encircling my upper-body was whirling and spinning. In 1985, I lay strapped down on a table as my CAT-scan progressed. Alan held my left hand, praying. We were praying that this test would be negative. The doctors had diagnosed a brain tumor.

Then in a split second, silence. Complete darkness. Alan squeezed my hand, I hadn't blacked out. The technician opened the door from her control room and said, "Power outage — I'll see what I can do." She dug into her purse and pulled out a tiny flashlight on her key ring. A single candle would have given out more light, I believe. There had been a major power failure in that section of town. The hospital did have a generator that was instantly called into action. All the available power was being routed to the operating room. Two patients were in the middle of surgery. My procedure was priority three at the time, and there just wasn't enough electricity for all of us. I didn't mind a bit. With that tiny flashlight, she disconnected my I.V., and unstrapped me. She led us to the waiting room where my mother was sitting in total darkness. We felt our way out to a hall and breathed in the lovely light pouring in from the windows. How many times had I cursed the darkness when the power would go out, when it really didn't matter? It was just merely inconvenient. Ever since that incident in the hospital, I'm led to pray for those whose lives are in jeopardy because of a power outage.

Power outages do happen. Freezers do break down. How do you handle it?

I went in our garage to get something from our freezer, and there was a puddle of water under it. It had stopped running. A queasy feeling started in my stomach. How much food was ruined? I opened the door and was so relieved, it was almost empty. We were going to mega-cook that coming weekend. I praised the Lord for His timing.

CAT-Scan Results

We had been there long enough for the test to prove negative. I did not have a brain tumor, I'm happy to say.

Alan, the engineer, investigated. We had let the freezer go too long without defrosting it. It couldn't run and automatically shut down. This lesson could have been very costly. But, the Lord was very gentle with us and we didn't have a high cost to pay in ruined food and work. We never again have let the ice build up so much on the coils.

But what do you do if there is a power outage? Don't panic. Don't open the freezer. If it is a short outage, the frozen food itself will help keep the temperature down. If you find out that the power is going to be out for very long, get some dry ice and put it in the freezer. It can help for many hours. If the electric company informs you it'll be days, contact your local grocer, butcher, or other frozen food handlers. They might allow you to store your food in their big walk-in freezers. I don't want to alarm you about outages, but have a plan in mind. In my ten years of marriage, we've never had a serious problem, except the one that was from our own carelessness and it wasn't very serious. (See new note on page 6-4: Overload.)

You've shopped, prepared, and cooked your food. Now what do you do with it? What are your options?

Options in Storage

We use a combination of storage devices/products to properly store our food: plastic bags, plastic containers, foil, and plastic wrap. Let's look at each of these:

Bags: On the market now are heavy duty bags that seal well. I personally like the zipper-type, though the twister-tie kinds can work well also. With both of these, make sure to squeeze all the air out of the bag before you seal it. This will help your food stay fresher and take up less volume in your freezer. Keep in mind that foods expand when frozen, so leave a little extra room for food expansion. You don't want the bag bursting. I've had some success using cellulose bags, I like the idea of their being better for the environment. I don't recommend using bags with piping hot food. Use your bags for food that is cool. Keep in mind that bags will take the shape you give them. Lay them out as flat as you can without stacking them until they freeze solid. Then you can stack them for economy of space. Be forewarned — don't leave a bag filled with liquid upright on a wire rack shelf. You'll be greeted with a frozen bag that is wrapped around the wire and almost impossible to remove from the freezer without tearing the bag. Once I was in a hurry and set a bag full of punch base upright on the wire rack shelf. The sides drooped down and the bag froze around the wire. I had to remove everything from that shelf, remove the entire rack from the freezer and let the item thaw on the counter before I could pry the bag off. Please learn from my mistakes. You could set the bag of food on a piece of cardboard until it freezes solid.

Plastic containers: Use the smallest size of container possible. Don't freeze air. Do leave a little head room for expansion. We already discussed in Chapter Four, the advantage to the environment of using a container over and over again, rather than throwing it away after one use. I often am asked my opinion of Tupperware® versus other similar products.

I'll tell you, I think Tupperware® is worth the extra price. I have tried other brands and you can keep them. It's very easy to crack a container, especially when freezing. I don't know how many times I've dropped a frozen dish on the concrete while reaching in my freezer. With Tupperware®, you're not out your money. You can get it replaced easily. Since I'm looking for good buys, that makes for a great buy. Tupperware® does lock in freshness and makes an airtight seal. If you're on a tight budget, "earn" your plastic by hosting a party.

Used containers: I also re-use plastic margarine tubs, etc. We've found that the 5-lb size tub is just the right size for one meal's worth of food for our size family. They're cheap/free. It's good stewardship to re-use them rather than just tossing them out. Be sure that their seal is still good. Depending on how you treat them, they can be re-used over and over. Foil pans can be reused many times. (See box.)

Foil: Don't be stingy with your foil. It just doesn't make sense to waste $6 worth of food for the want of a penny's worth of foil. It's worth it to buy the heavy-duty, wide rolls of foil for this system. I use foil for items that I'm going to bake rather than microwave. Use a strip and layer your casserole pan with a strip about thrice (3 times) as long as your pan. Load in your casserole; don't fill all the way to the edge. Make sure that your foil wrapping is smaller than the pan. Remember expansion. Bring the ends of sides of the foil together and fold them down an half inch. Keep folding and smoothing down toward the casserole until it is right on top of the food. For extra precaution, you might want to double wrap it in foil. I've had food poisoning and I've ruined food with freezer-burn. It's just not worth the risk to me. I take the extra effort now to assure quality food for my family. Once the item is frozen, you can just pop it out of the casserole dish and re-use your dish. When it comes time to heat it, it'll fit perfectly in your dish. This is a way to maximize that one casserole dish you have.

Clear Plastic Wrap: This personally is my least favorite choice, just because I wrestle with this stuff. It is great though for food that you'll be microwaving. Just as with foil, don't be stingy. Wrap and rewrap. Don't just let edges meet — interlock the edges. Fold them together.

Notes:

Proper Form

Most of the items in my freezer are stored in plastic bags. We use a variety of containers as "forms" to shape the bag as it freezes. Try children's shoe boxes, dry-goods boxes (e.g., cereal boxes). Fill the bag with your food, then set it in a container to freeze in that particular shape. Once it's frozen, remove the container. You'll be wasting less freezer room.

Foiled-Again

Since the early printing of this book, I've been reading reports about the negatives of aluminum (e.g., a possible link between aluminum and Alzheimer's disease.). Now, I rarely use foil. When I use aluminum pans, I use them as a form only and don't allow the food to touch the pan itself — I line the the pan with a plastic bag or wax paper, freeze the food, then remove it from the pan. I avoid aluminum pots and pans for the same reasons. My family is too precious.

Freezer Wrap: I don't even buy this product as the other alternatives work quite well. We have however, purchased a side of beef (see page 16-7) and the butcher wrapped the meat in this paper. It kept the meat very well. But then they double wrapped and folded the paper in a special manner. I watched closely. Ask your butcher to show you how. I give a demonstration in my workshops.

... Meat

If you're not in the habit of either cooking your meat immediately after purchase or rewrapping it, you're asking for trouble by leaving it in the meat trays as you purchase them from the grocer. That is not freezer wrapped. I've discovered through my seminars that some ladies just stick their meat straight from the grocer's into their freezer. The butcher's are wrapping it for sale — for display. That plastic wrap "breaths." It is made to allow in air so the oxygen can react with the meat and give it that red look that we think means fresh. So it is not airtight. It is not safe to freeze this way. If you can't cook the meat that day, re-package it, making it air-tight this time.

Freezing for Freshness

Freezing is one of the best ways to assure freshness in your food. In many cases, you're freezing the food the day you purchase it. Did you know that many fruits and vegetables lose from one third to two thirds of their vitamin C if not eaten until a day after picking?[1] Consider the alternative to the person who shops once a week. The food their family is eating has been sitting in their refrigerator for up to six days before they eat it. This system catches the food as soon as possible from time of purchase and freezes it at that fresher state. Clarence C. Birdseye discovered this concept while on a fur trading expedition to Labrador about 1915. He was so impressed with the flavor and freshness of the fish that had been quick-frozen, that he developed the first practical method of quick-freezing foods. We aren't able to quick-freeze at a commercial level, but we can surely quickly freeze.

For freshness, make sure that you have tight seals, that you burp them or force out any extra air, and that you seal all wrappings as stated in the above section.

Already have your freezer cold. I recommend you prepare it the night before by setting it at its lowest setting. See Chapter Six for more information on equipment. Your freezer can't adequately handle going from empty to full and freeze all the new food quickly enough. For a rule of thumb, never put more than one shelf's worth of un-frozen food in the freezer at a time.

We balance the already frozen food in my two freezers (side of refrigerator and individual unit) so each is about half full. The already-frozen food helps to keep the temperature down. As we cook, we put items in the freezer. Most of the items we include aren't hot. In other words, they're just room temperature (straight from the can or carton) when we are putting them in the freezer. That makes a big difference on how much work your freezer has to do. If you're pushed for space, let your food cool in the refrigerator first or in a bowl of ice water (good test to see if you really made the container airtight, or you'll end up with soggy food), then move it to the freezer. Even now that we're cooking for six months at a time, we have never had a problem freezing the food fast enough.

Space the food evenly throughout the freezer. Don't just fill one shelf full of food. Intermix the new food with the already frozen food. This will help the freezing also. Leave as much air around your new food as possible. It's the airflow that will help the food freeze quickly and evenly. After the food is frozen, you can stack and pack

Room Temperature

Don't let food stay out at room temperature once opened. You could get food poisoning.

the freezer tightly. Remember a well-stocked freezer runs better than a partially filled one.

Order versus Chaos

For the first four years we worked this system, we didn't even have a separate freezer. We used the one on top of the "frig." It took careful storing, but you'd be surprised at what you can fit in your freezer. By turning packages over, and re-stacking items, you can take advantage of every square inch of that space.

At first the food went in wherever it would fit. Now that we have more room, we go back to the freezer a few days after our work to organize the frozen food. We like to group the food by entree. I know where the food I want is and can quickly open the door and grab what I need without standing there searching with the door open. On the top shelf we'll store all the ground meat recipes. On the second shelf will be the poultry items. On the third shelf are all my breads. On the fourth shelf are all frozen fruits and vegetables. And in the lower basket are other meals, like fish, lamb, and beef. (Figure out a system that works for you.) This way I can easily glance and know what my inventory is.

Or, another way to organize your freezer is to stock it in order of consumption. Kind of a top-down approach. Intermix the food as you plan to serve them. On the top shelf place the meals that you'll eat first. Load it front to back as you plan to eat the food.

It is worth the time to organize the food in your freezer. Chaos costs you time and money. The longer you keep that door open hunting for food, the more energy it is costing and the more danger you're putting on the other food.

Labeling

"Daddy, this isn't how Mommy makes it," little Reed says as he is eating the breakfast Daddy has fixed him. They're having their last morning together just the two of them. In a few hours, they'll be heading to the hospital to bring Mommy and new brother Stuart home. Alan wants to make this a really special time. He doesn't want any sibling jealousy in his family. He makes Reed's favorite breakfast — French toast. He remembers that as a special treat, I would sprinkle confectioner's sugar over the top of the triangular pieces of cooked bread. Alan grabs for the container that he remembered having the confectioner's sugar. He doesn't notice the new label I'd put on the canister. He dusts the top of his masterpieces of French toastery with this white powder. Then he pours up the orange juice and carries the food to the table. Twenty-one month old Reed knows this is a special day as Daddy leads him in a thanksgiving prayer. Alan cuts up his oldest son's toast. Reed takes a big bite and drinks some orange juice. Alan has done the same. Then with white bubbles and foam coming out of his little mouth, Reed says, "This isn't how Mommy makes it." Alan agrees as a chemical reaction is going off in his mouth, too. He heads to the kitchen and grabs the "sugar" canister and sees the label for the first time — "baking soda."

That morning was memorable.

Artists sign their masterpieces. Clothing inspectors drop their number into pockets. Car dealers brandish their logos on your trunk. You, too, need to label your work.

Just as baking soda and confectioner's sugar look alike, you'll be surprised at how much foods, once frozen, all look alike. Unless you like "Surprise" for dinner each night, please mark your container with its contents and the date.

Grease pencils, for about 25¢ each, are wonderful markers for your plastic containers. The writing goes on easily and wipes off when you are ready to use the container again.

For plastic, foil, and other surfaces (possible uses all over your house), I chose the Penguin Freezer Wrap Marker by Sanford. I have tried dozens of markers and this one works better than any. I purchase mine at my local grocer's.

You can also use stickers or labels. You can find ornate labels in stationery stores to simplistic ones at business supply houses. Be careful, once frozen and condensation builds up on plastic containers, some kinds of labels just slide off. I only use labels on my glass canning jars (e.g., freezer jam).

Date your work. This is important. Be certain to put the date that you prepared this food on the container. You don't want to lose any food down in the bottom of your freezer and find it two years later. Dating food helps you control your consumption and ascertain that the food is still within allowable time frames.

About time frame charts for freezing — I must have more than twenty and they're all different. I've seen charts that say casseroles can only freeze for one month and others that state up to seven months. It's a combination of how well you're wrapping, how quickly you're freezing, and how finicky your taste buds are. We've had no failures up to six months, yet admittedly, some flavor is lost once in a while. In the recipe section, I've made a few notes on some items that are best eaten prior to six months.

Be sure to monitor the use of your food. Check your progress in the freezer. Don't, DON'T, **DON'T** forget to label your food.

Charting

I've mentioned how you must monitor your food, and you're wondering about ways to do this. In my industrial engineering courses, it's called inventory management. Businesses have all sorts of systems from the state-of-the-art, computer-managed ones to the old-fashioned, general-store system of "if it's not here, we'll order and have it in a week or two." You, too, can go formal or informal, but do something. There are several ways you can chart your inventory:

Poster: I have a friend who has a wonderful write and wipe board that is specifically designed to go on the freezer. She writes down the items as they go in the freezer, and wipes them off as they come out. She knows at any given time what is in her freezer without opening the door.

Clipboard: You could also use a clipboard and keep it on top of the freezer for the same method of writing down and marking through your inventory.

Calendar: Each day write down your menu on your kitchen calendar. This will help you balance out your entrees over the weeks and give you a quick reference on what you've done. Besides, it's probably handy and you don't have to buy anything.

As it goes: This is the open the freezer and see what's missing or see what's there approach. You'll really appreciate the time you spend organizing the contents of your freezer.

Mental Computer: Your mind is an amazing creation. You're able to recall, file, sort, re-arrange, and process information better than any computer. In one office which I worked, the secretary kept a mental inventory of the office supply cabinet. At any given time you could ask her how many boxes of paper clips were on the shelf and she knew. The only problem was the day she was sick and we all helped ourselves to the supplies. Her system was destroyed, because she didn't know what we took or where we put things back. Can you manage the ins and outs, the withdrawals and deposits made to your freezer? Or is everyone and his brother or sister, pulling things out? Adjust your inventory management accordingly.

My sister once was the type of person Erma Bombeck hates—perfect. I remember helping her cook in her kitchen and asking for a can of cheddar cheese soup. She said "It's in the pantry, four inches from the back wall, two cans deep on the third shelf." And it was. Her pantry was better organized than any grocery store. Her cans were in alphabetical order! It was a work of art. I've still never seen such organization.

A few months ago, I was again helping her cook and asked for something. She said, "Oh, I don't know, look around. It could be in the pantry somewhere, or maybe in the bag of groceries I haven't yet unpacked sitting on the chest freezer." Same lady, but what was the difference? Now, she has two beautiful children, and is back to being normal. Erma Bombeck would love my sister now.

Develop a style that works for you. Alan is an engineer and he has diagrams, 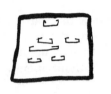 graphs and Gantt charts as his "to do" lists. If I let myself, I'd do well to grab a crayon and scribble on the back of a can label. Yet, I've had to train myself to be methodical. That's why I developed the forms in this book. I've had tours through my home just to see how we've organized. I'll develop these concepts of getting the house organized in Chapter Eighteen.

Portions

Remember to freeze in meal-size portions. You only want to thaw out enough food to eat in one sitting. Once Alan thought it would be a good idea to save containers and bags so he froze double portions. The problem with that is we'd either have to eat the same dish two nights in a row or re-freeze the extra portion. We didn't like either option, so now we are sure to freeze only one meal's worth of food in a container. Meal size portions are easier, yet you'll need more containers.

Some products can be frozen in bulk and retrieved in just the quantity you need for a meal. For instance, blueberries can be individually frozen (for procedure see page 14-2) then bagged together in gallon containers. Then, when you need just a half cup for muffins, you can reach in and pull out just that much.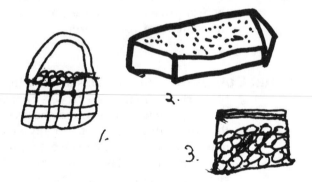

We also freeze some items in individual-size servings. This is wonderful for those times when you need a quick meal for one. It also is ideal for any family member that has to have his own special diet.

Don'ts

Just to remind you of some don'ts:

✘ Don't expect your 19 cubic-foot freezer to be able to freeze 19 cubic feet of room-temperature food overnight.

✘ Don't forget to label your food, including the date and contents.

✘ Don't let good food go bad because of improper wrapping or storing.

✘ Don't be stingy with your wrap.

✘ Don't lose track of your inventory.

✘ Don't forget to defrost your freezer before it needs it.

✘ Don't forget your Source, your sense of humor, and your calling.

This is the day which the Lord hath made; we will rejoice and be glad in it." — Psalm 118:24 (KJV)

CHAPTER THIRTEEN

Atypical Day or a Typical Day

My act was together. The house was clean. Dinner was prepared. The blueberry pie was in the oven. I was going to have time to soak in the tub before our dinner party.   I was thinking "Dinner parties aren't difficult, even for twenty." I ran upstairs to check on my two napping boys. They were sleeping peacefully. All was right with the world.

I started the tub, sprinkling in some bath salts, thinking that a nice bath would be wonderful. Then as my right leg broke the surface of the water, I heard a noise in the kitchen.   Then more noise. Then a loud crash.

I grabbed a towel, "daintily" rushed down the stairs and rounded the corner. How? How could a beautiful sleeping toddler do all this in a matter of minutes?

Stuart had crawled out of his crib, down the stairs into the kitchen, opened the pantry door (never mind the child-restraint hook), pulled out a gallon container of liquid cooking oil, and poured it over his head onto the floor. He continued by opening up every box of cereal in the cabinets and sprinkling them over the oiled floor! How? Why? Why me? Why now? What? What do I do first?

Of course, it was a brand new bottle of oil (now completely empty). Oh, but the sheer delight on Stuart's face — he was rolling, sliding and having a toddler field day on that floor.

Have you ever seen a greased-pig contest? At our church's Fourth of July picnic we had one, except we used greased watermelons.   I remember laughing so hard watching our deacons, Sunday School teachers and pastor wrestling an oiled watermelon to the ground. Just as they would get a good hold on it, it would slip out of their hands and land 20 feet away. **Then** it was hilarious.

Now I think getting a hold on a greased watermelon would be simple compared to grabbing my oiled toddler. My first task was how to even get across the floor to him without landing on my back, landing on him, or hurting us both. I grabbed a towel and a prayer and started nicely, "Stuart, darling, come to Mommy."

That started the game. (Remember, I'm dressed only in a towel myself.) Finally, after trying to walk on an inch of oil, and not making it, I got down and crawled. I don't know how much time it took to finally secure my precious bundle in my arms to bath him, but the timer was going off on the stove. My masterpiece of a blueberry pie, the pie I had sculpted with lattice work and carvings was done. But the oven was on the other side of the room. It burnt by the time I got back to it. I had something more important to deal with — my child.

My husband is a wonderful man and has to play many roles for me. Sometimes I like to give him an inkling of my state of mind by asking for a particular "role" when I call him. Like "Alan, I need to talk to the plumber." He switches into his plumber mode and gets ready to instruct me over the phone on the finer points of drains and PVC pipe. This call I asked for my priest and chemist husband. "That's a switch. What's up now, dear?" Once I got him to stop laughing, he answered my questions on how to clean up my child. I know how to clean up oil — boiling water. However, on a child a different method was needed. The pastor in him started praying for me and comforting me. He said he'd try to come home early, and would pick up a dessert on the way home.

It took four different tubfuls of warm water, and much rubbing and gentle drying, and every towel in the closet to get my little sweetie squeaky clean. Now I could dress myself, my Stuart was O.K.

By now the house had the most delightful aroma — burnt blueberry pie. The fire alarm sounded. Whatever happened to my restful bath?

I still had a kitchen to clean. By then the crispy flakes were soaky flakes. It took three rolls of paper towels, and seven pots of boiling water to break up the oilslick.

Somehow, I managed to be dressed, and have a clean house and dinner ready by the time the guests arrived. My fingers still looked like raisins, but the floor was so shiny!

The title of this chapter is atypical day or a typical day. Believe me that was an atypical day. But we do learn from days like that. And I don't know about you, but days like that certainly help me to appreciate typical days. Mundane sounds wonderful after that kind of excitement.

Yes, you can have dinner in the freezer, the salad already made, the table set to perfection and still have a disastrous dinner. Much depends on your attitude and your ability to flex. Some of it depends on the mood you set for your family and guests. That night my guests laughed with me over the story and then I heard some stories that would make my Crisco-kid story seem a trifle. But then when we look at our life from God's point of view, missing a bath is smaller than a trifle.

Now that you have done all this work, and have dinner in the freezer, how do you use it? What's the best way to utilize your meals? There are several approaches and I've used them all. Find a system that works for you. God gave you a temperament, a style, a flair. That makes you special. And remember of all the women in the world the Lord could have designed for your husband, He designed you as you are.

Your husband is the routine type. He wears the blue suit every Tuesday. You, however, are zany. That's where the balance comes in. He could never be spontaneous, but loves it when you are. Then you might like to cook with the "What falls out of the freezer when I open the door" decision-making model.

OR

Your husband is always embarrassing you. You identify with Mrs. Peter. Her husband, Simon (the Rock), was always saying the wrong thing to the right people. You're not shy, just conservative with your words. Your husband has never met a stranger. That's right. There's no one stranger than he is! Then you might like to cook with "What does the master plan suggest" decision-making model.

OR

Your husband is Prince Charming. He dances you off your feet. He brings you flowers. He always smells wonderful. You, on the other hand, never have had a firm grip on reality and love to live in fantasy land. If you just believe hard enough, he will sing "Some Enchanted Evening." May I suggest that you continue with this "treat him like you want him to be" idea and adopt the "What does hubby want?" decision-making model.

OR

Your husband is a cross between Steve Douglas (Fred MacMurray on "My Three Sons") and Andy Taylor (Andy Griffin in Mayberry). You, just like the "Pledge" commercials of yesteryear, wear chiffon evening gowns as you dust your grand piano. You're Mr. and Mrs. Average America, so you let your wonderful children decide as you adopt the "What do the Masses want?" decision-making model.

OR

Your husband has pointed ears and says things like "Live long and prosper." He's Mr. Logical. He's precise. He's never ~~wruung~~ wrong. He doesn't like surprises. You have better things to do than "worry your pretty little head about such matters," for "tomorrow's another day, my dear, Scarlet." You might want to adopt the "What's the master plan dictate?" decision-making model.

OR

You're like me and use the highly scientific model of "What am I hungry for?"

otes:

Considerate Considerations

Let's grab a little from each decision-making model and examine what you need to consider in planning tonight's dinner?

> » What is your day's schedule like?

> » How much thawing time do you have?

> » How much warming time do you have?

> » What other preparations do you need to do?

"What am I hungry for?"— I do keep in mind some of these questions, but if I'm to be honest with you, a great deal of the time it boils down to "What am I hungry for?" (Especially when I'm pregnant.)

"What do the Masses want?" — Give your kiddos a lesson in democracy. Bring it up for a vote. Warning: have a vote not a fight. Use this only when you have enough time to thaw and warm any of their choices. Of course, you nominate the candidates. Don't make this an open-ended, "What do you guys want for dinner?" Ask them, "Do you want mystery casserole number 1, Whatever's in container number 2, or What-do-you-call-it curtained in wrapper number 3?" (It helps if you look like Carol Merill or Vanna White.)

"What falls out of the freezer when I open the door" — This decision-making model is also known by, "What's in the front of the freezer?" This will definitely add variety to your life, if not surprise, especially if, when it fell, the label came off. This method works well as long as dinner didn't first fall on your foot and break your little toe. In that case, aren't you glad dinner is fixed and you can crawl into bed?

What does Hubby want? — Ask him his opinion. Then follow it. Don't ask him for his suggestion and then fix something else. That's a big no-no. My husband likes to know what's for dinner, he can dream about it all day.

What does the Master Plan suggest? — Use your master plan, or rotation schedule as a guide. Vary it according to the changes that have occurred. Is it raining today? Don't serve the casserole, serve the chili. Flex a little.

What does the Master Plan dictate? — This decision-making model is for those of you who thrive on order. I've only been able to last a week or two following a master schedule to the letter, so I stopped writing them.

What is a master plan? In addition to planning a list of entrees that you'll eat for the next months (see sample menu, page 8-2), you can assign them days. Use a calendar or a chart and write in what meals you'll have when. Honestly, this makes sense and is probably a good idea.

For example, if you're going to have spaghetti eight times in four months that means approximately every other week. Write down spaghetti every other Thursday. Write down chili the other Thursdays. Put down Turkey Mandarin the first Sunday of each month. Continue through your list spacing meals throughout your time frame so that you have an excellent balance of meats and textures without any repeats in a given week.

If that is too much of a straight jacket for you, you might want to use an index card system. I tried this for one year and it worked fairly well. On the front of index cards, I write down a menu. The entree, the accompanying side dishes (favorites or optionals), what recipe books I'll need to refer to, and any comments. On the back I write down the ingredients I'll need, highlighting any unusual ones that I might not carry on hand in the pantry (e.g., pimento pieces). Then I use this in conjunction with my other lists.   I can move the cards around in any order I want and for as many days as I want. The cards are small enough to keep in my purse for shopping.

We live in a society that screams for instant everything. From gratification to breakfast, we want it in an instant. I usually balk away from all that hype, but I do want to add in my own nomination — instant creativity. This is my lifesaver as I'm sinking down for the third time. I've written a book (in your hands) on kitchen management—on being prepared. And yet, there are days I don't even think about dinner (that is OUR dinner, I've been too busy writing about YOUR dinner) until I hear Alan's key in the door. Presto chango. I want instant creativity. I praise the Lord for my microwave, grab something out of the freezer and zap it, then greet him and find out how his day was.   I'm thrilled that I did think about tonight's dinner months ago when we mega-cooked, so today I could write.

Thawing

Of course, instant creativity is not the best way to handle dinner. But it does work. We've covered your inspiration, your decision-making models for choosing what to serve. What do you do from there?

How do you get dinner out of the freezer and onto the table?

Thaw, Ma'am, thaw.

The best (healthiest, safest) way is to take out tomorrow's dinner tonight while you're straightening the kitchen. It can thaw slowly and evenly in the refrigerator.

Leave it out on the counter all morning. This is an option only because I know you'll try it. I don't recommend it, though I've done it, too.   The problem here is that the outer edges are thawed and starting to get room temperature while the

Thawing

Depending on how you stored the food, thawing times vary. An entree one inch thick is going to thaw quicker than one five inches thick. You might have to take a frozen entree out and thaw it in the refrigerator two days ahead. The setting of your refrigerator will also influence the thaw time.

middle is still frozen. Room temperature is a favorite of little germs and things to grow in. This is not a healthy idea. Try to plan around this one.

We now have two microwaves and I wonder how I lived for five years of married bliss without one. Both of ours have a defrost setting. Know your machine and rotate your dish. This will not work well if you wrapped your dinner in foil. You'll have to unwrap it, or better yet choose something else to cook.

Many of our meals that are in oven-proof containers, or can be easily put in one, can bake from their frozen state at a lower temperature and for about twice as long as it would take to bake normally. Don't pre-heat your oven, just stick your dish (covered) in the oven, heat it at 50° - 100° F less than what the recipe calls for, but at the stated time in the recipe check it (this will usually be your halfway point). Depending on if you need the top to brown (e.g. home-made pot pie), remove the cover.

Heating

That last suggestion also explained the heating as well as the thawing of some dishes. Other things you need to consider, when heating your already thawed foods, are:

» Containers (you can really save washing by using bake 'n serve dishes).
» Pre-heating versus cold oven. If it's not a baked good (cake, bread, etc.) there is rarely a need to pre-heat your oven. Save energy and let the food warm up gradually as your oven does. In fact, your casseroles will come out smoother, your meat will be more even, and vegetables won't be as soggy.
» I can't give you much advice on microwaving, though I know how to use my ovens. Both of my ovens cook differently. My first question, when my children ask me how long to zap something is "Which microwave?" because I have two different instructions depending on the machine used. In the recipe section, you'll notice I'm very vague about the micro-waving instructions. Get to know your machine and experiment. Remember to always undercook. You can't un-zap your food.

Accompaniments

Earlier I told you that some of my meals are captioned "Some Assembly Required" and that some require more side dishes than others. You need to consider this when you're scheduling your time. With some meals you're going to want to serve a starch, a vegetable, a salad and bread. With some meals all you'll need to add is a salad.

Even many of these side dishes can be prepared ahead. I've had delicious vegetable casseroles. My sister fixes a wonderful broccoli/corn casserole that I'll include in the recipe section. (See page 16-20.)

We like fresh produce, but sometimes it's impossible to get. So I really appreciate the vegetables that I blanched and froze when they were in season.

Other ideas for freeze-ahead dishes are in Chapter Fourteen.

Presentation

Food has to look good to taste good. Kids know this. They can just look at something and know it's yucky. We taste with our eyes, too — so spend a little time on your presentation.

Keep in mind there are two aspects to presentation: the food itself and the table setting. (Chapter 18 has a section on table settings.)

Take a minute and add a sprig of herbs to the side of the platter (Use the same herb as you used to season the dish). Sprinkle the top of a casserole with grated cheese, bread crumbs, or Paprika. Arrange the asparagus in a fan. Curl the carrot sticks. Make a cucumber boat. Have fun. Children love this. Look for more ideas in the recipe section. Obtain ideas from the style that restaurants use to showcase their meals.

Yippie-Hallelujah

What are you like when you wake up? Some people jump up singing. Some people can't find their own toes. I start waking up at five a.m., listen to radio programs for a while, have a quiet time and finally drag myself out of the covers around seven a.m. It isn't pretty.

But do you want to be greeted with an, "Oh, don't you feel well?" I know I don't. So we started something here in our family.

"Oh, no little Joey's up. Rats!" Have you ever heard a mother say this when her little one wakes from his nap? I don't know about you, but I know I certainly don't want to be greeted like that. So we started something in our family.

"Yippie-Hallelujah!" "Oh, delight!" "Oh, rapture!" "My little sweetheart is up!" Though inside I might be saying, "Couldn't you go back to sleep for another hour" — I don't say it. Because I know I wouldn't want to hear it myself. Instead, we all greet each other warmly. Instantly, our attitudes warm up to our words. Little three-year-old Trent will come stumbling out of his room, still clutching Gnarly, his beloved stuffed bear, still kind of cranky. But a word or two of encouragement and those sleepy eyes are filled with twinkle and merriment.

Then he's hungry. He's always hungry.

My mind doesn't work well before 10 a.m, and I'm not too sure it works that well after 10 a.m. So we made up a schedule of breakfasts. This way I don't have to think. It's the master plan decision-model, but for breakfast and lunch. By supper, I'm ready to put on a magazine-cover dinner, but early in the morning, when the children are starving and I don't think I could eat a thing, we just look at the chart on the refrigerator and I can go into automatic pilot. We keep it simple — for me. Reed has learned to make oatmeal, so on Tuesdays he's in charge. Stuart can mix a mean bowl of cereal so he does Mondays. Trent can pass out fruit, so he's our snack guy. Bethany Kay (toddler) is in charge of sunshine — she is to dispense it. On Wednesdays, I fix an old-fashioned breakfast, eggs and toast (and if we had any leftovers from Tuesday's lunch of baked potatoes, I make hash browns). Thursday, we dive into piles of French toast or pancakes (health-food versions). By Friday, I'm usually awake and bake fresh muffins. Saturday and Sunday, depending on our day's plans and how late we sleep, can be anything from Dutch Baby Pancake Puffs to "Eat an apple in the car and don't drip it on your church clothes."

Similarly, we have a plan for lunches. This way I can homeschool right up to the wire without having to concern myself with lunch. The two older boys are becoming quite adept at several of our menus (e.g., baked potatoes from the microwave, peanut butter and home-made jelly sandwiches or banana sandwiches, grilled cheese sandwiches, and yogurt).

Adopt a menu plan that suits your family. Don't try to keep up with the four-color ads in magazines. Fix food that fits your budget — monetary, caloric, and dietary. Keep in mind that in most cases (meat is an exception) the closer the food is to the form God originally made it, the healthier it is (e.g., raw carrots are better for you than cooked carrots, fresh apples are better for you than apple pie).

With a little forethought your typical days can be calm and peaceful and you can spend your mental energy on something more important than figuring out an answer to your children's cries, "I'm hungry! What's there to eat?"

With that in mind, let's look at more applications (other than entrees) of this "Dinner's in the Freezer!" idea. Chapter 14 will offer you some more ways to use planning and preparing ahead.

CHAPTER FOURTEEN

Applying the Principles

I can imagine what he thought. I had answered his knock on our door in tears. My face was red and swollen from uncontrolled crying. Our neighbor was dropping by to give us an invitation to a party. He had just left his counseling course at the seminary and upon seeing my weeping was ready to console me and have one of his first attempts at counseling. Had I just had a fight with Alan? Had I just received bad news from my family? How had Satan attacked me to bring on such a reaction? I could barely speak. So I signaled him in and pointed to my kitchen where sat a 50-lb sack of onions that I had been peeling and chopping to freeze for future use. We both burst out laughing as we realized the comedy of the situation.

Since then I've learned a few tricks in peeling onions to help stop the weeping, plus I've heard all sorts of suggestions from others:
  » Cut while running water from the faucet.
  » Keep your mouth full of water.
  » Hold a toothpick in your mouth. (Wood is supposed to absorb the fumes.)
  » Cut the onion all but the root. Leave it intact as long as possible.
  » Use the food processor — even better — outside in the backyard!
  » My 100% guaranteed method to stop your onion tears — charm your husband into doing it.

In addition to the aforementioned onions (and earlier chapters — entrees) you can use this "Dinner's in the Freezer!" method to bulk buy and prepare many dishes, desserts, ingredients and extras. This chapter will help to start you thinking of different tasks you're doing in your home everyday that could be done ahead. I'll be the first to admit that this list is not exhaustive. It's only the tip of the iceberg, or just one shelf in your freezer.

Be creative. "Mass-production" cooking, or even tripling recipes, can be applied to many other cooking jobs besides just entrees.

Breads

If you're baking a loaf of bread, why not bake two? You have the bowl out; it takes just a few more minutes to crack another egg, add another cup of flour, etc. Besides you already have the oven hot. Or why not bake ten loaves? Quick breads freeze well. Plus you'll have an "instant" gift loaf, a special bread for dinner, and a "care" package for that new mother, etc.

A friend, Karen Jones, grinds whole-wheat flour for me every other week. I bake loaf bread, rolls, pizza, etc. What I don't bake on my baking day, I go ahead and shape the dough and freeze it. Then, when I want to bake it, I just thaw it out and let it rise, then bake it. I have found that by shaping the dough into small balls (1"-2" diameter), freezing each ball separately, then (once frozen), moving the hard balls to a bag, I can reach in and pull out as many dough balls as I need. These balls work great in Monkey Bread, Quick Bread Baskets, Clover rolls, etc. (explanations in recipe section).

Frozen bread dough is available in your grocer's freezer, but home-made is much less expensive, fresher, and more nutritious.

Pies

Do you love homemade pies? I know I do, but I don't always have the time to make fresh pastry. Sure, the local grocer has frozen pastries, but they are in a tin pan, have "added ingredients," and up to 85% of the price is for the convenience. Take an hour one day and mass-produce pastry circles. They freeze well and you can separate a stack with wax paper. It costs just pennies. You control the ingredients. The taste is 100% better. When it comes time to bake the pie, just "peel" off a pastry round, lay it in your glass dish, fill it with your pre-prepared filling, and top with your second pastry round. If you don't have the space to freeze the flat pastry circles, try freezing the dough in balls to be rolled out later.

What pre-prepared filling? The one you made one afternoon when fruit was in season. Grandmother canned, but do you? Honestly, today's methods are so simple. I like the idea that I can leave all that sugar OUT of my family's desserts. Savings? Last year I purchased directly from the farmer, so I knew they were fresh. The blueberries were at an incredible price — 24 pints for $12.00. That's 50 cents a pint. I was sure I had a bargain, but I checked the local grocer on my way home. He was offering blueberries that were days older than mine for a real bargain — $2.75 a pint. I saved $54!

I made some pie filling and canned it. Homemade blueberry preserves are wonderful and easy to make. The rest I froze using cooking sheets and T.V. table trays. Be creative, use flat boxes, whatever you have. You might have to turn them upside down. I layered the berries out and froze them individually. For ease, line container with waxed paper. Then when the berries were solid, I poured them into a large container. Since they were frozen separately, whenever I want to make muffins, etc.,

I just open the container and scoop out any amount I need. They aren't frozen together in one big clump as they would be if I had just dumped fresh blueberries into a bag.

The recipe section has some pie recipes that freeze well after being made, and some that are quick and easy to make fresh on the day you will serve the dessert.

Cakes

Many cakes freeze well. I'll bake a large cake, cut it into fourths, serve one-fourth that night and freeze the others for festive desserts in subsequent weeks.

Produce

The method of freezing pieces separately works well for most **berries, bell peppers, mushrooms, onions,** etc. If you can't prepare the whole meal, at least prepare the produce when it's fresh. It will save time by dicing, slicing, etc. and freezing ahead.

Make your own produce rinse, **Brown Away,** to keep your fruit from browning: Mix one cup of water and one tablespoon of lemon juice and pour this over your cut fruit.

When you're preparing **strawberries,** wash them before you remove the leaves and stem. If you remove the stem first then wash them, the water will make your strawberries turn mushy. For a salad, serve your strawberries still partially frozen. This gives them body. Or use them in their soft form for recipes like muffins, quick breads, coffee cake, punch, frozen drinks, etc. I've never been able to freeze them so that they are appropriate for strawberry shortcake.

Melons can be frozen also. Ball them or just chop them into bite size pieces. Freeze separately. Set them on a tray without any pieces touching. Freeze them quickly by putting this tray on an empty shelf of your well-stocked freezer. They should be ready to bag in 1-2 hours. Test them to make sure they are indeed hard or solid. Then just pour or scoop them into a plastic bag. Immediately, place them back in the freezer. Melons are best fresh, but are still yummy out of the freezer. They are better if you only allow them to thaw partially.

With a little effort, you can freeze **white potatoes** already prepared for recipes. Potatoes are a food item that can be bought very, very inexpensively in mass quantities. The problem is eating them before they spoil. Go ahead and peel them (or leave them unpeeled), slice them or cube them, then freeze them. Blanching them before freezing helps keep them from browning and keeps them fresher. These potatoes once thawed work very well as mashed potatoes, scalloped potatoes, au gratin, German potato salad, etc. Without rapid freezing techniques it is difficult to premake your French fries; however, try it. Your potatoes will be a bit softer than fresh.

Blanching

With blanching, the boiling stops the maturing process and the ice stops the cooking process. You'll be pleased with the intense colors this process brings out.

To blanch:
Lower the prepared (cut and washed) vegetables into a pan of boiling water. I use a collander to submerge the produce into the water. Allow it to boil for several minutes (e.g., 3-10 minutes). I use a blanching chart from the Ball Corporation (see Appendix C). Move the vegetables to a pan of ice water. Allow it to cool for the same amount of time that it boiled. Then the vegetables are ready for freezing.

Notes:

Orange Potato Swirls

For festive meals, I make orange potato swirls. Slice oranges horizonaly 1/5 of the way down. Scoop out the orange pulp and reserve the juice. These oranges become bowls. Make a batch of creamy white mashed potatoes. Also make a batch of mashed sweet potatoes (I use apple sauce and the reserved orange juice to soften). Double load a pastry bag half (on one side) with the white potatoes, the other half with the sweet potatoes. Squeeze the potatoes through a wide tip into the prepared orange bowls — the pattern with be orange and white swirls. You can make these ahead by freezing the oranges ready to fill or already filled. Bake for 15 minutes in a 350° oven.

Peter, Peter, Pumpkin Eater Seeds

The seeds you scoop out of the pumpkin make a tasty treat. Wash them. Spread them out on a cookie sheet. Sprinkle with your favorite spices (we like to use the same spices as we'd use in a pumpkin pie, some families like salt). Bake them in the oven on a low temperature (250°-300° for 30-45 minutes). They make a good addition to home-made granola mix.]

Pumpkin Pie Custard

For an alternative to the tradional pumpkin pie at Thanksgiving — bake the pumpkin filling in a pie pan without the pastry shell. It bakes the same. Yet, you have just cut approximately 100 calories off a piece of pie (depending on how large of a piece you cut).

Sweet potatoes freeze very well. When they are in season, they are a real buy. They are a wonderful source of fiber and flavor. Peel them, cut them into serving sizes, blanch (5 minutes in boiling water and then 5 minutes in ice water) drain, then freeze in meal size containers. Try using sweet potatoes instead of white potatoes the next time you make "French Fries." [I don't fry them, I bake them in the shape of French fries until crispy.] Also make mashed potatoes with them. It's a welcome change. My family loves sweet potato cakes. Form a cup of mashed potatoes (mash them with apple sauce instead of butter for a healthier dish) into a patty. Freeze enough patties for each member of your family, then separate them with wax paper. Try sweet potatoes in many of your white potato recipes. (e.g., hash "reds" instead of browns) Sweet potatoes are not just for your Thanksgiving dinner.

In the Fall, **pumpkins** are very inexpensive. We buy several large ones in early November, when the stores have marked them down after their big "jack-o-lantern" push. Use a large spoon and scoop out all the seeds. With a very sharp knife, cut up the pumpkin. Be sure to peel off the outer layers. Since I'm going to use my pumpkin just like the pumpkin you might buy in cans, I boil it in a little water until it's soft, mash it, then freeze it in 1-, 2-, and 3-cup containers. I use this pumpkin for pies, muffins, quick breads, even in meatloaves, and for many desserts. To give you an idea of the economics, from two pumpkins ($1 each) we "put-up" enough pumpkin to make 50 pies (or batches of muffins, etc.) Comparing that to the same amount of canned pumpkin, that's a savings of more than $50 for just a few hours work.

If you haven't already been buying bushels of vegetables, it's worth your consideration. You can buy a year's worth of green beans for less than $10 directly from the farmer at a market. A few hours of processing (blanching and freezing) and you'll have quality vegetables for side dishes. Yellow squash, peas, carrots, etc., blanch and freeze well. And, as stated earlier in the book, your vegetables will be healthier frozen so close to picking than if you had bought them during your once-a-week shopping trip and served them six days later.

Have you read the label on your tomato sauce can lately? You might be surprised at how much salt is processed in. While I was pregnant with my second son, I was even more watchful than usual about salt. I didn't consume salt if at all possible. Then one night I had dinner at a friend's house and by the time we prepared to leave, my feet were so swollen that I had to borrow her bedroom slippers to wear home. Trying to put my own shoes on was like the scene in Cinderella when the ugly step-sisters tried to force their huge feet into that dainty slipper. Yet, it was my shoe. What had happened? I had enjoyed seconds of her spaghetti. Yes, she had cooked with canned tomato paste and sauce. The same thing I had done many times. That evening convinced me of the advantages of canning my own tomatoes. I control the salt.

Canning is not difficult. I was a bit apprehensive at first. But once I started canning, I found the rewards outweighed the effort. Since the subject of canning needs an entire book's worth of instructions, I'm not going to go into detail on that process in this book. If you're interested in canning, I highly recommend that you refer to the Ball Blue Book (see Appendix C). However, I have included a beginning canner's recipe for apple butter (see page 17-4).

Salads

You've been cooking for years — think how you could pre-prepare any of your salads. Frozen salads are delicious. By using airtight containers, you can turn your own refrigerator into a salad bar, then assemble the pre-cut veggies in each night's salad. Does your family like gelatin salads? Mine does. They definitely make ahead well. In the recipe section is a frozen salad recipe that my sister makes in September and serves for Thanksgiving dinner. She usually keeps two or three of these in her freezer at all times and grabs one whenever she needs a "covered dish." (See page 16-33.) By having fruit frozen you can make a delicious fruit cup even when fruit is out of season.

Soups

It's healthy. It's a great source of nutrients and fluid. It's a real budget stretcher. It's a delicious use of left-overs. It's an easy way to dress up a dinner. It's soup. Whenever we dine at an oriental restaurant, soup is an automatic part of the dinner. What would a formal dinner party be without a soup course? Yet, how often do we consider adding a soup course to our Tuesday night dinner of meatloaf? Soups freeze well. To save space in the freezer, store it in it's concentrated form. Why freeze 6 cups of water? Do you think soup is only for cold weather? Try it in the summer. Or try a cold soup.

While I was working at Walt Disney World I picked up this trick. Every time I've served this chilled apple soup, I've received raves. Buy the most attractive apples you can find. With a knife, cut a slice off the top. With a spoon (and/or a knife) cut and scoop out the core and center section of the apple. You'll be making a "bowl" out of the apple. Make certain you don't puncture the peeling, you want the outer shell of the apple intact. With the scooped out apple (free of core) make an apple sauce. You might want to add more commercial applesauce. Spice it as you would an apple pie (cinnamon, nutmeg, cloves). Freeze the apples (and their lids, that first slice off the top) until they are hard. Depending on when you'll serve these treats, you can freeze the soup (the applesauce mixture) or just refrigerate it. When it comes time to serve this beautiful and tasty course, remove the frozen apples from the freezer, spoon in the chilled soup (thawed, if previously frozen), top with the lid. Serve immediately. This is very attractive and makes any occasion festive.

Meats

Do you love grilled dinners? If we had the time, I'd want grilled food every night. But we don't have the time or necessarily the weather for this luxury. So whenever we do heat the grill for one meal, we go ahead and grill enough meat for at least two or three more meals. We then freeze the grilled meat until the night we want to

---

Apple Bowl Pudding

Note: to make the "soup" more of a dessert — mix in the following with the applesauce: cornstarch diluted in apple juice, some fructose (or sugar) to taste, and some milk. This will make it like an apple pudding soup. The amounts depend on the size apples you're using, but roughly for six medium-size apples, I'd add in 2 cups of commercial apple sauce, 1/4 cup cornstarch diluted in 1 cup of apple juice, 1/2 cup fructose, 1 cup milk, and spices (1 Tbsp cinnamon, 1 tsp nutmeg, 1 tsp cloves — we like the flavor, you might want to use less). Cook these ingredients until the mixture is thick. Serve same as the soup.

serve it. We thaw the meat and either warm in the oven or the microwave. That wonderful smoked flavor is still there.

Has your husband ever been busy with something else in the yard and let your dinner catch fire? One thing you can do to help prevent that roast from turning into charcoal wrapped around raw meat is to start the cooking ahead of time. Microwave the meat 75% of the way you like it. Then hand it over to "Mr. Chef." He'll only have to grill it the last few minutes. You'll still have that wonderful grilled flavor. However, by microwaving it, you'll be able to cook off most of the fat. It's the fat dripping down that causes the shooting flames that burn your steaks. This pre-cooking saves grill time and will enable you to cook three meals worth of meat with the same coals as you'd use to cook one meal's worth.

Condiments, Spices, Stock Items

Bulk buying can really pay dividends with pantry items. Your condiments (ketchup, mustard, relishes, pickles, etc.) can be bought in large gallon containers. Since my children can't physically carry a gallon jar of salad dressing, we spoon up a little in smaller containers for day-to-day use. Be careful to refrigerate items that need refrigeration. Many prepared mustards don't have to be refrigerated. Read the label, or call the 800 number that is printed on many groceries for proper handling instructions. We buy our rice in 100-lb bags for a per-pound cost that is 1/10th of the per-pound cost of a 2-lb bag. In other words, the 100-lb bag is the same price as five 2-lb bags. Rice stores well. We keep ours in a plastic drum (see page 4-5 & 12-3) out in our garage and just refill the pantry-sized container when needed. We buy our spices in bulk, in restaurant-sized containers.

Once you start exploring the large or industrial-sized container you'll be amazed at the prices. Very often the gallon size is actually cheaper than the smaller size containers. For instance, in one store the #10 can of cling peaches is less than the 15 oz size can (difference also in store-brand vs. name brand). I am often asked, "Where in stores are the big cans?" For some reason, some groceries don't stock their large quantity items next to their smaller can little brothers. You'd think the #10 can of peaches would be next to the 15 ounce can peaches next to the 8 ounce size cans, etc. But some grocers pull all the big cans and boxes and stock them all together on a separate shelf — one shelf of nothing but industrial-size quantities. Don't give up looking in your store. Ask for help. They might take you to an old, out of the way shelf back behind the garden hoses, but the savings will be worth your search. Your hunt will yield a real treasure. Stop thinking of buying just enough food for one week. Be willing to buy enough ketchup for a year. It does cost more at first, but you can have "free" ketchup for nine months of the year (comparing the cost of buying the same quantity in smaller containers). Examine your pantry for items that you could bulk buy for real savings. To give you some more ideas:

- » cornstarch
- » baking soda
- » baking powder
- » yeast (I store it in the refrigerator in an air-tight container)
- » honey
- » B-B-Q sauce
- » salad dressing mix
- » bouillon powder
- » carob powder (or cocoa for you chocoholics)
- » corn meal
- » some flours (rye and oat flours seem to have good shelf life)
- » milk solids (powdered milk)
- » _____
- » _____
- » write your other ideas in the notes column

Last-Minute Helpers

Has this ever happened to you? Sunday in church there's an announcement that after the service that night there will be a fellowship, and all the ladies are asked to bring an entree, a dessert, or a finger food. My Sunday afternoons are special, and

I don't want to spend them cooking. I also don't want to drop by the local grocer's deli section. So this is when planning ahead really helps. Just thaw one of the entrees from the freezer. Grab a loaf of carrot bread. Take ten minutes and bake a "fresh" pie. Or thaw some miniature cream puffs, and stuff either with pudding (for a dessert) or tuna salad (for finger food). Or, are you on the hospitality committee? Punch? Keep a punch base (frozen "slush") in the freezer. Then all you need to add is the juice or soda and you are ready to go.

Breakfast and Lunch

Does your husband leave for work before you get up? Could he take a lunch to work and save that cost? Or are mornings hectic and busy? Why not freeze

---

Quick Label

Save time by not copying down instructions when you are making labels — when you store your supplies in air-tight containers, rip off the box top/front or cut off the instructions and slip them into the container with the food. It serves as the label and keeps the "recipes" with the main ingredient. Example: Cut the back off the pancake mix bag on which the instructions are printed and slide it between the mix and the container side. If you're using a clear container — it will show through and serve as the container label.

Carob

Carob is a wonderful substitute for chocolate. I use it interchangeably with chocolate in recipes. Start weaning yourself off chocolate by substituting carob little by little in your recipes. For instance, we make hot carob instead of hot cocoa. Your body will appreciate the fewer calories and less caffeine.

Supfast?

Have you ever fixed breakfast for supper? On a Sunday night or a weeknight, my family loves a pancake or French toast dinner. They think it's a special treat. AND it fits right in with my "restful" Sunday evening.

breakfast and a "bag" lunch ahead? Try breakfast treats like pancakes, waffles, coffee cakes. Many lunchbox items freeze well and thaw between morning and lunchtime. Many sandwiches (of course, no lettuce or mayonnaise), fresh cut and frozen vegetables (e.g. carrot sticks), and/or home-made T.V. dinners (if he has access to a microwave unit) freeze well.

My attitude was not loving. I flopped down the "sandwich" on the table. "Here's your lunch," I muttered. I was full of resentment. I didn't think my parent's rule that if mother wasn't home, I had to fix lunch was fair. I only had twenty minutes for lunch before I had to get back to my next class at high school. My brother, however, had an hour before he had to get back to his job. I was wondering why he couldn't fix his own sandwich. Then, Gary asked a question that transformed my attitude for the rest of my life. As he lifted up the two dry slices of bread and looked at the single slab of baloney, he said, "There's no love in this sandwich. Where's the love?" He was right. I had served him two slices of animosity wrapped around a slab of selfishness. That sandwich didn't even have a teaspoon full of love in it.

Gary could teach Dagwood Bumstead what a sandwich is. Mom would just put a little of this and a lot of that on his sandwiches — a C.O.R.D. sandwich. It took time, interest in him, and a knowledge of what he liked. She made love sandwiches.

I picked up this unlovely sandwich and went in the kitchen and filled his sandwich with "love."

My mother had always made mealtime a delight. The main ingredient in every meal was love. She made lunch an island of joy in a rough sea of a day. While many of our peers chose to lunch at fast-food joints, all of us chose to drive home. Not only would we receive proper food, but we'd be re-fueled with encouragement, enthusiasm, and hugs.

I remember one day when I was ill and home from school, I noticed for the first time what my mother's days were really like. She'd wake up early. She'd prepare wonderful breakfasts for all seven of us over a span of two hours as we would head off to school or work. Then she'd work on laundry — mountains of smelly, stained clothes. She'd vacuum between handling loads of wet clothes. Then, just when she'd have a minute to herself, the first lunch wave hit. Again, during a span of two hours, she'd prepare lunches for all of us rushing in and out. As I lay on the couch, I was startled to see one of my sister's friends pop in for lunch. My sister wasn't even there. This girl knew that our home was open and that she was welcome. My mom prepared her a lunch and served her a side order of compassion. Mom's afternoon was even busier. She did, admittedly, take a break. Her doctor had ordered her to take "ten." She'd set a timer for ten minutes and lay down with her feet elevated, but as soon as the alarm rang, she was up and going again. I remember that day clearly. Before that day, I had thought she led a life of leisure, of luncheons, of showers, of circle meetings, of ladies' clubs, and of shopping trips.

One thing that always amazed me about my mother was her behavior with my dad. Maybe that's why they're still in love with each other after more than forty years. No matter what she was doing, no matter where she was — she could be in the middle of rolling out pastry, she could be in the middle of a telephone conversation, she could be hip-high in a craft project, no matter — five minutes before my dad was going to be coming through the door, she'd go to her room, comb through her hair, put on fresh lipstick, change her dress, make herself physically and emotionally beautiful before greeting him at the door. The rest of the evening our home was filled with joy.

So whatever you choose to serve for breakfast and lunch (AND dinner), be sure to include **love** on the menu.

Collecting Ideas

Collect your ideas from everywhere.

Get ideas from the freezer department at your local grocer. If "they" can freeze it, so can you.

Notice how and what restaurants are serving. You can gather ideas for presentation of food, food combining, and techniques. With a little experimentation you can adapt these creations for your home.

I have never met a lady that isn't complimented when you ask her for a recipe. Think about yourself. If you invited a friend for dinner would you feel honored if she asked you for your secret? It's a true compliment. It seems not only polite, but smart. You'll be receiving a proven recipe — one that you know you like.

What you can do with this program is simply up to you. If you don't like tuna, use salmon, or shark or whatever. But try.

Examine your own life and consider ways you can streamline your work, budget, and supplies to economize and utilize your equipment.

Along with the idea of adding love to your menu, in Chapter Fifteen, we'll look at the gift of hospitality. We'll also examine some household management helps and some holiday celebrating ideas in Chapter Eighteen.

🍐 *Distributing to the necessity of saints; given to hospitality. — Romans 12:13 (KJV)*

🍐 *Use hospitality one to another without grudging. — 1 Peter 4:9 (KJV)*

CHAPTER FIFTEEN

Practicing Hospitality

The savory smell of Mama White's home cooking traveled throughout the white frame house and shady yard. The large country-styled kitchen was the hub of activity, with Mama White directing traffic. Aunt Ginny was kneading the creamy-colored bread dough on the floured table which creaked with each downward thrust. Aunt Bettie was occupied with the rumbling electric mixer's churning of the creamery butter and sugar that was to add the final touches to the red velvet cake cooling in the window sill; but she was not too occupied to slap the hand of the little one whose finger had a glob of stolen icing on it. Two of the grandchildren darted through the screen door, leaving it to bang shut, and raced through the obstacles of the busy aunts. Then they sped into the dining room, knocking into Aunt Charlotte and sending all the silverware which she was carrying to the floor. The children halted with fear in their eyes upon hearing the crash and bam! They stooped to help the irritated aunt collect the spoiled utensils. She marched them straight to the white enamel sink, where they remained until every last spoon, fork, and knife was washed and dried and their silver surface shone.

The radio crackled as Uncle Walt twisted the knob, trying to get the afternoon's football game. Several uncles sat on the comfortable chintz furniture in the airy living room, browsing through that morning's paper. Uncle Billy, who had the comic section, nudged Uncle Bill C. and pointed to "Peanuts," and they both roared with laughter. On the large covered front porch Aunt Ula and some nieces sat in the creaking gliders snapping and shelling peas, fresh from the garden.

The side yard was dominated by a capacious oak tree which already contained ten grandchildren racing among its wide, sturdy limbs. Cousin Kenny scrambled up the ladder leaning against the enormous gnarled trunk of the tree, while Cousin Clark, with a howl of pure delight, leaped to straddle the sack swing. The dried moss in the croaker sack squeaked as his weight forced the swing out and away from the "launching pad." As the rope grew taunt, the powerful limb drooped, sending vibrating impulses to the tiny branches further down and causing the leaves to quiver, as if in delight with the joy it was giving the slim boy. As the swing completed its arc, the frolicking boy caromed off and ran to the rustic ladder for his next ride. As the swing neared the tree on its return flight, another whoop was heard as Cousin Debbie leaped out into the air. Daddy White, amid adoring grandchildren, went about the mundane task of choosing mouth-watering strawberries in the two-acre garden, in such a manner that caused it to appear absolutely fascinating to his wide-eyed audience.

As a load of late-comers rattled up the dirt drive, Mama White, wiping her floury hands on her crisp apron, rushed to the back porch to greet them. The four doors flew open as the occupants simultaneously tumbled out to go through the informal receiving line. Everyone hustled to greet the newest arrivals with hugs and kisses and, "Boy, how you've grown's." Suddenly, a squeal from the kitchen rang out over the happy talk in the yard. Cousin Diane shouted, "The potatoes are boiling over!" Aunt Eloise rushed to the rescue.

Beyond the drive under a clump of oaks, Uncle Clyde and Uncle Jack relieved each other turning the hand crank on the ice cream freezer, spewing slivers of ice on the grass smelling freshly mown. Nearby two large watermelons bobbed in an old galvanized wash tub, while Cousin David jabbed at them with a twig.

Moochie, our tiny dog, ran yelping through the stacks of corrugated drainage pipe stored nearby with the neighbors' cat in hot pursuit. Cousin Paul called encouragements to the dog and joined in the chase. Cousins Mark, Gary, Kim, and Steve had a rambunctious game of "King of the Mountain" going on top of the pipe. In the middle of the yard, a horseshoe sailed through the air and fell with a clunk upon contact with the old, rusty iron stake. Dad and Uncle Tom had won their third game in a row. Uncle Bill M. flung his arms in the air in a futile gesture of defeat, and ambled off shaking his head; then suddenly with inspiration, he hollered, "Baseball anyone?" And from everywhere relatives emerged and ran to the clay road to get the game started. The first ball fouled into Mama White's prize croton bush. All the players froze as they saw Mama White step on the back porch with the dinner bell.

Do you have some similar wonderful memories? I hope so. I'm convicted about what I'm doing or not doing to give my own children similar memories.

As we studied in Chapter Seven, the Lord knows that meal time is a very teachable time for us. It can be a joyous time. For proper digestion, it must be a happy, peaceful time.

Don't save the "parties" just for guests. Throw a themed dinner party for "just" your family. Treat your children as guests. Invite your husband to a special evening. All the suggestions that follow for dinner parties, decorating, etc., can also be used for your "regular" nights at home.

Welcome

How do you make your guests feel welcome? Just by being in that mind set of wanting to make them feel welcome is the right start. If your mind is on how well **you**'re going to do, how good **your** home looks, how good **your** food tastes, chances are excellent that **your** guest will be uncomfortable. But if your mind is set on how **they** are going to enjoy the evening, how comfortable **they** will find your home, how much **they** might enjoy eating, you'll be well on your way. Don't be concerned about what they are going to think of you. Don't think of you. Think of them.

There are many things you need to do before offering hospitality by a dinner party, be it for one or fifty. Give yourself as much time as you need to plan ahead. Sometimes you only have minutes to prepare for company, so the more time you've spent thinking through hostessing concepts, the easier it'll be. The more often you do entertain company, the easier it becomes. Practicing hospitality makes perfect. What follows are a few ideas that you might want to consider, followed by an example.

The Theme

You don't have to adopt a theme for the evening, but it can help make your planning easier and more fun. Don't choose something too complicated or too difficult. It may be as simple as a picnic theme, or as elaborate as a black-tie dinner. But make it fit your family's style. We've had immense fun with themes. Using themes need not cost any extra money. We often make decorations with construction paper.

We collect ideas for themes from everywhere. Here are just a few theme ideas:

- » Hobo dinner: Eat off tin plates. Use newspapers for table cloths. Use rags for napkins. Serve bread baked in cans, etc.)
- » Black-tie dinner: Use your best china and silver. Dress in your best clothes. Decorate with tuxedo-styled decorations (easy to make with

"Air Assault and Pepper"

Do you like international recipes? We do. There's something about trying to duplicate the food of a country to make it "real" for our geography lessons. In addition to the cookbooks labeled international, look at garage sales, etc. for military wives' cookbooks. These books are full of the recipes these wives have collected from living all over the world. And many of the wives are from other nations and add a taste of their own culture.

See Appendix D for information on ordering the cookbook written by the Officers Wives' Club of Fort Campbell, KY. It is named "Air Assault and Pepper" in honor of the 101st Division.

black and white paper). Then, in your best tureen, serve beans and franks.

» Travel log: This is our favorite. We visit a particular country for the evening. So far, we've "visited" Japan, Germany, England, the Middle East, Mexico, and Latin America without ever leaving the dining room. We coordinated these meals with our homeschool studies.

» Progressive dinner: Instead of progressing from house to house we progress from room to room. This works well when you have a small house and many guests. Use one of your children's rooms for a make-your-own nametag greeting place. (Supply with markers, and other art supplies.) Serve the appetizers in your son's room, the salad in your daughter's, the main course in the dining room, and the dessert in the living room. Each time we do this, the families enjoy it — especially the children.

» Celebrate the state where your guests are from. Serve home-state food. If you have many guests, seat them according to geographical region. Give them name tags the shape of their home-state. This is really fun and keeps conversations going, especially if you're going to have guests that don't know each other.

» Make your own kabob party. Set up buffet-style bowls with all sorts of different shish kabob fixings (pineapple, pepper, meat, onion, etc.) and have your guests involved in making their own kabob. Then head for the grill to cook it.

» Make your own pizza party. Similar to the kabob party, but give each guest his own pizza pan or plate already prepared with the dough and let them top it any way they choose.

» A trip to the sea is another way to be creative. Decorate with sea shells and serve fish. Use clam shells as plates.

» Have an indoor picnic. Spread the cloth out on the living room floor and serve picnic food out of a basket. This is particularly welcome in January.

» Obviously, work with the holidays and observances. We recently had a party on Flag Day and used flags as the theme.

I'll stop here. Theme ideas alone could fill a book.

The Invitation

Expressing that sense of WELCOME starts with the invitation. People can hear the genuineness in your voice. Are you asking them because you feel obligated to or because you truly want them over to your home? Pray before you call for the love of the Lord to shine through. During this call, ask if any of your guests have any allergies or special medical needs. This can really help you with planning your menu. There's nothing like serving coconut pie to someone that's allergic to coconut to remind you to ask next time about medical conditions. Ask if there's anything else you could do to make them more comfortable. One of the world's best hostesses in my opinion, Betty Kearney, keeps a highchair for her guests with small children, though her children are grown. When your youngest child outgrows your highchair, you might want to think about keeping it for use when you entertain young families.

Written invitations aren't just for parties. Use a blank notecard and mail it to reconfirm the up-coming dinner with a family. It adds to the idea that you're looking forward to the dinner and that they are indeed special. This is also an excellent lesson in etiquette for your children. Teach them the proper wording. Let them create their own invitation.

Menu Planning

Planning the menu need not be difficult. Let your theme work for you. Listen for your guests' favorite meals. While I was pregnant with my first child, my husband was talking to his mother, "Oh, she's doing better today. She's eating bell peppers with blueberry yogurt." [It tasted delicious at the time.] It was just a comment. But my mother-in-law, Virginia, noticed it. The next time we visited her, she had purchased blueberry yogurt and bell peppers to make me feel welcome. I thought that was very considerate. That was true hospitality.

Decorating

Since you've saved time in the kitchen by having dinner in the freezer, spend a little more in the dining room setting a special mood. Think a minute about restaurants and how much fun the atmosphere is. With very little cost you can decorate your table with a theme. For example, we use a red checker table cloth for spaghetti meals. It transforms our room into an Italian restaurant. Make it a memory.

A simple thing like lighting a candle can transform a routine meal into a treat. My boys ask for candlelight dinners. There's something about low light and a flickering flame to calm down a hectic day.

You don't have to invest in fresh, professionally-arranged flowers for your dinner. Be creative and use items you already have on hand.

Let your children make the centerpiece for your table setting. Take them around the yard and pick flowers and leaves (ferns) and let THEM arrange them in a vase. Or let them pick a figurine from around the house to decorate the table. This idea from my sister has helped involve our children, but also makes them feel special about their own abilities and about being a valuable member of the family. Don't just make centerpieces for company dinner, make it for a family dinner. For example, use some camping equipment as the center-piece and serve hiker-friendly food (grilled meat, pot of beans, dried fruit, etc.). You can have fun with a camping theme for dinner.

Do you ever go to garage sales, flea markets, or bargain houses? Whenever I do, I look for "themed" dishes to add atmosphere to my table settings. For instance, a black enamel bowl for Oriental meals, an old-fashioned crock pot for beans, a tropical-styled dish/plate for Polynesian meals, an "Old World" bowl for goulash, etc. Many of my special, mood-setting dishes were purchased for about one dollar each.

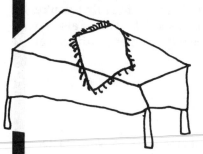

A low-budget way to add flair and variety to your table settings is by dressing up your classic solid-colored table cloth with a yard square of fabric with hemmed or frayed edges depending on the formality desired. I look on the bargain table at the cloth store, and can pick up remnants for a dollar or two. A Scottish plaid, an African print, a bright primary-colored print, or a dainty rose print draped at the diagonal over a solid-colored cloth can change the look of your whole table setting.

This next hint may sound formal, but really it's more fun than formal. My sister, Kay, a very creative lady, gave me the idea and we've been using her inspiration ever since. We like to make place cards for just us and for company meals. It's amazing how special a dinner guest feels with his own place card. Many times it's a "school project." A folded-over piece of white cardboard with a sticker, a drawing, a cut-out, or an artificial flower works well. It's a little thing, but it can make a quick dinner just sparkle or make a special dinner shine even more. Again, involve your children. Entertaining/hospitality is not something just Mommy and Daddy do.

Even young children can set the table. It becomes a math lesson when counting out "X" number of spoons. Besides, many children can benefit with reinforcement of lesson about learning systems, order, etiquette, and practice in discerning right from left.

My boys (Bethany's too young to help now) love to turn our home into "Chez Bond," a restaurant extraordinaire. They pretend to be waiters, hosts, and bus boys. Reed drapes a dish cloth over his forearm and writes down our "orders." Stuart balances trays of food. Trent struggles with my chair. It is excellent training for them in servanthood and in manners. Though we practice strict table manners in our home, it never hurts to add restaurant eating practice to our training.

Addressing the other senses

Decorating addresses the eye-gate. But what about the ear-gate? We've been slowly collecting dinner music. I rummage through racks of records at bargain houses to find international records. Many areas of the world have distinctive music styles. Movie makers have used this technique of music filler to set the mood even before "talkies" by employing organ music to add atmosphere. We have Hawaiian, Italian, German, etc., records that add background music for the evening. Put on a classical album. Set up a Christian tape. You'll notice the difference.

I really notice smells, do you? The smell of fresh bread baking is one of the most wonderful smells on earth. While some people like the smell of a new car, I much prefer the smell of a new baby. Smell is something that is rarely noticed when it's pleasant. Oh, but when it's NOT pleasant, everyone will notice. We all know the smell of something burnt. Some of us more than others. It can ruin the "taste" of even good food. Clear the air quickly — run your exhaust; open the door; set a little pot of boiling water on the stove and drop in a few drops of lemon extract/juice, cinnamon sticks/oil, or your favorite spice; microwave or bake an apple.

The nursery smell was getting to me, so I purchased one of those room scent enhancers that are advertised on television. After several days of horrible migraines, we finally tracked it down to the potpourri-maker in the nursery. We threw it away and within an hour my headache was gone. It was artificial. Forced. Phony. Contrived. I've learned that lesson, and now use only natural solutions as mentioned in the previous paragraph and by keeping the negative smells down in the first place. One product, we regularly use is our Rainbow cleaning system[1] to clean the air.

What to wear?

Have you ever attended a party over-dressed? Or under-dressed? It's horrible. The invitation stated that Alan should wear his dress uniform and four-in-hand tie which is equivalent to a tuxedo in civilian wear. From my up-bringing, combined with etiquette books and military protocol books, my attire should be formal (long skirt) since the party was after five. I was looking forward to my first reception as Alan's new bride. I worked for hours making a black satin, full, floor-length skirt to go with my black satin blouse. It would be stunning — basic black and pearls. His brigade commander was having a Christmas reception at his home. That evening, Alan looked dashing in his uniform. I straightened my hair, lifted my skirt to go through their door. The first thing I noticed was that all the other wives were

in street length dresses, regular dresses, not even party clothes. I wanted to hide. The Colonel's wife greeted me that minute with a smile and compliment on my dress. I couldn't turn and hide in the car. What had I done wrong? It was after five wasn't it? I found out that all the wives had gotten together at their last meeting (before I had joined the group) and "voted" not to wear formal clothes, but just street clothes. No one had told me. My hostess went out of her way to assure me that I had dressed correctly. But I still felt odd.

If you want to give a semi-formal dinner, tell your guests. If you want to throw a hoe-down-style dinner, tell your guests. When we have theme dinners we sometimes even wear costumes, or theme dressing. For instance, I bought a dress from Mexico at a garage sale for 50 cents and wear it sometimes when we have chili. I have a dress that conjures up the image of Western Europe and wear it for some meals. Our children love to dress in their church clothes for dinner, so Alan leaves his suit on from work, I'll don an old long dress and we have a delightful time. While another night it might be shorts and bare feet for a casual dinner. Then, of course, their are those nights we have come-as-you are feasts.

The day of the dinner

This is the most important "hint" I want to share with you. The most crucial preparation you can do for your family meals, and/or hospitality times, is praying over your home. Start at the doorway and walk through your home. Do some Spiritual cleaning. Ask the Lord to bless your guest and your family. Ask Him to permeate each room, each conversation, and each thought. I'd rather have a spirit of peace fill my home, and dinner a little late, than strife and a magazine-cover-table-setting. Proverbs 17:1…

"Better is a dry morsel, and quietness therewith, than an house full of sacrifices [prime rib] *with strife."* (KJV)

Sample Dinner

Before our Bethany was born, Reed and Stuart planned this dinner party for a couple of our friends. We had been studying the country of Germany, so we turned out our own Oktoberfest. We called and invited this couple, then followed it up with an invitation the boys made. They colored a Bavarian-theme picture on the front of a card and we had fun writing the words:

DOS JONES (Not their last name)

ARE WILKOMMEN

DOS KUM

UND ENJOY

DOS FRIENDFEST

(DATE)

AT THE HAUS OF THE VON BOND'S

DA KIDDERS WOLFGANG (REED), HANS (STUART) UND CLAUSE(TRENT) ARE READY TO OOMPAH!!

They made decorations out of construction paper including posters of the German flag and pictures of children in traditional German clothing. We used the colors of the German flag for the tablecloth and napkins (red, yellow, and black). They made place cards and napkin-ring decorations. The boys dressed in shorts with suspenders, knee socks and dress shoes. They looked the part. We served German potato salad, Rinderrouladen (beef), Himmel und erde (potatoes) and for dessert, a Black Forest cake. We put on an album of Bavarian music. The boys tried to speak with German accents and remembered several German words. It was a fun evening.

Being the Guest

"You served Jim Travis cheesecake?" my friend said astonished. "Wow, you must have a wonderful recipe."

"No, I replied, I just used one of those mixes," I answer sheepishly.

"I guess you didn't know, Jim is famous for his cheesecake. He's won awards for his speciality," she tells me.

I think back to when we had Jim and his wife, Carra for dinner. Not once did they give the slightest indication that my feeding mix cheesecake was anything out of the ordinary. They ate it and even said it was delicious. That's like Horowitz complimenting a first year piano player's "Chopsticks."

When you entertain guests like that, it's their gentility that makes the evening a success. An intricate part of being an enjoyable hostess is your being a gracious guest.

I appreciate the lesson on humbleness that the Travis' taught me that evening.

Bring Home the Meaning

Attach meaning to your meals. I've written up background stories for my recipes. The children love to hear them over and over again. By ascribing a narrative or a history to your oft-repeated meals, your children gain a sense of continuity, family, and specialness. It makes even a Tuesday evening meal more than just calorie consumption. It makes it a time to bond together as a family.

Share with your children the stories, the lives, and the memories that you have when you serve your grandmother's recipe in the tureen that your aunt gave you for a wedding present. You'll never be at a loss for dinner conversation. The emphasis isn't on the material good, but on the love and thoughtfulness of the gift. For instance, I have a lovely silver butter dish that's been in my family since the 1800s. My boys love to hear stories, and imagine all the places that piece has been. Their ancestors were using it for butter even before there was electricity! Think of

Christmas in June

Dinnertime is a wonderful time to read those letters from friends and relatives. Pick a Christmas card and letter from a dear friend and re-read it on hot nights in June.

the history lessons: the years it might not have been used because of shortages of butter (e.g. wars, the depression). It is round with a section for ice, then a glass tray for the butter. Great, great, great, great grandmother didn't have a refrigerator.

If you don't know many stories about your family, there's no better time than now to start collecting them. Time goes so fast, and before we know it, these stories get lost. Next time you visit your great aunt, record (tape, camcord, or write) her stories.

If everything you have is modern, first generation to you, you still have stories of who gave them to you and the occasion of the gift. For instance, my mother dropped the entire stack of her wedding china plates while she was a newlywed. She was left with only the serving pieces. So we always heard the now hilarious story of how dad found out about the accident. She was serving dinner for some company, when Dad came in and asked her why she had set the table with the everyday dishes. She had been meaning to tell him about that. . . . You have stories, too. Dredge them up. Give your children a sense of belonging — belonging to something very unique — your family!

Dine Together

"Tell us, tell us, what was it like at Jill's house?" our dorm-mates surrounded Linda (not her real name) as we returned from our weekend trip to my home. I decided a weekend home would be nice so I invited a friend down the hall to join me because tension on campus flourished after Ted Bundy attacked a sorority near campus in 1978. We had had what I considered a normal weekend. My family members were their usual selves. My mother didn't do anything out of the ordinary for us.

"It was wonderful. They eat together just like in the sorority house — table manners and everything! Like in the movies with china and silver and all. They were polite to each other. They talked to each other and there wasn't even a television on," she says with the words pouring out of her mouth at a rapid pace. The others are asking questions, fascinated.

I dragged my suitcase to my room trying to clear my head. What had we done differently? We were just who we were. Then I thought about my friend. Her parents were divorced. She lived with her mother who worked. She only ate "formally," as she called it, for Christmas dinner.

"Her mother even wore an apron when she was in the kitchen," I heard as I started to unpack. The response from the others in the dorm was both upsetting and reassuring. I was reassured and comfortable that my family was intact, happy, and loving. We like each other. I was upset because I realized that even back then (late seventies), I was a rarity. I was from a family that ate their meals together.

I started reflecting on other families I knew and visited. One family I dined with often ate every meal off T.V. trays with the T.V. set blaring. In one family, the mother left the pots on the stove and everyone dished up their plates and ate when they felt like it. They ate with their father at the table maybe once a month. Another family had gone so far as to build a house that had two separate living areas. One for the children and one for the father — the mother spanned both. The father would live in his area. The children were only allowed in the living room and the dining room on Christmas day! She was to have them all fed and out of sight so that he and she could dine in peace later in the evening. All the children of these families would love to dine at our house, even to the point of inviting themselves over.

It alarms me how dinner-time has faded out of American life. It's been replaced with "soup for one," the evening news or syndicated re-runs, drive-thru windows, and dinette tables (without leaves for expanding for extra seating).

Mealtime can be special, even the best time of the day. As wife and mother, you can do so much to add to the joy of this time.

I had one friend who's father had a policy I admired. If I mistakenly called during their reserved dinner hour, he would answer **all** phone calls politely, but firmly, "Hello. We're dining now. Please call back after 7:30." Nowadays, we have our answering machine to catch the calls during dinner. It's our commitment to our family. Otherwise, we'd rarely dine together. One of us would be on the phone chatting. If you don't have an answering machine, would you be willing to turn the ringer off? If it's important, they will call back. And if your area is anything like ours, we average 10-15 calls a week from telephone solicitors trying to sell us everything from vinyl siding to bowling memberships. They invariably call during dinner. I don't want them interrupting my husband's story of how his day went or our children's report of their day in school.

Decorating with Flare

Remember balance. I look to my parents as an example of this. She's an artist. He's an inventor.[2] She looks for aesthetics. He looks for function. I remember his grand idea of rigging the sprinkler system up through the bird bath. The bird's loved it. It saved water. It kept her lovely rose garden gently watered. Functionally, it was wonderful. Aesthetically, it was downright odd. Her lovely rose garden's harmony was contrasted with this PVC pipe sticking out of her porcelain bird bath. I remember her lovely cuckoo clock from Germany that had stopped and was irreparable. She kept it hanging in the living room for its decoration. Dad thought

this was illogical, so he gutted it, nailed it to a tree, and so turned it into a bird feeder. The Lord knew what He was doing when He paired these two together. I have joked with them that if Mom was to buy a chair, it would be the most beautiful chair she could find, but not comfortable. Dad would choose the most comfortable chair available, but it would be ugly. But by using the strengths God has given each of them, they have developed a wonderful blend of beauty and function. Through more than forty years of marriage, they have worked together to produce both functional and lovely homes, projects, and products. Likewise, look for a balance in maintaining your home. Comfort is a mixture of beauty and function. Make your home comfortable.

Why decorate for someone else? It's your family that lives there 24 hours a day. If you like navy, but aqua is the "in" color this year, use navy. Magazines are filled with beautiful ideas for decorating. If you like variety, use themed party ideas, or decorate for the season. The simpler the decoration, the easier you can adapt the setting. Some wall and window decorations are so elaborate that if you used anything but a white tablecloth with them, the walls would scream in pain. When you are designing your rooms, keep in mind how you want to use them. If you want to only use one tablecloth in your dining room, then the matching wallpaper, curtains, and carpeting will look beautiful. But how will your Christmas decorations work in the same room? Just remember how you are going to USE the room rather than how you want the room to appear. Balance.

"God! Amen!"

"Thank you for dinner, Lord. Thank you for the rolls. Thank you for the chicken. Thank you for . . ." Reed was praying — then nothing — just silence. I peeked up from my folded hands and saw Reed moving his food around on his plate. "Fourteen peas. Thank you for potatoes . . ." he continued on.

I learn so much from my children's prayers. We had a very dear friend who had diabetes. Every time we visited home and saw her, she'd captivate Reed with her stories. He loved her dearly. I received a prayer request that her kidney transplant from several years ago had gone awry and that they needed another donor. I explained it to my young children. Reed was especially concerned about his dear friend, Miss Brenda. Every meal, every time he prayed, he'd add in "And Lord, Miss Brenda needs a new "ken-dee." Would you please give her one?" This prayer went on for months. Then we received the phone call that Miss Brenda had died. How was I going to tell my children? I knew the next mealtime, Reed would be praying for her. I was fighting back the tears as I pulled him on my lap and told of Miss Brenda. "Then God answered my prayer," he said. "She has her new ken-dee now."

Mrs. Doty, our toddler's Sunday School teacher, pulled me aside and said. "Stuart's talking. He said three words, 'Jesus, sister, amen.'" His first three words together and he asks the Lord for a sister. "Just thought you'd like to know," she says with twinkle in her eyes. I smile and say I'd like that one answered, too. (God answer was evident — Bethany Kay.)

I can't think of anything that can make or break an enjoyable dinner than beginning it with prayer. We pray before all our meals, even before snacktime, and even in restaurants. We hold hands, bow our heads and pray. We've had waiters/waitresses interrupt our prayer, not even knowing what we were doing. We've had waiters/waitresses thank us for renewing their faith. We've been questioned and have received some looks. My favorite was when I heard a lady say to her husband, "See that family praying? Remember when we used to do that?"

Sometimes the children pray, sometimes we all pray, sometimes only Alan speaks. But we acknowledge Who provided the meal and ask Him to make it nourishing (with some meals it's more of a miracle than others). Sometimes we pray for other requests, but always for any guests.

Alan and I keep well abreast of the news and discuss current events with our children. I shouldn't have been surprised when our boys tacked on a P.S. to our evening prayer one night, "Lord, please do a miracle in General Noriega's life." That prayer convicted me. We had lived in "his" country and had seen first hand some of the horror of his reign. I wanted him to "get his" after Operation Just Cause. I had not been praying for his spirit. But the boys had learned the lessons we were teaching them well (even if I, the teacher hadn't) about prayer. Throughout Operations Desert Shield and Desert Storm they prayed the same prayer for Saddam Hussein. You can imagine their thrill when we read in the news about Noriega's profession to faith. Since then their prayer list has expanded dramatically.

All of our children are learning that prayer is an integral part of life. Not just before the meal. They even ask during the meal if they can pray to say thanks. They pray after the meal. They pray throughout the day.

Prayers don't have to be memorized. I think they're more "real" if they're not. Yet, my father says the same prayer that his father stated before every meal and probably his father before him. The Lord knows its meaning even though He's heard it thousands of times before. Encourage your children to branch out into their own wording. Please don't teach them that prayers have to rhyme.

I still admire my son Stuart's prayer when he was a little guy. He had down all the essential elements of a great prayer. When his daddy asked if he'd like to say the dinner prayer for us, he said in his "deep voice" and with as much sincerity, enthusiasm, and animation as anyone could muster, "God! Amen!"

Average can (or other containers) categories

#10 can	Net wt. approximately 6 to 7 pounds
#2-1/2 can	Net wt. approximately 3 1/2 cups
#2 can	Net wt. approximately 2 1/2 cups
Standard or regular soup can	10-3/4 ounces
Family size or large soup can	26 ounces
Extra large can of soup (ready to serve)	50 ounces

I have purposely not filled this chart in so you can customize it with the stables, cans, sizes available in your area, and with your preference as to brands. Filling this in will help you when making out your lists for multiple amounts. For instance, you might want to write down the sizes that mushrooms come in.

Part IV

Recipes

Introduction and Notes

In my collection of recipe books (now more than 70), the formats, styles, and presentations of recipes are so varied and different. Some give so little information that you have to guess your way through it. Some give such detail that they tell you how to boil the egg. Some use double-talk or are confusing — "Add the egg. Before you add the egg, mix in the flour." Don't you just love the "cook until done" directions? What does that mean — 10 or 50 minutes?

Here, true to form, in recipe-ese, are some of the recipes we use in our "Dinner's in the Freezer!" method organized in different formats:

>   a) Suggestions/hints for ubiquitous entrees. (You already know how to make meatloaf.)

>   b) Entrees presented in dual form — as given to me and adapted. (This is done as an example for you. You can compare the two styles as you learn to re-write your own recipes.)

>   c) Entrees using the worksheet format. (We are purposely not printing all the multiples and conversion amounts. This is so you can write in the conversion amounts according to the size, volume and/or weight amounts available to you. Or, in other words, so you can personalize the recipes.)

>   d) Basic recipes for you to multiply according to the size of your family. Some will be noted if they are best made one at a time.

WARNING: DO NOT use any of the recipes in this book without first reading the explanations and text of this book.

The list of recipes is printed on the following pages.

Recipes Listing

Chapter 16: Freezer Recipes
A Word or Two on:
Ground meat recipes:
Goushed meats 16- 1
Cooked ground meat 16- 2
Other meals:
Chicken 'n Dumplings 16- 2
Lentil Soup 16- 2
Stir-fry 16- 2
Chicken Cordon Bleu 16- 3

Entrees:
Aunt Eloise's Casserole 16- 4
Mrs. Thomas' Casserole 16- 5
Super-Grandma's 3-bean Casserole 16- 6
Turkey Mandarin 16- 8
Sweet 'n Sour Meatballs 16- 9
Miss Betty's Tuna Casserole 16-11
Shrimp Jambalaya 16-12
Evan's Mom's Casserole 16-13
Y'all Soup 16-14
Ahoy Dinner 16-15
Harvest Fest 16-16
Chuckwagon 16-17
Mount Vernon Pie 16-18
Curry Turry or Great Scott Casserole 16-19
Speckled Rice 16-20
Kay's Broccoli & Corn Casserole 16-20
Swiss Steak 16-21
Crab Newburg 16-22
Almost Plum Nearly 16-23
Red Square 16-24
Kielbasa Amore 16-25
Spring Chicken 16-26

Side Dishes:
Zucchini or Carrot Bread/Muffins 16-27
Cookies Anytime 16-28
Pastry 16-29
Tidbit Cream Puffs 16-30
English Muffins 16-31
Panama Punch 16-32
Gator Bowl Salad 16-33
Frozen Cranberry Salad 16-33
Pudding Pops 16-34
Crazy Carrot Cake 16-35
Balmy Breezes Pie 16-36
Healthier than Thou Fruitcake 16-37
Home-made Tortillas 16-38

Chapter 17: Quick Recipes and Easy Recipes

Quick-as-a-wink Coconut Pie 17- 1
Quick Monkey Bread 17- 2
Bread Dough Ideas 17- 2
Quick Quiche 17- 3
Fruity Tuity Stuffing 17- 3
Deb's Dip 17- 4
Shawberry Dip 17- 4
Apple Butter 17- 4
Pizza Bread 17- 5
Lemon Sauce 17- 6
Dragon Sauce 17- 6
Fool Proof Sweet 'n Sour 17- 7
Graham Crackers 17- 7
Wassail 17- 8
Merry Pop-ins 17- 8
Master Mix 17- 9
Dough Enhancer 17-10
Grace's Treats 17-10

Chapter 18: Extras and Whole Home Management

Personal Care 19- 1
    Models' Facial 18- 2
    Nail Treatment 18- 2
    Soap Management 18- 2
    Hair Care 18- 2
    Miscellaneous Personal Care 18- 3
Children's Projects/Gifts 18- 4
    Children's Modeling Clay 18- 4
    Easy-bake Clay 18- 5
    Scented Soap Balls 18- 5
    Cinnamon-Applesauce Ornaments 18- 6
    Gift Ideas 18- 6
Money Laundering 18-10
    Soap, Suds, and Duds 18-11
    Wrinkles Beware 18-12
    Scheduling 18-13
    The Immaculate Order of Perpetual Folding 18-13
    Mending 18-14
Health Manners 18-15
    Diaper Rash 18-15
    Diarrhea Treatment 18-16
    Swimmer's Ear Treatment 18-16
    Sore Throat Gargle 18-16
"Mom, where's my _____? 18-17
    Control or KAOS 18-17
    The First Mate's Log 18-19
Mrs. Clean 18-20
Wrap-up 18-21

Index of Bonus Recipes, Tips and Explanations

More or Less 16- 3
Buying a Whole Side of Beef 16- 7
Easy Egg Drop Soup 16-10
Idea for Homeschoolers 16-13
Poultry Sauce 16-23
Fire Engines 16-24
Cooking Spray 16-28
Florida Cracker Lemonade 16-32
Banana Split Salad 16-37
Cake Cones 16-38
Average Can Categories 15-14
Brown Away 14- 3
Peter, Peter, Pumpkin Eater Seeds 14- 4
Orange Potato Swirls 14- 4
Pumpkin Pie Custard 14- 4
Apple Bowl Pudding and Chilled Apple Soup 14- 5
Equivalent Amounts 11- 8
Smoothy-Frothy 6- 7
Some Basic Measurements 6-12

Write here any other tips, boxes, or charts that you would like to quickly reference along with its corresponding page number.

He that gathereth in summer is a wise son: but he that sleepeth in harvest is a son that causeth shame. — Proverbs 10:5 (KJV)

CHAPTER SIXTEEN

Freezer Recipes

A WORD OR TWO ON:

Ground meat recipes:

I'm not writing up recipes for hamburgers, chili, meatloaf, etc., because I give you credit for already having a favorite recipe. However, I'd like to suggest some helps in making mass quantities:

Goushed Meats:

We mix 20 to 30 pounds of ground meat at one time. Alan does this and our boys help. Kids love getting their hands into the meat mix. Make it a game.

You can really save by buying a large quantity of meat. For example, the last time I needed ground meat, I called or checked six different meat markets. By ordering 50 lbs of ground turkey all at once, I saved more than $1 a pound off the grocery store price.

Do this sequentially (This saves times and is more efficient):

- Mix for hamburgers — form some of the mix into hamburgers, label, and freeze (if you'll be microwaving these use your finger and leave a hole in the center. They will cook more evenly.) Example of what to put in the mix: ground meat, spices, eggs, and/or sauces.
- Add ingredients to the remaining meat mix for meatballs — form some of this mix into meatballs, label, and freeze. (Or form, cook, label, and freeze. See page 16-10.) [Example: you might want to add some baking mix, more spices, and/or some cereal — all according to your tastes.]
- Add ingredients to the remaining meat mix for meatloaves — form into loaves, label and freeze. [Examples: tomato sauce, more eggs, additional spices, cereals, grated cheese, flour, etc.] OR you may want to cook them now, then freeze. See page 9-8.

Tell Them Why

I'm now buying 80 pounds of ground turkey at a time and receiving major discounts. When you make your calls you'll want to point out to the butcher why he can afford to lower the price for you.

They will not be spending as much preparing it since you will accept it just as it comes off the truck in 10 pound logs. They save money several ways:

1) They will save labor in not having to divide and package the meat into one pound packages. A good butcher takes about five minutes per pound to repackage — for 80 pounds that saves them more than six hours of labor costs — more than $40!

2) They will save the material costs of the package tray and the wrapping, also wear and tear on the equipment. This savings varies from store to store.

3) It increases their order and might qualify them for a better rate from their supplier.

It certainly might help to point these benefits out to your butcher when you call — he may give you an even bigger discount.

Extra benefit for you In some cases you will be eliminating one more thawing and re-freezing of the meat, since you can accept it as originally frozen. They won't be thawing it to repackage

16 - 1

Have you tried adding wheat germ or soybeans to your meatloaves? Not only is adding cereals to your hamburgers stretching the meat dollar, it is adding better nutrition. Other things to stretch your meat mix are bran flakes, granola, oatmeal, and/or grated vegetables (e.g., zucchini, eggplant, etc.).

Use your ring molds to form your meatloaf. Freeze. Pop out and bake. Fill the center with vegetables or mashed potatoes. Not only does it look attractive enough for company, but kids love it.

Cooked Ground Meat:

Spaghetti Sauce: Use your favorite variation. Save money by purchasing a family pack of meat. Use either fresh produce from the farmer's market (big savings, e.g., bushel of tomatoes for $5) or use the #10 cans from the store. The sauce freezes or cans well. Use for spaghetti, lasagna, manicotti, pizzas, and/or your favorite Italian dish. These meals can be completely prepared ahead and just warmed up on serving day. Or you can make the pasta fresh and serve it with the pre-prepared sauce on the day you wish to eat it.

Chili: Use the same savings ideas here. Save money by using dried beans instead of canned. Remember in your plan to allow for soaking time. Chili can be eaten as "soup" or used as a meat base for tacos or other Mexican dishes. Our children like "Mexi-ghetti" — use chili in place of traditional spaghetti sauce and mix it with cooked spaghetti noodles.

Beef Stroganoff: A budget version is made by browning the ground meat and adding cream of mushroom soup (or golden mushroom soup) and sour cream. Use your Dutch oven and make six meals worth. Divide, label, and freeze. Serve over rice, noodles, mashed potatoes or toast.

Others Meals:

Chicken Dumplings: This meal freezes well. Use your own master mix for the dumplings. Again, substitute and make turkey 'n dumplings if the price is better than chicken. Or look for the grocer's special on chicken. Chicken à la king is also a good option.

Lentil Soup: Or your favorite soup. Soups freeze well and make hearty meals. Try C.O.R.D. soup, or Soup Surprise, or make up your own catchy name. Just keep a jar in the refrigerator for all those tiny amounts of table scraps "too small to save," then once a week throw all these left-overs into a pot of broth for a delicious soup. To conserve space in your freezer, freeze only the concentrated soup. When you are warming it to serve, add the extra water. Don't take up valuable freezer space freezing water.

Stir-Fry: We like oriental food, and it cooks up quickly. Save the time, and dollars, by pre-preparing ingredients. Then on the day you'll serve it, just pull out cut bell peppers, cut meat (store and freeze a cup of chopped chicken, turkey, or beef), etc.

Make Your Own Soup

You know me, "Never pay retail." Recently for a mega-cooking session, I was not able to find my cream of ____ soups at a discount. It would have cost me more than $26 to buy all the cans at the local grocery. I refused and figured if they can make it, I can make it.

For casseroles, making your own soup works surprisingly well. Here's what to do:

Make up a sufficient batch of your favorite white sauce, as healthfully as you desire. You may use your non-milk substitutes, or vary it as you deem for your family. As the sauce thickens, sprinkle in bouillion powder until you reach the concentration or flavor you desire. Just taste as you go. Use chicken broth or bouillion powder for cream of chicken soup. Vegetable powder makes for a wonderful cream of vegetable soup. Your creativity is the limit. Excellent powders are available through co-ops. To jazz it up a little , you can add scraps or leftovers like chicken broth and tidbits, or finely diced vegetables.

I've tried this several times and we even like the soup well enough for a first course soup. It definitely works well in casseroles and look at the savings!

<u>Chicken Cordon Bleu:</u> This makes a special meal and is really easy. Just roll flattened chicken breast around a slice of ham and cheese (e.g., Swiss) jelly roll fashion. Brush chicken with beaten egg and roll in bread crumbs. Secure with a toothpick. Freeze. Then, thaw and bake, grill, or pan fry. Try other recipes for as much pre-preparing as possible. The more work <u>you</u> do, the more money you save. Also, the larger the quantities you buy, the more you save.

I want to encourage you to try your favorite recipe. Be creative. The Lord has given you such talent! Use it in the kitchen.

More or Less

In the recipes that follow, the code MOL means **more or less**.

With ingredients like salt, meat, sugar, butter and/or garlic you can adjust the amount you use according to your preferences. Other ingredients will be noted also.

Salt:
> » I don't like the taste of salt so I greatly reduce the amount in the recipes or leave it out all together. One way to reduce the amount of salt is to wait to season your food at the table. If you salt the dishes while cooking, the taste isn't as strong once it's on the table. If you sprinkle salt on at the table you'll need less salt to get the same taste. Remember salt is a preservative and can toughen meat if added too early.

Meat:
> » One way to greatly affect your food budget is by varying the amount of meat in the recipes. You can increase the amount of meat or decrease according to your budget.

Sugar:
> » I avoid sugar for my family. I've tried many substitutes and the only one that I can recommend is granulated fructose. It is the natural sugar that comes in fruit. In recipes, you can usually substitute one half the amount of sugar called for by using fructose. If you do use sugar, you can start cutting back by using less and less sugar in your cooking.

Butter:
> » For most recipes that call for sauteing an ingredient in butter, I steam it in the microwave instead. For most bean and meat dishes, I will greatly reduce or totally eliminate the butter from the recipe.

Garlic:
> » It has been my experience that garlic doesn't multiply precisely in mega-recipes. Instead of using the regular x6 means multiple by six, I cut it by one half. Your personal preference might be different. Test it to find a balance that your family will enjoy.

Cold Oven Versus Pre-heating:
(Reprinted from page 13-6 as a reminder) *If it is not a baked good (cake, bread, etc.) there is rarely a need to pre-heat your oven. Save energy and let the food warm up gradually as your oven does. In fact, your casseroles will come out smoother, you meat will be more even, and vegetables won't be as soggy.*
This same idea adapts for most recipes that aren't required to rise. Please note, you will have to adjust the overall baking time slightly. Learn your own oven's rate.

Recipe: Aunt Eloise's Casserole

Background: This recipe was a delicous "covered dish" at a family reunion. We liked it so much, we asked for the recipe. To give you a feel for how to convert a single-meal recipe to this mega-cooking style, I'm printing the original version and then the recipe as I adapted it.

As given to me by my aunt:

1 hen or 2 fryers (about #5)
1-1/2 stick oleo
2 large bell peppers
1 lb can stewed tomatoes
6 oz Pepperidge Farm croutons
   (Cheddar and Romano cheese flavor)

2 Lg onions
1 pound thin spaghetti
1 can English peas
1 pound Velveeta
4 oz Monterey jack cheese w/jalapenos

Boil chicken until done. Remove. Bone. Reserve broth. Saute onions and peppers in oleo. Cook spaghetti in 1-3/4 qt of chicken broth. (DO NOT DRAIN) Grate cheese. Mix all ingredients. Top with croutons. Makes 2 - 9" x 13" pans or 3 lg Corningware-type dishes.
   Bake 25-30 minutes at 350. **Freezes well.**

Adapted for larger quantities:

10 to 15 pounds of cooked turkey meat, cubed (I cook one extra large bird and use the meat for several
   recipes)
10 large bell peppers (chopped)
1 #10 can stewed tomatoes
10 large onions (chopped/diced)
5 to 8 pounds thin spaghetti (whole wheat noodles are yummy)
1 #10 can English peas (or use regular green peas)
1 large block of Velveeta (I buy it in 5 pound blocks)
2 pounds Monterey jack cheese (our children don't eat jalapenos)

Fit these steps into your overall plan:

1. Cook turkey, bone, and cube approximately 10-15 lbs for this recipe. Save drippings for broth to cook spaghetti.

2. To save calories, cook (zap) peppers and onions in microwave rather than sauteing in oleo or butter.

3. Cook spaghetti in broth and additional water, if needed. (Cook in batches depending on the size of your pots.) Keep about half of the broth.

4. Open all cans, jars, etc.

5. Mix all the ingredients together, including 1/4 to 1/2 of the broth.   (This mixes much better if spaghetti is hot, because the cheese melts as you mix.)

6. Divide into meal-size portions. Label. Freeze.

7. Thaw, bake at 350° for 25 to 30 minutes (or microwave).

Recipe: Mrs. Thomas' Casserole

Background: Susan Thomas served us this recipe while we were at a church camp. I had never seen my son Stuart, then 1 year old, eat so much of anything in his life. Five years later it is still his favorite recipe. He's been known to have fifths. It multiplies well because of the moistness of the casserole.

Here's the basic recipe:

1-1/2 lbs ground chuck
1 c. chopped onions
1 (1 lb) can corn, drained
1 can cream of chicken soup

1 can cream of mushroom soup
1/4 cup chopped pimento
1-1/2 teaspoon salt
1/2 teaspoon pepper
1 (10 oz) pkg noodles- cooked

Brown meat and onions until meat is done and onions are tender. Add all other ingredients. Mix. Pour into a 2-1/2 qt. casserole dish or two smaller dishes. Bake at 350° for 30 minutes. Yields 12-15 servings.

Adapted for larger quantities:

1 family pack of ground turkey or beef (approximately 10 to 12 pounds)
5 to 6 cups chopped onions (Use less if your family doesn't like onions.)
1 #10 can kernel corn, drained
2 large cans (26 ounces) cream of chicken soup (or use six regular 10-ounce size.)
2 large cans (26 ounces) cream of mushroom soup (or use six regular 10 ounce-size.)
1 large carton (3 lbs) of sour cream (Adds flavor, and freezes well.)
1 large pkg. (40 oz) noodles-cooked (Try whole wheat noodles.)
3 4-ounce jars pimento (Optional depending on your family's tastes.)

Fit these steps into your overall plan:
Steps that can be done ahead or assembly-lined: (1 and 2)

1. Brown meat in microwave or skillet, using strainer to drain fat.

2. Cook onions, either saute or steam in microwave. (Should be approximately 2 to 3 cups cooked.)

3. In large mixing container, mix all soups and sour cream evenly.

4. Add in all other ingredients, mix well.

5. Divide, label, and freeze.

6. Thaw, bake at 350° for 30 minutes (or microwave).

Side dishes: Since this is a complete meal casserole (starch, meat, dairy, vegetable), all you might want to add are dinner rolls (or a quick bread) and a salad.

Servings: This version yields our family six meals.

Recipe: Super Grandma's 3-bean Casserole

Background: When my eldest son, Reed, was 2, he drew a picture for his Great Grandmother Hileman. I explained that she was his great grandmother, his daddy's grandmother. His answer was, "She's more than great, she's SUPER!" I had to agree, so the name stuck. This is one recipe Alan asked his new bride to learn how to cook, so Grandma Hileman, who is one the best cooks I've ever known, mailed it to me. She has mastered the art of hospitality so that she can make you feel special. My husband was raised on this casserole and now, his children are.

Here's the basic recipe:

1/2 cup ground beef
10 bacon slices (chopped)
1/2 cup onions

Brown and cook until onions are tender.

Get ready in 3 qt roaster:	1/3 teaspoon salt
1/3 cup packed brown sugar	1/2 teaspoon chili powder
1/2 cup ketchup	1/2 teaspoon pepper
1/4 cup barbecue sauce	1 cup kidney beans (drained)
2 tablespoons prepared mustard	1-16 oz can pork and beans
2 tablespoons molasses (dark)	1-16 oz can butter beans (drained)

While meat and onions are cooking, get remainder ready in 3 or 4 quart casserole dish or roaster pan. Mix well.

Bake at 350° for 1 hour or more. Good warmed up.

Adapted for larger quantities:

5 pounds ground beef or turkey (mol)
2 to 3 lbs bacon (We've had wonderful success using turkey bacon and sugar-free bacons.)
4 to 6 cups onions (chopped, raw) or 2 to 3 cups cooked onion
1 cup granulated fructose (or if you must, 2 cups white sugar)
5 cups ketchup (There are sugar-free and salt-free versions available.)
2 1/2 cups of your favorite BBQ sauce
1/2 cup prepared mustard (experiment to find your favorite, e.g. yellow, brown, dijon.)
1/2 cup molasses (Blackstrap is healthier than regular.)
Salt, if you desire
2 Tablespoons chili powder (as hot as you like it)
2 Tablespoons pepper
10 cups (approximately) kidney beans (Save money by preparing them yourself, or buy a #10 can of pre-cooked beans.)
1 #10 can pork and beans
1 #10 can butter beans (Or substitute Great Northern beans.)

1. Brown turkey and bacon in microwave (or skillet). Drain and chop bacon. Either cook onions or scoop out 2 to 3 cups from already prepared onions.

2. In large container, mix all the liquid ingredients. Then stir in beans and meat, mixing well, but gently. (You don't want to mash the beans.)

3. Bake before freezing. I use my large turkey roaster and bake at 350° for one hour.   Then divide, label and freeze.   Be careful about choosing containers since mixture is HOT.

4. Thaw, warm in oven 15 to 25 minutes at 350° or microwave.

Serving suggestions: We occassionally use this casserole as the entree or sometimes we use it as a side dish (with hamburgers, etc.) It is very hearty.

Buying a Whole Side of Beef

Have you seen the ads presenting a year's supply of beef for an average of $2 a pound?

It sounds wonderful, doesn't it? We had friends that declared that they love buying a whole side of beef once or twice a year.

We tried it one year and declared we would never do it again. Yes, if you would normally buy the same meat that comes in the package but on a weekly basis, buying it all at once is a big savings.

We discovered that for the same $119 a month (that's what the figure calculated out) otherwise we could have purchased more food for our family and the meat we prefer.

We would rather eat ground meat recipes all week and then have top quality steak once a week than mediocre meals all week long. By purchasing the whole side, you have lots of medium range beef (beef that must be tenderized and served in dishes that are very labor intensive, and yet, it still can be tough to chew).   We ate the ground meat quickly, the steaks didn't last long, and we were stuck with high priced, medium range beef.

Before you sign up for a butcher's special, please examine your family's eating habits.

<u>And</u> it took up loads of freezer space. **AND** I still had to cook each of these mid-range beef cuts each day. I have better things to do. . . .

Recipe: **Turkey Mandarin**

Background: This recipe is very colorful and delicious. It's a favorite of mine for entertaining. You can completely prepare it ahead and warm it up. Once while living in Panama, we invited our minister of music and his family to Sunday dinner. I thought I had everything timed and ready. The casserole was made. I had popped it into the oven while we ate the appetizers and the salad. Then we had one of those wonderful, never anticipated power-outages. I always enjoy entertaining fellow Christians. They always understand and are helpful. He just drove the casserole to his house, baked it in his oven and brought it back. Even after all that, his wife asked for the recipe.

Here's the basic recipe:

1 can Mandarin orange sections
1 can cream of chicken soup
1/2 cup turkey stock (or use chicken broth)
1/4 teaspoon salt

3 cups cooked regular white rice
6 to 8 slices cooked turkey
1/2 cup slivered toasted almonds

Preheat oven to 350°F. Lightly grease shallow 1-1/2 quart baking dish.

To make sauce: Drain orange sections, reserving liquid; set orange sections aside. In small saucepan, combine reserved liquid with soup, turkey stock, and salt, mixing well. Bring to a boil, stirring constantly.

Place rice in prepared baking dish. Arrange turkey over the rice in a single layer. Arrange orange sections over turkey. Pour sauce over all the layers of ingredients; sprinkle with almonds.

Bake, uncovered for 25 minutes, or until mixture is hot and bubbly. Makes 6 to 8 servings.

Adapted for larger quantities:

1 large can (24-ounce) Manadrin oranges (or 3 regular 8-ounce cans) [For 6 x recipe use 6 reg cans.]
1 large (26-ounce) can or 3 regular (10-ounce) cans cream of chicken soup [For 6x recipe use 6 to 9 cans (9 cans make a thicker sauce, but it costs more).]
3 cups chicken broth [For 6x recipe use 6 cups]
salt (if you wish)
15 to 18 cups cooked whole grain rice (it's healthier than white)
8 cups chopped cooked turkey MOL (bite-sized chunks if you'll be serving to children. You could use slices, but it stretches for more servings with chunks.) [For 6x recipe use 12-20 cups]
Almonds, optional (We use water chestnuts for the crunch, since I'm allergic to nuts).

This recipe can be adapted different ways, depending on your style and use:

(Follow the above instructions to make sauce.)

1. Make the sauce, divide, label freeze. Separately bag rice, turkey, and oranges. Then thaw and assemble right before warming.
2. Make the entire casserole and freeze. Thaw and bake.

I've used both methods. #1 is more work on the day of serving, but the rice is less gummy.

> **Hint:** When substituting whole grain rice for white rice allow an extra 20 minutes cooking time. If your family only likes white rice, try weaning them slowly to whole grain, mix 1/4 cup of whole grain rice with your cup of white rice. Then 1/2 cup, etc. Soon they'll be eating only whole grain and thinking that white rice is bland.

Recipe: Sweet 'n Sour Meatballs

Background: For a mission banquet at our church in Panama, about ten of the ladies were given this recipe to prepare. Though we all had the identical recipe, the dishes looked so different. The size of the pepper, pineapple chunks, and meatballs made each unique. Even the tastes were different. God made us all individuals, and every woman I've ever met added her own flair to her cooking. So enjoy this recipe with your own portion of flair and style.

As given to me by Ginny Kessel and Donna Shelton:

Meatballs: 2 pounds ground beef, salt, pepper (onion salt and garlic powder, if desired) to taste; 1 egg (if desired). Mix and form into 1" balls (try to get 32-40 from 2 lbs to get 8-10 servings of 4 each). Brown in large skillet until "done." Remove from pan and drain off all but small amount of fat. Saute 1 green pepper, cut in 1" strips, until crispy-tender. Remove from pan.

Sauce:
   2 cans (16 oz) pineapple chunks, drained and juice reserved
   2 tbsp. cornstarch or flour
   1-1/4 to 1-1/2 cups reserved pineapple juice
   4 tbsp. vinegar (white or cider)
   2 tbsp. sugar (granulated or light brown)
   1 tbsp. soy sauce

In large skillet or saucepan, dissolve cornstarch in juice. Add remaining ingredients. Bring to boil, stirring constantly, until mixture becomes thick. Add meatballs, pineapple chunks and green pepper. Heat through. (If sauce seems too thick, thin with juice or water.)

Adapted for larger quantities:

1 family pack of ground turkey (or beef) — about 10 pounds
4 to 5 eggs, and seasoning to suit your tastes
5 bell peppers (red or green)

1. Kids love to "goush." Let them mix the ingredients, and with a proper lesson, they can form the balls.
2. Brown meatballs in skillet or microwave. Drain off fat.
3. Prepare bell peppers (either cut now, or use previously sauted peppers). Note: we like our peppers crisp, so I don't saute them, I add them to the recipe raw.

1 #10 can pineapple chunks, <u>save juice</u>
3/4 cup cornstarch
9 cups of reserved juice (You might have supplement with juice from a separate can.)
1 1/2 cups vinegar (your choice white or cider)
3/4 cup sugar (we use granulated fructose)
1/2 cup soy sauce

4. Mix cornstarch with juice BEFORE heating. Mix well, dissolve. Bring to a boil until thick.

5. Add other ingredients and heat through.

6. Divide into containers, label, and freeze.

> Tip: For years I've had problems with gravy chunks. One day I learned this secret. In a jar place liquid in first then add flour or whatever, shake and the majority of clumps are gone! — Kathryn Sleigh, TX

To complete the meal:

Thaw.
Heat in saucepan on medium, or microwave.
Either cook rice now or thaw previously cooked and frozen rice. Or use noodles for a change.

To make this dinner even more special:

- Make a quick egg drop soup. There are sweet 'n sour or duck sauce recipes on pages 17-6 and 17-7. They are wonderful with egg rolls.
- Serve egg rolls. (They can be purchased inexpensively in large quantities from warehouse stores.)
- Use any special dishes with an Oriental theme. Set out some chopsticks.

Note: You can vary the size of the meatballs to suit your family. It seems to stretch farther if you make small meatballs (1/2" to 3/4" in diameter rather than the 2" size). You can save by cutting back and not using as much meat as the recipe calls for.

> **Hint:** Go ahead and form, then brown more meatballs for other recipes and freeze. They make great appetizers with a sweet 'n sour sauce, or gravy sauce (e.g. Swedish Meatballs). Use them to make a quick stroganoff, or add to your spaghetti sauce.

Easy Egg Drop Soup

Prepare chicken broth — adjust volume to your family's appetite. I make one cup per person. (Bouillion powder or cubes work well.)

Mix in 1 tablespoon cornstarch per cup of broth. Stir until it is evenly dissolved. Cook, stirring until broth is thick. (Note: It is much easier to mix in cornstarch to cold liquids, so add cornstarch before you heat the broth.)

Add in grated vegetables (e.g., 1/4 cup of grated carrots per 3 cups of soup). This can vary according to what you have in stock. Don't add too many vegetables. This should be a thin soup. Use one to three different grated vegetables to add color.

Simmer at least five to ten minutes.

Just a few minutes before serving, beat one egg in a cup. Bring soup to a boil. Stir the boiling soup until a vortex or whirlpool forms. Drop in beaten egg. Stir or whip with a whisk for one minute. The egg will cook in strings. Serve immediately.

Recipe: **Miss Betty's Tuna Casserole**   From: Betty Kearney

Background: Two dear saints from my church, Leona Lee and Betty Kearney, ministered to us with this delicious casserole one Sunday afternoon. I had been confined to bed for a few days after a threatened miscarriage of my second son. Seven months later, Stuart was born with no damage. Until this casserole, I had never met a tuna dish (except tuna salad) that I liked. "You would not believe what I've eaten under the name of tuna," says my husband. We enjoyed this so much that it's been a standard in our meal plan. The tuna mix freezes well. This recipe is a short-cut/easier version of the original.

x 1	x 5	Ingredient	x 1	x5	Measurement
2	10	eggs	1/6	5/6	dozen
1/2	2 1/2	teaspoons salt (mol)			
1/2	2 1/2	teaspoons pepper			
1-1/4	6 1/4	cups salad dressing (type used as sandwich spread or mayonnaise substitute)			
2	10	cups bread crumbs	4-5 slices	2 loaves	whole bread
1 sml	1 #10	can of peas and carrots OR #10 can of just carrots OR fresh chopped carrots	1 lb	#10	can
1	5	cups chopped bell pepper	2	10	peppers
1/4	1-1/4	cups chopped pimento	1/2	3	4-oz jars
2 Tbs	1 to 2 cups	finely chopped onion	1/2	2 to 3	onions
14 oz	66.5 oz	tuna (water packed is healthier than oil packed OR use canned salmon)	14 oz	66.5 oz	can

Steps:

Steps that can be done ahead or assembly-lined: (1 and 3)

1) Chop bell peppers and onions. You don't have to pre-saute, but you might want to, depending on your family's tastes. Do you like your peppers and onions very soft or still firm?
2) Mix all moist ingredients and spices.
3) If you make your own bread crumbs, be sure to have enough.
4) Open cans and mix in all other ingredients. Suggestion: mix all but carrots and peas, then gently add them in. This way there is less possibility of crushing the shape of the vegetables.
5) Divide, label, freeze.
6) To finish: Thaw. Bake in casserole dish in 350° oven for 20 to 30 minutes. Meanwhile either make fresh mashed potatoes or use instant. Pipe, spoon, or drop potatoes on top of tuna meat. Your creativity can make this very attractive.

Notes/Comments: Betty's orginial recipe instructed us to separate eggs, and use only yolks for the tuna mix; then, when ready to serve, whip the egg whites until they are like meringue, fold in 2 Tablespoons of mayonnaise and spoon in the center of the casserole with the potatoes around the edge. Then return to oven to broil a few minutes to crisp the meringue. This is delicious and so attractive. However, because we're freezing this, you might as well put the whole egg in the mix. Sometimes I do separate two eggs and make the meringue depending on the time I have. Note: we use salad dressing instead of mayonnaise because it freezes better. Also note the changes made in the shopping list amount to correspond with standard store sizes.

Side dishes: rolls, fresh salad and/or _____

Servings: The x5 recipe yields our family 10 meals.

Note: In this recipe I calculated in the "personalize" columns to give you direction in filling out the other recipes.

Recipe: **Shrimp Jambalaya**   From: Hand-me-down type recipe

Background: I love seafood. But I do want to caution you to be very careful with it. I was hospitalized for several days with severe food poisoning from eating bad shrimp. The grocer's freezer had broken, the shrimp had completely thawed, then they re-froze it and sold it. My husband and I feasted on the shrimp, so obviously, the "ruined state" of the shrimp wasn't noticable. I don't want to scare you. I just want you to know that if your seafood thaws — cook it then. Do not re-freeze raw shrimp. Once it's cooked in a recipe, you can re-freeze with no deleterious effect.

x1	x2	x3	x5	Ingredient			Personalize
1	2	3	5	cups cubed cooked ham			
1	1	2	2	cloves garlic (or use powder) (mol)			
2	3	4	5	tablespoons butter (mol)			
2	4	6	10	cups chicken broth			
1	2	3	5 (or 1 #10)	cans (16 oz) tomatoes			
1/2	1	1-1/2	2 1/2	cups chopped onions			
1/2	1	1-1/2	2 1/2	cups chopped bell pepper			
2T	1/4c	1/3c	2/3c	Worcestershire sauce			
dashes to taste				cayenne pepper and/or Louisiana hot sauce			
1	2	3	5	lbs shrimp, shelled and deveined			
1	2	3	5	cups raw rice (to stretch — double rice amount. Also double chicken broth (or water))			

Steps:
Steps that can be done ahead, or assembly-lined (1)

1) Chop ham, bell pepper, and onion.
2) Brown ham with garlic in butter. (This step can be eliminated if you use already cured/cooked turkey ham.)
3) Add remaining ingredients, except for shrimp and rice. Boil.
4) Add rice and shrimp.
5) Reduce heat, simmer covered, about 20 minutes (check rice for tenderness).
      *** If you use brown rice allow for 40 minutes cooking time.***
6) Divide, put in containers, label, freeze.
7) Thaw, warm in microwave or stove top.

Notes/Comments: Like spaghetti sauce, jambalaya is a dish that is cooked hundreds of different ways. Each family has their own version. Use this version as a model for you to experiment with to find your family's own taste (e.g., sometimes I add some lemon juice).

Serving Suggestions: I serve it over a bed of rice (if I didn't double the rice in the original cooking) along with a salad, bread, and vegetable side dish.

Servings: The x5 recipe yields our family eight meals.

Remember: Monitor your freezer. Don't lose a month's worth of food because you forgot to defrost. Keep the door closed. Check it, especially if it's out in the garage or in the basement.

Remember: Monitor the contents in your freezer. Don't lose food in there.

Recipe: **Evan's Mom's Casserole**   From: Gail Meade

Background: Role models are so hard to find. So we were thrilled with Evan. He is a young teenager with character. We could feel safe enough with him to ask him to babysit our young sons. When Gail gave us this casserole along with a baby shower gift, our boys' named it after their friend Evan. [I thought that the hostess of my baby shower for Bethany had a brilliant idea that you might want to consider the next time you hostess a shower. They suggested that each guest also bring a frozen casserole with their shower gift. I loved it.]

x1	x 5	Ingredient			Personalize
1	5	lbs ground meat (cooked)			
1	5	onions, chopped			
1	5-6	cans tomato soup			
1 reg.	1 #10	can green bean, drained (or use frozen or fresh)			
1 teas.	2 Tbls	dill weed			
1 teas	2 Tbls	onion salt or powder			
1/4 cup per meal (mol)		cracker crumbs (optional)			
1/4 cup per meal (mol)		Parmesan cheese (optional)			

Steps:

Steps that can be done ahead or assembly-lined: (1 and 2)

1) Brown ground meat.
2) Chop onion.
3) Mix all the ingredients, GENTLY (except cracker crumbs and cheese).
4) Divide, put in containers, label, freeze.
5) Thaw.
6) Place in casserole dish, sprinkle top with cracker crumbs and Parmesan cheese.
7) Bake (350° for approximately 30 minutes) or microwave (compensate according to your own oven).

Serving Suggestions: I serve it over a bed of rice along with a salad, bread, and a vegetable side dish.

Servings: The x5 recipe yields our family eight meals.

Idea for Homeschoolers:

When the Meade's daughter, Kristyn, graduated from high school homeschool, they gave her a graduation ceremony. They decorated our church activity room with personal items from their home. They set up displays of photographs of Kristyn from birth to that day. They displayed her awards, samples of her work, and mementos. Bob, the dad and "Superintendent of the School," gave a heart-warming presentation. He combined humor in giving his graceful daughter awards. Years of love and caring poured out of these parents as they blessed their daughter and released her for the future the Lord has for her. The gathered friends of the family, and relatives (some had flown in for the ceremony) stood and issued a blessing on Kristyn and thanked her for the positive impact she had had on our church and families. After the ceremony, we were greeted with a beautiful reception of cakes, punch, etc. I had never enjoyed a high school graduation ceremony so much. It was personal. They had combined the best aspects of a coming-out party, a graduation, and a Blessing Service.

Recipe: **Y'all Soup**   From: Ideas from dining in some Southern restaurants
Also called "Feature from the Black Legume."

Background: When I worked at Disney World, I loved to eat the **black bean soup** that was prepared lavishly on the "Empress Lily." Since that time, I've had similar versions of this Southern staple soup. I started experimenting trying to duplicate the tastes and textures of the restaurant versions. This version is a passable one. And probably a tad bit less expensive to prepare. We have tried several names: I liked "Empress Soup", but the children didn't. Stuart calls it "MUD SOUP" because it does resemble mud in appearance, but not in taste. Alan liked "Feature from the Black Legume" and so that is the most popular name around here. Please feel free to rename it.

x1	x5	Ingredient			Personalize
1/2 c	2 lb bag	black beans			
1	5	onions, chopped			
1/2 c	2 to 3 c	ham, chopped			
1/2 c	2 lb bag	black-eyed peas			
just a dash		hot sauce			
1-teas	2 Tbls	onion salt or powder			
2 strips	10-12 strips	bacon cooked and crumbled (optional)			

Steps:
Steps that can be done ahead or assembly-lined: (1, 2, 3, 4 and 5)

1) Sort beans and then soak them overnight.
2) Cook beans and peas according to package instructions [OR cover with 5 inches of water, bring to a boil, then simmer for 2-4 hours until desired tenderness is reached.]
3) Cook, drain and crumble bacon.
4) Chop onion.
5) Chop ham into 1/4" to 1/2" cubes.
6) Mix all the ingredients, GENTLY, to avoid mashing the beans.
4) Divide, put in containers, label and freeze.
5) Thaw.
6) Place soup concentrate in sauce pan. Add water mixed with cornstarch (e.g., 1 Tablespoon per cup of water added). Adjust the amount of water you add according to how dense you like your soups — e.g., 1-10 cups of water. Heat, stirring occasionally as mixture thickens. When thickened and hot, serve.

Serving Suggestions: I serve it as soup, or as an entree with a side dish of rice. Side dishes needed: a salad, bread, and a vegetable. Old Southerners always serve this with a bowl of freshly chopped onion for diners to sprinkle over the top.

Servings: The x5 recipe yields our family eight meals.

Hint: This is a meal that I place frozen in my crock pot, set it on low, add water (mixed with cornstarch) to the fill line. Then I can leave for the day on a field trip, or for appointments, and when we rush in the door late in the day — dinner's on the table in five minutes.

Recipe: **Ahoy Dinner**   From: Trying to find another fish dish

Background: While I was developing this recipe, we were studying a unit on the telephone and Alexander Graham Bell. Our children were thrilled when they learned that with the early phone systems, people answered the phone "AHOY," instead of the common "Hello" of today. They had fun answering our phone with an "ahoy!" So in deference to them we named this casserole "Ahoy Dinner." If you really stretch the concept you can grasp for a connection — tuna, ahoy, ships, etc. Now everytime we serve this dish, the children remember facts about our communication unit. [One of my personal favorite anecdotes about Bell is that he complained about the telephone in his later years while working for the deaf. Its ringing interrupted his research. How many times have we been interrupted with a phone call! — ah, those telemarketers.] When you're personalizing recipes to make them "yours," get ideas from everywhere. There's no need to call it something that will scare the kids off.

x1	x 5	Ingredient			Personalize
1	5	can mushrooms (4-oz size)			
1 (10 oz) can	1 (#10) can	tomatoes (or use fresh or home-canned)			
1 cup	5-10 cups	raw rice			
10 oz	50 oz	frozen, canned or fresh cooked spinach			
2 (7-oz) can	1 - 66.5 oz can	tuna (drained)[we prefer water packed]			
1/2 cup	3 to 5 cups	bread cubes or crumbs (home-made suggested)			
1 cup	5 cups	Cheddar cheese, grated			
1/2 tsp	1 Tbls	dried oregano leaves			
1/2 tsp	1 Tbls	dried basil leaves			
1cup	3 cups	celery, chopped			
1	3 to 5	small onions, chopped			
3 cloves	6 cloves (more or less)	garlic, finely chopped or use equivalent amount of powder			

Steps:
Steps that can be done ahead or assembly-lined: (1, 2 and/or 5)

1) Chop celery, onions, garlic. (If you like, make your own bread cubes.)
2) Steam onion, celery, garlic until tender; OR saute onion, celery, garlic in some hot oil.
3) Add mushrooms, tomatoes, spices, to onion mixture in a large saucepan, or Dutch oven.
4) Bring this mixture to a boil. Reduce heat and simmer for 1 hour. Stir occasionally.
5) Cook rice and spinach, (while tomato mixture is simmering or do well ahead).
6) Gently mix rice, spinach and tuna into tomato mixture.
*** You can either freeze toppings separately, or go ahead and assemble the casseroles ready to bake.

Separately:
7) Divide, put in containers, label and freeze.
8) Thaw, place in casserole dish.
9) Sprinkle bread crumbs and cheese on top.
10) Bake at 350° for 30 minutes

Pre-assembled:
7) Line casserole dishes (see page 12-3 for directions on envelope fold) with enough plastic or aluminum foil. Fill dishes with tuna mixture, sprinkle with cheese and bread cubes. Wrap.
8) Freeze. Once frozen solid, pop casserole out of dish and put immediately back in freezer. (Reuse dish for other recipes.)
9) Thaw first and bake 350° for 30 minutes; OR bake directly from frozen state at 300° for 1-1/2 hours. (See page 13-6.)

Servings: The x5 recipe yields our family

Recipe: **Harvest Fest**   From: Playing around in the kitchen

Background: Autumn is such a glorious season. We love the gardens' bounty in the fall. This recipe seems to play on the advantages of this time of year.

x1	x 5	Ingredient			Personalize
6	30 or family pack	pork chops			
1	5-10 (or a #10 can of prepared)	apples, pared, slices or rings			
1/4 cup	1 cup (mol)	brown sugar or fructose			
1/2	2-5 cups	raisins			
1 Tbls	1/4 Tbls	grated orange peel			
1/3 cup	2 cups	orange juice			
1 (1 lb) can or approx. 6 fresh	1 (#10) can or approx. 30 fresh	sweet potatoes			
Dashes to your preference		Optional — Spices you can add: cinnamon, cloves, nutmeg			
1/2 teas	1 Tbls	Worcestershire sauce			

Steps:
Steps that can be done ahead or assembly-lined: (1)

1) Prepare apples.
2) Trim meat, wipe off.
3) Brown chops, (takes about 15 minutes on each side).
4) Divide chops into appropriate servings for your family, and temporarily place each "meal" in a container.
5) Distribute apples, potatoes, and raisins among the chops.
6) Mix all other ingredients. Pour this orange juice mixture evenly over chops.
*** You can either bake now then freeze, OR freeze and then bake.

Bake, then freeze version:
7) Bake the casseroles at 350˚ for 20 minutes.
8) Cool in refrigerator.
9) Wrap in foil, plastic wrap, or place in a container.
10) Freeze.
11) Thaw and warm 15 minutes at 350˚; OR bake frozen at 300˚ for 45 to 60 minutes.

Freeze, then bake version:
7) Wrap casseroles.
8) Freeze.
9) Thaw and bake at 350˚ for 20 minutes; OR bake frozen at 300˚ for 1 hour.

Servings: The x5 recipe yields our family five meals.

> **Remember:** The Lord gave you a wonderful sense of smell. Use it. If food smells bad, it is bad. Don't risk your family's health — toss the food out. Check for color. Check for freezer burn. Check for ice build-up on the food. If you are monitoring the contents and making certain that you have properly sealed the container, you shouldn't have to throw any food away.

Recipe: **Chuckwagon**   From: Attempt to duplicate a Fort Worth treat

Background: A recipe from our five years in Texas — the state of "yee-haws," cowboys, and bandanas.

x1	x 5	Ingredient			Personalize
2	10	cups dried lima beans (mol)			
2 teas	3 Tbls	salt (mol)			
1 lb	5 lbs	link or miniature sausages			
2 Tbls	3/4 cup	onion, grated			
2/3 cup	3 cups	corn syrup (dark or light)			
1-1/2 Tbls	1/2 cup	prepared horseradish			
1 cup	5 cups	ketchup OR half ketchup and half BBQ sauce			
2 teas	1/4 cup	Worcestershire sauce			

Steps:
Steps that can be done ahead: (1 and 2)

1) Soak beans and cook until tender.
2) Grate onions.
3) If necessary, cook sausage. Drain well.
*** You can either mix all the ingredients, bag and freeze; OR bake it now and freeze it pre-cooked.
In large oven container (e.g., turkey roaster), mix all ingredients.

Freeze, the bake version:
4) Gently mix all ingredients.
5) Divide, store, label and freeze.
6) Thaw, bake at 375° for 30 minutes; OR bake frozen, at at 300° for 1 to 2 hours — check every 30 minutes.

Bake, then freeze version:
4) Gently mix all ingredients.
5) Bake in a large roaster at 375° for 30 minutes.
6) Divide, store, label, and freeze.
7) Thaw, warm in at 350° oven for 15 minutes, or microwave.

Recipe: **Mount Vernon Pie**   From: Trying to duplicate a restaurant dish

Background: On the grounds of George Washington's estate museum is a lovely restaurant.   I ordered a pot pie. I was used to the tiny ones that you can find in the grocer's freezer in those small aluminum pans.   The waitress, dressed in a Martha Washington style outfit, served me the most delicious pot pie I've ever eaten. It was home-made herbal pastry filled with large chunks of vegetables, meat and thick gravy.   You probably already have ideas from dishes you've been served in restaurants. Experiment. Try to duplicate them. The results can be wonderful.

x1	x 5	Ingredient			Personalize
2 shells [1/2 teas. dillweed]	10 shells [1 Tbls dillweed]	pastry pie shells (see page 16-29) to make an herbal crust, add dill weed to your flour when you make the pastry mix.			
2	10	cups cubed meat (chicken, beef, or your choice of meat)			
3	15	potatoes (cubed)			
4 to 5	20 to 25	carrots			
1 stalk	3 to 5 stalks	celery			
1	5	cups green peas (fresh, frozen, or canned)			
2	10	whole cloves			
1 to 3	5 to 15	cups gravy (homemade, from mix, or packaged)			
1/2 teas	1 Tbls	Worcestershire sauce			

Steps:
Steps that can be done ahead or assembly-lined (1, 2, 4 and 6)

1) Cook and cube meat.
2) Make gravy.
3) Chop onions, celery, potatoes and carrots.
4) Cook vegetables until tender, but not soft. (Microwave or boil.)
5) Gently mix vegetables, meat, gravy, spices and Worcestershire sauce.
6) Prepare pastry. Roll out into appropriate shapes to fit your pans (e.g., I use 8" pie pans because they fit perfectly into a gallon plastic bag for freezing).
7) Lay one pastry round in bottom of pan. Fill with meat mix. Top with pastry and crimp edges.
*** You can bake then freeze; OR freeze then bake:

> **Quick Cut** — Being lazy, I look for shortcuts. Cook the stew meat in the size chunks as they come in the package. Allow them to cool in the refrigerator. Then cut them into small cubes with a handy pair of kitchen shears. This is MUCH easier than trying to cut raw meat into the same small sized cubes. By using 1/2" or 1/4"cubes, the meat "stretches" for more servings.

Bake, then freeze version:
8) Bake all the pies at one time at 425° for 30 minutes.
9) Cool in refrigerator.
10) Wrap in foil or plastic wrap for freezing, OR slide into a plastic bag and seal.
11) Freeze.
12) Thaw and warm 15 minutes at 350°; OR bake the frozen entree at 300° for 1 hour.

Freeze, then bake version:
8) Wrap pies.
9) Freeze.
10) Thaw and bake at 425° for 30 minutes; OR bake the frozen entree at 300° for 1 to 1 1/2 hours. Check after 1 hour.

Tip: Place little foil "tents" over the pastry edges to keep them from burning.

> **Quicker pot pie:** One alternative to making the above pie is to use a convenient package of mixed vegetables. Purchased in a large package, it can be comparable in price to fresh.

Recipe: **Curry Turry or Great Scott Casserole**   From: Robin Scott

Background: One day during my recovery from the complications of giving birth to Bethany Kay, I was having a particularly rough time. My leg just wasn't working, and one thing after another was not going right. I had not recruited help for that day and that was the day I needed it. I prayed for guidance, strength, and HELP! Robin, a friend and mother of six, called and said that she had had a real burden for me and was coming over with a dinner and could help for a few hours — a real answer to prayer. She did several loads of laundry for me, straightened up the house, and our children had a wonderful time playing together. I just lay in bed and praised the Lord for giving me good friends. This is the dish she served us that night. She had even set the table and had everything ready for Alan and our children to sit down and eat.

x1	x 5	Ingredient			Personalize
4 to 5	20 to 25 (mol)	chicken breasts, or same amount of turkey			
1 bunch or pkg	5 bunches or pkgs (equivalent)	broccoli (frozen or fresh)			
2	10	cans (10-ounce) cream of chicken soup			
1/2	3	cups salad dressing (or other substitute for mayonnaise)			
1 Tbls	1/3 cup	lemon juice			
1/2 tsp	1 Tbls	curry (If you like curry, use more.)			
2 Tbls	1/2 cup	chicken broth			
4 oz	20 oz	herb-flavored corn bread dressing			
Dashes to your preference		butter, melted (optional)			
2 to 4 cups cooked	10 to 20 cups cooked	optional, a bed of rice. (In step #4, start with a bed of rice, then add the meat, etc.)			

Steps:
Steps that can be done ahead or assembly-lined: (1 and 2)

1) Cook chicken (or turkey).
2) Cook broccoli.
3) Mix together soup, salad dressing, lemon juice, curry, and broth.
4) In your lined casserole dishes, layer the following: meat, broccoli, sauce, dressing and butter.
*** You can either bake now, then freeze; OR freeze and then bake.

Bake, then freeze version:
5) Bake the casseroles at 350° for 20-25 minutes.
6) Cool in refrigerator.
7) Wrap in foil, plastic wrap, or place in a container.
8) Freeze.
9) Thaw and warm 15 minutes at 350°; OR bake frozen at 300° for 1 hour.

Freeze, then bake version:
5) Wrap casseroles.
6) Freeze.
7) Thaw and bake 350° for 20-25 minutes; OR bake frozen 300° for 1 to 1-1/2 hours. Check after 1 hour.

Side dishes: bread and fruit salad

Servings: The x5 yields our family seven meals.

Note about the dressing: For a crunchy texture — don't cook the dressing, just sprinkle the bread cubes/crumbs over the top. For a softer texture — cook the dressing and layer on top. Either version is savory.

Recipe: **Speckled Rice**   From: More playing around in the kitchen

Background: Just another meal — no story.   The children like this colorful dish.

x1	x5	Ingredient			Personalize
4 oz	1 pound	Pepperoni, sliced			
1 reg pkg.	5 pkgs or commercial size	Uncle Ben's wild rice mix, or similar rice			
4 oz	1 pound	Ham			

Steps:
Steps that can be done ahead or assembly-lined: (2)

1) Cook rice according to package directions
2) Chop pepperoni into quarters. Chop ham into bite-size cubes.
3) Mix pepperoni and ham into rice.
4) Divide, label, freeze.
5) Thaw, warm in microwave or stovetop or oven. SIMPLE!

Serving Suggestions: Fresh vegetables, salad, and whole-grain bread.

Servings: The x5 recipe yields our family five meals.

Recipe: **Kay's Broccoli and Corn**   From: My sister, Kay Black

Background: Kay is often asked for this recipe, it is that good.

x 1	x 3	Ingredient			Personalize
1	3	cans cream corn (16 oz size)			
10 oz	2 heads	fresh broccoli or equivalent frozen			
1	3	eggs, beaten			
1/2cup (12)	1-1/2 cups (36)	crackers (your choice)			
1	3	onion, chopped			
1/2	1 1/2	teaspoon salt			
dashes		pepper			
1/4	3/4	butter			
1-1/2 Qt	9" x 13"	Oven-proof dish			

Steps:
Steps that can be done ahead: make graham crackers and/or crust
1) Cook broccoli (on stove or in microwave).
2) Cook onion (either saute in butter or cook in microwave).
3) Gently mix broccoli, corn, eggs, salt and onion.
4) Pour in oven-proof casserole dish.
5) Mix butter and cracker crumbs, so that crumbs are equally moistened. Sprinkle over vegetables.
6) Do NOT preheat oven. Bake at 350° for 35-40 minutes.
7) You can divide, label and freeze before you bake it or after.

Servings: The x3 recipe yields for our family 4 meals of side dishes.

Recipe: Swiss Steak   From: Playing around with the microwave

Background: I thoroughly enjoy eating. Don't you? This recipe is one use for middle-range meat. By cooking it with the microwave it becomes tender.

I **use** my microwave. All my friends had microwaves for years before we saved enough to buy one. I appreciate the way I can cook food without adding fat and that steaming works so well. The quickness of this method is a definite benefit. You'll have to adjust this recipe to suit your own microwave. It can be adapted for cooking in a skillet.

x1	x 5	Ingredient			Personalize
2 lbs	8 to 10 lbs	boneless beef round steak [shop around for a family pack of meat at bargain prices]			
1/4 cup	1 cup	flour (use your favorite)			
1 tsp	1 1/2 Tbsp	salt (or none at all)			
1 cup	2-3 cups	celery, sliced very thinly			
1	5	onion, thinly sliced rings			
1	5	bell pepper			
1 (small-10-oz)can	1 large or 4 to 5 small cans	tomato soup			
2/3 cup	3 cups	water			
1	3	Tablespoons Worcestershire sauce			

Steps:
Steps that can be done ahead, or assembly-lined: (1, 2, 4 and/or 5)

1) Trim fat off meat; pound flat. Cut into appropriate sizes for your family.
2) Mix flour and spices. Coat meat with this flour mixture.
3) Place coated meat in microwaveable dish(es).
4) Chop bell peppers, onions and celery.
5) Either saute or microwave vegetables until tender.
6) Mix vegetables with remaining ingredients.
7) Pour vegetable mixture over meat. Cover dish with lid or with plastic wrap.
8) Microwave on high (100%) for 5 minutes. Then cook for 40 to 50 minutes on medium setting (50%). My microwave has a revolving tray. If yours doesn't, be sure to turn the plate every ten minutes. Adjust the cooking time according to your oven.
9) Divide, label, and freeze.
10) Thaw and warm in oven. (You can thaw it via microwave if you are rushed for time)

Notes/Comments: This microwave method really helps make the meat tender. In that way you can use a cheaper cut of beef. This recipe can be done in an electric skillet, but my experience has been that the meat will not be as tender.

Side dishes: Since this is just the meat dish, you'll still need to prepare a starch, vegetable salad and bread.

Servings: The x5 recipe yields our family five meals.

Recipe: **Crab Newburg**   From: Attempt at duplicating a restaurant meal

Background: Warning: This is not the most healthful of meals, but sometimes we like to splurge in the calorie arena. And this recipe is a delicious dive into "not-the-most-healthful-of-eating." We've had wonderful success with imitation crab meat. It's affordable and is better (lower in calories) than real crab.

x1	x 5	Ingredient			Personalize
4 oz	2 lbs	crab meat (can use shrimp, or scallops or similar type of seafood—it also works with poultry)			
1/4 cup	1 cup	bell pepper (diced)			
2 Tbls	1/4 cup	butter or margarine (optional)			
2 (10-oz) cans	10 (10-oz) cans	Cheddar cheese soup OR homemade cheese sauce			
2 Tbls	1 small can (6 oz)	tomato paste			
dashes		hot pepper sauce			
1 cup or 1 can	5 cups	mushrooms (slice fresh) or sliced canned			
1 small can	3 to 5 cans	pimento (strips or pieces)			
2	10	eggs			
1/3 cup	1 2/3 cups	heavy cream			

Steps:
Steps that can be done ahead, or assembly-lined: (1 and 2)

1) Chop peppers. Slice mushrooms.
2) Either saute mushrooms and peppers in butter or steam in microwave.
3) In a large saucepan, blend soup, tomato paste and pepper sauce. Add mushrooms and bell peppers.
4) Add crab meat and pimento.
5) Heat through.
6) Meanwhile, in a separate bowl, blend eggs with cream.
7) Gradually, stir in one cup of hot crab meat mixture into eggs. Then carefully mix all of the egg mixture into the rest of the crab meat mixture. (By doing this separate step, you help keep the eggs from cooking into lumps, making for a more even sauce. It increases the eggs' temperature gradually.)

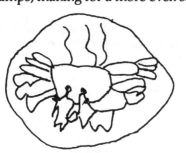

8) Cook slowly on low heat until thickened.
9) Divide, label, and freeze.
10) Thaw, heat through. Serve over rice, pastry shells, or toast. (See page 17-2 for a quick way to make pastry shells.)

Servings: The x5 recipe yields our family five meals.

Aside: Fresh vegetables are, of course, healthier than canned. If possible, for all these recipes, make your own tomato sauce and prepare your own fresh vegetables.

Recipe: **Almost Plum Nearly**   From: Experimenting

Background: On a "great explore," as Winnie the Pooh would describe it, my parents were out on a Sunday drive with some dear friends, the Kiers. On old country roads and rambling through the back woods they came across the relics of a farm. Leaning against a rotten fence post was a sign. It read "Almost Plum Nearly Farm." The name appealed to our family. It's an old country expression for as close to perfection as you could get.

x1	x 5	Ingredient			Personalize
1 jr jar	5 jr jars	plums, baby food (see note below)			
1 1/2	7-1/2	cups chicken broth			
2 Tbls	3/4 cup	cornstarch			
2	10	Tablespoons orange juice concentrate, frozen			
2	10	Tablespoons honey			
1 tsp	1 1/2 Tbls	Worcestershire			
3	10 to 15 lbs	pounds chicken or turkey (use pieces, slices, or chunks)			

Steps:
Steps that can be done ahead, or assembly-lined: (prepare poultry and/or plums)

1) Mix all ingredients except poultry.
2) Cook, stirring until thickened.
3) Pour mixture over poultry.
4) Divide, label and freeze.
5) Thaw, heat through.
6) Serve over rice or noodles.

> **Fresh plums** work wonderfully with this recipe. Simply peel and chop them removing all pits. Cook them until soft and puree them in your blender. Be careful, if they are hot your blender may overheat. Let them cool first.

Servings: The x5 recipes yields our family five meals.

Note: One of the recipes that I read (to glean ideas for this recipe) called for a can of whole pitted purple plums, drained. The recipe instructions included forcing the plums through a sieve to get them to a state that could be used in the sauce. I tried that once. The can of plums was expensive, plus it required extra work to prepare. Since then I've used the baby food plums (junior size) and have had wonderful success. The baby food plums are inexpensive and 100% plums compared with the "adult" plums which were packed in a sugar syrup. Now if eating baby food isn't your style, you can go the regular plum route.

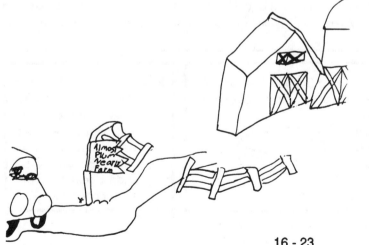

> **Another idea:** For another delicious sauce to serve over poultry: mix one cup of orange marmalade or apricot preserves with one package of dry onion soup mix and one cup of Russian or Western dressing. Follow the same steps as above (multiply out for larger servings).

Recipe: **Red Square** From: Eastern Europe Study Unit

Background: We were studying about the U.S.S.R. and more specifically Russia. They seem to be on the news now daily. As part of our studies I wanted to give the children a taste for their food. First, we talked about going hungry and being in long food lines. Then we discussed the high cost of meat. We combined several recipes for goulash and made a dish. Because it came out red in color and the food was cubed, the boys loved the idea of Red Square. Besides, that fit in with the geography lesson.

x 1	x4	Ingredient				Personalize
5	20	beets				
2-3	10	potatoes - whatever kind is cheapest				
1/2	2	pounds stew meat chopped into tiny cubes				
3-4	12-16	carrots				
1	4	onions				
1/2 tsp	1 Tbls	each of the following spices: Tarragon, basil, cumin, salt, and pepper.				
1	2	bay leaves				

Steps:

Steps that can be done ahead: (1 and 2)

1) Clean, peel, and cube vegetables.
2) Brown meat.
3) In a large dutch oven, boil vegetables in water. OR use crock pot.
4) Add in meat and spices.
5) Simmer, covered, on very low heat for one hour. Test vegetables for tenderness. If they are tender yet firm, serve OR . . .
6) Divide, label, freeze.
7) Thaw, and heat.

> Don't forget to remove the bay leaves.

Note: The beets turn everything red. The potatoes appear red. The carrots appear red. So don't think you've done something wrong. Remember this is a very simple dish, born out of the poverty of poorer countries.

Servings: The x4 recipe yields for our family four meals.

Tip: Do you ever use a full soap pad (steel wool type) at one time? Cut them in half with your kitchen shears into a more workable size. This way you don't waste half of it and you also sharpen your shears.

Hint: Leftover mashed potatoes? Make "Fire Engines" —partially slice a hotdog in half length-wise (don't cut clear through), scoop mashed potatoes in well/groove, then layer on slices of cheese. Bake in oven until cheese is melted. [There are turkey hotdogs available.]

Remember: Double check for airtightness. Don't do all this work and then have to throw it all away because you didn't seal the container correctly.

Recipe: **Polish al Fredo** From: Mixing two cuisines

Background: We experimented with two distinct ethnic cuisines: Polish and Italian. This recipe is a mixture of the two. I hope you like it.

x1	x2	Ingredient			Personalize
1/2	1	pound vegetable curly noodles (or could use regular)			
1/2	1	cup chopped carrots			
1/2	1	cup chopped zucchini			
1/2	1	cup chopped bell pepper			
1/2	1	pound Kielbassa or Polish sausage [mol]			
1/2	1	Tablespoon onion powder			
1/2	1	Tablespoon garlic powder			
1/2	1	cup half 'n half cream			
2 Tbls	1/4 cup	Parmesan cheese			

Steps:
Steps that can be done ahead: (1 and 2)

1) Prepare vegetables, wash, and chop.
2) Cut sausage into slices, then cut each slice into four small pieces.
3) Saute vegetables in a skillet with a small amount of butter or oil.
4) Add onion and garlic powder.
5) In another pot, prepare noodles. Bring water to boiling, add noodles, cook for 6 to 8 minutes or according to package directions.
6) Add noodles and sausage to vegetables.
7) Cover skillet and let simmer for 20 minutes.
8) Add half 'n half cream and cheese. Stir. Let cook another 5 minutes to thicken.
9) Serve, and/or divide, label and freeze.
10) Thaw, warm, and serve.

Note: One alternate way to prepare this is to make only the sausage/vegetable mixture, freeze; then on the day of serving, prepare the noodles and serve the two together.

Servings: The x2 recipe yields our family three meals.

Tip: Children love to "paint" your pans. Just have them do the greasing of your baking pans using a pastry brush and the shortening as paint. Even when Trent was 21 months old he could do it. It gets them involved and saves you from the messy task.

Recipe: *Spring Chicken*   From: OWC Fort Campbell Cookbook

Background: This was in the cookbook that the Officers' Wives Club of Fort Campbell, KY published in 1982. Permission granted to print here. For more information, see Appendix D. Used by permission. We've found it more fun to rename recipes so to encourage our young eaters. Chicken Casserole, the original name was kind of boring and didn't excite the children. So we looked at it — when cooked it has the soft colors of Springtime. So we made a play on the words calling it "Spring Chicken."

x 1	x 3	x 6	Ingredient				Personalize
3	6-9	9-18	Cooked, diced chicken (mol)				
4	12	24	Boiled eggs, chopped				
2	8	16	Cups cooked rice (cook in chicken broth)				
1	2	3	Cups chopped celery				
1	2	3	Onions, chopped (mol - see note on page 8-10)				
1	3	6	Cups salad dressing				
1	3	6	Cans mushroom soup				
1	3	6	Cans water chestnuts				
2	6	12	Tablespoons lemon juice				
1	3	6	Cups bread crumbs (mol) (optional)				

Steps:
Steps that can be done ahead or assembly-lined (1, 2, 3 and 4)
1) Bake, chop turkey.
2) Cook, peel, chop eggs.
3) Cook rice.
4) Chop celery and onions.
5) Open cans, chop waterchestnuts.
6) Supervise, mix ingredients (except bread crumbs).
7) Divide, sprinkle each top with 1 cup bread crumbs, label, freeze.
8) Thaw and Bake in 350 °F, 40 to 45 minutes.
9) OR bake frozen, Bake in 300 °F, 1-1/2-2 hours. Check after 1 hour and stir.
10) OR zap in microwave 20 minutes on medium high, covered. Check after 10 minutes.

Notes/Comments: Sample recipe, details explained in Chapter Nine.

Side dishes: Home-made bread and fresh fruit cup.

Servings: Each multiple serves six, so "x6" will make 36 servings.

This recipe is repeated here so that you can personalize it.

Tip: One sure way I know to chop eggs without ending up with mush is by using a pastry knife. The blades slice the eggs evenly. My food processor turns them into puree, so I like the ease of the pastry knife or pastry blade.

Recipe: **Zucchini or Carrot Bread**   From: Adapted from three recipes

Background: A friend called me after her son's birthday party to tell me how well my boys had behaved. "I offered them some candy, and they said, 'No thank you, Mommy will give us a muffin when we get home instead.' I want your muffin recipe. How have you taught them to prefer good food?" This is my boys' favorite bread/muffin recipe. They literally like it better than candy.

x1	x4	x10	x12	Ingredient			Personalize
1 1/2	6	15	18	cups grated zucchini and/or carrots (any combination)			
1/2	2	5	6	cups oil (Safflower is preferable)			
1/2	2	5	6	cups honey (brown sugar or molasses can be substituted)			
2	8	20	24	eggs			
1 tsp	4 tsp	3 Tbls	1/4 cup	vanilla			
1 1/2	6	15	18	cups whole wheat flour			
1/2 tsp	2 tsp	5 tsp	2 Tbls	baking soda			
1/2 tsp	2 tsp	5 tsp	2 Tbls	salt (mol)			
1-1/2	2 Tbls	5 Tbls	1/3 cup	cinnamon			
1/2	2	5	6	cups raisins			
1/2 tsp	2 tsp	5 tsp	2 Tbls	nutmeg			
1/2	2	5	6	cups chopped nuts (optional)			

Steps:

Steps that can be done ahead, or assembly-lined: (1)

1) Grate carrots and zucchini.
2) Beat together oil and honey. Beat in eggs and vanilla.
3) Sift dry ingredients and add to liquid mixture. Stir in nuts and/or raisins.
4) Bake in greased 9" x 5" x 3" loaf pans (or muffin tins or mini-loaf pans) at 350° for 45 to 60 minutes, or until test done. (Approximately 12 to 15 minutes for medium-sized muffins.)
5) Cool in pan 10 minutes. Invert onto wire rack.
6) Wrap, label and refrigerate or freeze.
7) Thaw and serve.

Servings: This recipe yields a dozen medium-sized muffins or one large loaf per multiple or a combination thereof. For example: Normally, x10 yields 6 loaves and 48 muffins. Note: By not filling the pans as full and by using smaller sized pans, I am able to stretch the x10 recipe to bake 6 small loaves (7" x 3 1/2" size), 36 medium-sized muffins, and 48 mini-muffins and 8 mini-loaves.

Tip: Measure oil in measuring cup first, then measure the honey. Both will pour out quickly without the honey sticking to the side of the cup. (Illustration: In 4-cup measuring cup, fill with oil to the 1 1/2-cup line then pour in honey to the 3-cup line.)

Hint: A food processor is a major help in the grating of the carrots and zucchini. Or you can use your blender. Check your manual. Mine requires a cup or two of water with the vegetables to grate. You just have to allow time for draining the water. Or you can burn some calories by using a hand grater.

Recipe: **Cookies Anytime**   From: Adaption of recipes and experimenting

Background: It is rare for me to serve these cookies and not be asked for the recipe. The dough is similar to those expensive, yet convenient slice and bake cookies you buy at the grocers'. Save a lot of money, and make your own ready-to-bake dough. You control the ingredients, so you can use whole grain flour, and substitute fructose for sugar. Then, when you need cookies quickly, just grab a roll out of the freezer, slice, and bake. Or for an extra treat, roll out and cut into your child's favorite shapes.

x1	x2	Ingredient			Personalize
1-3/4	3-1/2	cups whole wheat flour (or your favorite flour)			
1/2	1	teaspoon baking powder			
1/2	1	teaspoon salt (mol)			
1/2	1	teaspoon baking soda			
1/2	1	cup sugar (or less fructose — see page 16-3)			
1/2 (1 stick)	1 (2 sticks)	cup butter, margarine, or other substitute			
1	2	eggs (or equivalent egg substitute)			
2	4	Tablespoons milk			
1	2	teaspoons vanilla extract			
5 doz	10 doz	Approximate yield of cookies depending on the size you make			

Steps:

1) Sift flour with baking powder, salt, baking soda, and sugar into large bowl.
2) Cut butter into flour mixture until similar to coarse corn meal.
3) Stir in eggs, milk, and vanilla. If easier, use a hand mixer.
4) Either wrap in rolls for slicing (use wax paper or plastic wrap); OR place in an airtight container. Either refrigerate at least 2 hours, or freeze.
5) To form:
   From frozen dough: Thaw partially. Slice into 1/8" circles; roll out to 1/8" inch thick and cut with favorite cutters; OR simply spoon out in cookie-sized mounds. Dough works better when it's very cold. Keep unused portion in refrigerator while you work.
   From chilled dough: Slice, roll, or spoon out out as above.
6) Bake on cookie sheets (there is no need to add extra grease). Spraying with cooking spray helps with clean-up. Bake 7 minutes at 375°. Cool on wire racks.

Notes/Comments: I've tried multiplying this recipe by four, but found it was more dough than I could handle to mix well. You might be more coordinated than I am. Try to find your own level. I usually run through the recipe 2 or 3 times to get 4 to 6 times the recipe or 20 to 30 dozen cookies (10 to 15 rolls).

Tip: You can also mix in nuts, raisins and/or chips (e.g., chocolate, carob, or butterscotch).

Hint: I used to love a commercial brand of cooking spray (a girl's name) because it helped in clean-up, cut calories, and it came in a pump. (I don't like aerosol sprays since they kick up my asthma.) For some reason, I haven't been able to find it in pump form anymore. So I read the ingredients on the can and have mixed equal amounts of liquid lecithin and vegetable oil and poured it into my own pump sprayer. It's less expensive and works well. Be sure to shake it well before each use.

Hint: Before running errands, we fill a thermos full of ice water to take with us. Whenever my sons get thirsty, we just pour up some of the water. This has saved us time and money by not having to "drive-thru" for a soft-drink. Besides, water is much better for all of us.

Recipe: **Pastry** From: Practice, practice, practice

Background: Pastry making is an art that can be easily mastered. The trick is don't try so hard. A dear friend had tried to make pastry, but it was always tough, so once we set up side by side and she mirrored each step that I did. We found the problem, she was overworking the dough. She was making it much more work than it needed to be. Handle the dough as little as possible for a tender crust.

x1	x2	x5	Ingredient			Personalize
2	4	10	cups flour			
1/2 teas	1 teas	1 Tbls	salt (mol)			
2/3	1-1/3	3-1/3	cups shortening			
1/3	3/4	1-3/4	cups cold water (approximately)			
1	2	5	Yields enough pastry for double crusts			

Steps:

1) Mix flour and salt.
2) Cut in shortening until mix has consistency of small peas. (Use forks or a pastry knife.)
3) Add cold water a little at a time until mix is barely dampened. You probably won't need the full amount mentioned above.
4) Form into balls. Place in air-tight containers. Chill.
5) Roll out a ball onto a floured sheet, board or cloth. Stack the flat pastries, separating with sheets of waxed paper.
6) Freeze in air-tight container.
7) To make a pie: just peel off a pastry round. Let thaw and form in pie pan. Follow directions for pie.

Notes: You could also freeze the pastry dough when it is in the form of the balls, just reverse steps 5 and 6.

Suggestions:

- Make your own turnovers, pirozhkis, or pockets with this dough. They are very expensive pre-pared and available in the grocer's freezers. However, you can make your own for much less.
- Use this recipe to make your own pot-pies. See page 16-18. Try adding a dash of herbs into the flour for the meat pies.
- You can pre-make and bake tart-size pastries and freeze. Then just thaw and fill with quiche fillings, meat salad, jelly, or other fillings.
- If you're cutting back calories, try making pies, but leave off the bottom crust. For instance, each Thanksgiving I make one of the pumpkin pies crust-less for the diet-watchers. It makes a pumpkin custard. I simply pour the filling into an empty pie pan and bake it with the others. Delicious.

Hint: One requirement of cooking that I personally found difficult was sifting. I used a sifter that left my hand cramping after just sifting a few cups. Then I learned the trick of simply using a fine gauge metal strainer, and stirring the flour until it sifts down. I can now sift five pounds of flour in minutes, without hand cramps.

Hint: Use your cookie cutters for more than cookies. Make sandwich puzzles. Cut a shape out of a sandwich (the puzzle piece), leaving the form as the puzzle. For a snack, cut cheese slices with your cutters (e.g., giraffe shape cut-out of yellow cheese with raisins for spots). I'm not skilled at cake decorations, so I make cookies to decorate the tops of cakes. I use alphabet-shaped cookies to spell out "Happy Birthday." Cut your biscuits out with cookie cutters (e.g., heart shape).

Recipe: Tidbit Cream Puffs

Background: These bite size cream puffs are very easy, and freeze well. They are great for quick desserts or appetizers. They are always a hit, even if your husband accidently fills them with the wrong filling. Alan once filled them with dip instead of pudding. Both bowls were in the refrigerator and he grabbed for the first bowl he came across. The puffs were still gobbled up quickly. I try to keep a bag full of about thirty of them in the freezer at all times for quick serves.

x1	x2	x3	Ingredient					Personalize
1/3	2/3	1	cup butter or margarine					
3/4	1-1/2	2-1/3	cups water					
3/4	1-1/2	2-1/3	cups sifted flour					
1/4	1/2	3/4	teaspoons salt					
3	6	9	eggs					
30	60	90	yield: number of puffs					

Steps:

1) Preheat oven to 400°. Grease or spray cookie sheets (1 pan for each multiple).
2) In a saucepan, heat butter and water to boiling.
3) Quickly stir in flour and salt. Beat with spoon until mixture forms a ball and leaves the side of the pan. Then remove from the heat.
4) Beat in eggs, one at a time. Make sure they are well mixed.
5) Drop, by teaspoonfuls, onto prepared cookie sheets. OR to make them "fancy" load a pastry bag (see hint below) and using a decorator tip, squeeze the dough out into fluted mounds.
6) Bake 30 minutes. Cool on wire rack.
7) Divide, bag, and freeze.

To Serve:

8) Thaw as many as you'll need.
9) Slice in half horizontally.
10) Fill with a pudding or cream for a dessert. Or for appetizers: fill with a meat salad (e.g., tuna, crab, ham) — either mayonnaise based or cream-cheese based. Or fill with ice cream and make your own ice cream sandwiches.
11) Replace pastry top.

Note: Use this recipe or use your favorite cream, puff/eclaire recipe, just spoon the dough out by teaspoonfuls.

Hint: Orange marmalade makes a great and quick sauce to coat meat or chicken. Orange juice is a wonderful marinade for meats or chicken.

Hint: Pineapple juice is a natural meat tenderizer. Use it as a marinade.

Hint: It might sound silly, but many baby foods work well for quick sauces. For example, baby plum pudding makes a delicious meat sauce.

Hint: To help with clean-up, to keep filling/icing fresh, and for quick storage, I use a zipper-type storage bag for a pastry bag. Simply cut a small piece out of one of the bottom corners. Fit your tip through it as you would your pastry bag. Stuff the bag with the filling/icing and "zip" it closed. This way if you are interrupted while working (with four children, I am always interrupted), you can lay it down without the icing pouring out; or you can place it all in the refrigerator until you can finish it. This also works if you need to store icing. For instance, when you have icing in different colors and only need a tiny bit for the current project, you can store or freeze the extra for the next decorating session.

Recipe: **English Muffins**   From: Adapting several versions

Background: If you've never had home-made English muffins, you're in for a treat. Warning: you may never go back to store-bought ones. With this one recipe I learned the folly of trying to double a recipe too many times. I had more dough than I could physically knead, and had to "draft" my husband for help. Kneading dough was not what he expected when he came home from work, but he was again a sweetheart. Once he tasted them, he offered to help anytime. Just a word to the wise, know your limits (physical ability, storage space, dish capacity) and you can save some wasted work.

x1	x 2	x3 (very difficult)	Ingredient				Personalize
			cornmeal				
1-1/4	2-1/2	3-3/4	cups very warm water				
1	2	3	pkgs dry yeast				
1 teas	2 teas	1 Tbls	fructose or sugar				
2 teas	4 teas	2 Tbls	salt (mol)				
4	8	12	cups sifted flour				
1/4	1/2	3/4	cup butter softened				

Steps:

1) Grease large cookie sheets and sprinkle with cornmeal.
2) Mix sugar in water; dissolve yeast in sugar-water mixture.
3) When yeast is frothy, add salt and 2 (4 or 6) cups flour. Beat vigorously with a wooden spoon until batter is smooth (2 to 3 minutes).
4) Add butter and 1 (2 or 3) cups flour; continue beating until batter is smooth. Gradually, add in remaining flour gradually then beat until batter is smooth, sticky and thick.
5) Turn out onto a well-floured pastry cloth, board, or sheet. Coat all sides of the dough with flour. Cover with bowl and let rest 5 minutes.
6) Knead dough five minutes until smooth. Roll out 1/4 inch thick. With a biscuit cutter, or a large can, cut into muffins. Place onto cookie sheet coated with cornmeal.
7) Let rise in a warm place, covered with a towel about 50 minutes until double in size.
8) Bake muffins on ungreased griddle or skillet until golden brown, about 7 minutes on each side. Cool on wire rack.
9) After they have completely cooled, freeze in air-tight containers.

Suggestions: In addition to just slicing and eating the muffins, try making eggs benedict, use them for hamburgers buns, chicken a la king, or as the "crust" for a personal pizza. My favorite is a Polynesian delight: spread a split muffin half with salad dressing (e.g. sandwich spread), add a pineapple ring, and top with 1 teaspoon of shredded coconut. Broil 1 minute.

Hint: Most recipes in standard recipe books that call for all-purpose flour would be better (healthier) if you substituted whole-wheat, oat, or other whole-grain flour. Better yet, grind your own flour fresh.

Tip: When you use whole-grain flours, instead of flouring your pastry cloth or kneading board, **oil** your hands and cloth or board. This is much better than flouring for making the dough not stick while kneading.

Tip: When I'm making yeast breads, to help the dough rise, I set the bowl or trays on my clothes dryer and time my laundry so that I'm doubling the use of the heat: to dry the clothes and to give heat to the dough.

Recipe: **Panama Punch**   From: Donna Shelton

Background: Donna first served me this punch at a church function while we were stationed in Panama. It was not only delicious, but I liked the fact that she had made it days before, and just had to add soda before serving. I've experimented and varied the ingredients, so try it with your favorite juice.

x1	x 2	x3	Ingredient				Personalize
5	10	15	ripe bananas, mashed				
1/2	1	1-1/2	cups lemon juice				
1 sml	2sml	1 large	can orange juice frozen concentrated (prepared as directed) or the equivalent of fresh				
1-1/2 OR 3	3 OR 6	4-1/2 OR 9	cups fructose OR sugar				
3	6	9	cups unsweetened pineapple juice				
To be poured over punch base the day of serving:							
16-24 oz	32-48 oz	48-72 oz	clear soda like ginger ale or lemonade				

Steps:
1) Mash bananas.
2) In saucepan, warm juices and stir in fructose or sugar until dissolved.
3) Stir in mashed bananas.
4) Pour into forms (air tight containers or ring molds).
5) Freeze at least 12 hours. Will keep for months in the freezer.
6) To serve, remove from freezer about 2 hours ahead of time. Thaw to a mush texture. Pour into punch bowl. Pour soda or lemonade over mixture.

Servings: Approximately: 10 cups for x1, 20 cups for x2, and 30 cups for x3.

Suggestions: Don't just save this for company. Freeze small amounts and make a cool refreshing drink for your family. I have a friend who especially enjoys this drink. Whenever she comes over, I make her a pitcher-full. It's nice to have it ready in your freezer. I have formed it in a decorative ring, and only thawed it for 1 hour to dress it up. Also, the base makes great popsicles for the children. Just pour it in your molds or into cups (place a popsicle stick in cup).

Question: If you had food and drink prepared, would you be more apt to entertain, to practice hospitality, to invite those visitors to your church over, or offer some help to the family moving in on the block? Give it a try and see if it helps you to be more hospitable.

Florida Cracker Lemonade: To get more juice from your lemons, place them in very hot water for 10 minutes, or microwave for thirty seconds. This is a wonderful experiment for you and your children. When we tested this old secret, we squeezed 1/3 cup from the cold lemon and 2/3 cup from the hot lemon. I often am asked for my lemonade recipe. If you are only used to "crystal versions" of lemonade, it is a special treat, to drink some made from real lemons. Juice your lemons for all their worth, then heat the juice in a sauce pan and add in 1 teaspoon of fructose or 2 teaspoons of sugar per lemon sqeezed. Stir until dissolved. In a pitcher, add the juice mixture to 2 cups water per lemon used. Slice a lemon very thinly and float rings in the juice. Adjust the ratios according to your palette for tartness or sweetness.

Recipe: **Gator Bowl Salad**   From: Idea from my Aunt Ginny

Background: Some twenty years ago, my Aunt Ginny encouraged me and showed me the value of pre-preparing. It was her year to hostess the White family reunion: seven siblings and beaucoup grandchildren. She had us all for the entire week-end. I remember having a wonderful time. I believe she did too. She had already prepared all the food ahead of time. She only had to warm it up. She was organized. One of the dishes she served she called "Batman Salad." She was a master at the art of renaming recipes to entice children. That was when the campy television series was out. So we all dug into the "Batman Salad." Madison Avenue could learn something from mothers on positioning products. I don't remember what all was in the salad, so I re-invented it and named it for my father's favorite team, the University of Florida Gators- it's orange and blue.

4 (4-serving size) packages of orange-flavored gelatin

1 12-ounce container of whipped topping (or make your own. I use a sugar-free version)

1 20-ounce can of crushed pineapple and juice

1 48-ounce container of sour cream

1 48-ounce container of cream cheese

1 16-ounce package of mini-marshmallows

12 to 24 ounces of blueberries or more

2 cups of grated coconut

1) Fold gelatin powder into whipped topping. Set aside.

2) In a separate bowl, cream together sour cream and cream cheese.

3) Gently stir together gelatin mixture, cream cheese mixture, pineapple, coconut, and mini-marshmallows. Ensure all ingredients are evenly dispersed throughout mixture.

4) Ever so gently, fold in blueberries. Do not overmix or the salad will turn solid blue.

5) Divide into meal size portions. You can eat this after it has chilled for five hours. And/or you can freeze servings and partially thaw in refrigerator.

Note: If you want even more contrast of the orange and blue, you can add orange food coloring to the salad before you fold in the blueberries. You can use more blueberries for a richer looking and tasting salad. It also is attractive if you fold in some Mandarin oranges.

Servings: This version makes enough for eight meals for our family. You can certainly pare this recipe down to make a smaller amount. Just divide everything by four.

Recipe: **Frozen Cranberry Salad** From: My sister, Kay

Background: Kay serves this year round. She keeps two or three in her freezer for dinners, parties, and covered-dishes. It is delicious.

1 20-ounce can crushed pineapple (#2 can and juice)

1 can whole cranberry sauce

1 8-ounce package cream cheese, softened

pecan pieces (optional)

1 regular pkg (12-ounce) miniature marshmallows

1 small container of whipped topping (2 cup size)

Steps:

1) Blend cream cheese until soft.

2) Add all ingredients except marshmallows.

3) Gently fold in marshmallows.

4) Freeze in mold.

5) Serve frozen. Let stand at least a few minutes before serving.

Recipe: **Pudding Pops**   From: Much Trial and Error

Background: My children love popsicles, pudding pops, and other frozen treats. But, they are expensive and laden with sugar. So I started experimenting and have found a combination that they love, is reasonable in cost, and I can control the sugar.

Basically, make your favorite pudding recipe, only use 1 and half times the milk required. Make your favorite gelatin recipe, only use 1 and a half times the water. Evenly mix the two together and pour in cups or molds. You could use sugar or sugar free mixes. However, I like to make mine from scratch:

For Pudding: (this is great as banana pudding by just adding slices of bananas)
1/4 cup cornstarch
2/3 cup fructose (or sugar)
1/4 teaspoon salt (optional)
2 cups of milk, scalded for regular pudding **OR**
  3 cups of milk scalded for pudding pops pudding
3 slightly beaten egg yolks
2 Tablespoons butter
1/2 teaspoon vanilla
For Gelatin:
Either 1-6 oz package of gelatin mix **OR**
  2 packages of unflavored gelatin
Water or juice (depending on flavors desired) use amount of liquid according to package directions except for the pudding pops use 1 and a half times the liquid called for.

1) In a double boiler, mix cornstarch, fructose (or sugar), and salt.
2) Gradually add in milk. Cook until thickened (about 10 minutes), stirring constantly.
3) To avoid having the eggs lump, slowly add a small amount of hot mixture to the egg yolks in a separate container. Then mix this egg mixture into the hot milk mixture. Cook five more minutes.
4) Add butter and vanilla. Stir. Remove from heat. Allow to cool.
5) Follow directions on package of gelatin except use 1 & 1/2 times the liquid required. (Either use unflavored—and add your own juice or flavoring—or use a pre-packaged type.) It should normally yield four cups. However, since you'll be using 1 & 1/2 times the water (or juice), the yield will be about 6 cups.
6) While still liquid, evenly mix gelatin and pudding. You can also add mashed bananas for more flavor, or any other pureed fruit.
7) Pour into cups or popsicle molds. Freeze. Enjoy.

Servings: This recipe yields approximately 35 pudding pops.

Suggestions:
- By varying the juice and fruit, you can make all sorts of delicious combinations.
- To make frozen yogurt pops: try adding in some yogurt in place of the pudding or in addition to it.

Hint: Make visiting children feel special. Save money. Help the environment. All by using an idea from my sister, Kay. She bought one package of disposable plastic cups (sturdier than paper ones) and marks each cup with a child's name. She keeps the stack in her pantry and whenever the child visits again he/she can re-use the same cup. This saves going through dozens and dozens of paper cups on subsequent visits. She has cups made for nephews, nieces, friends' children, her children's friends, etc. As one visiting child said as he ran to her pantry to get his own cup, "I'm special at the Black's. I have my own cup. They want to me to come back again and again."

Recipe: **Crazy Carrot Cake**   From: Searching

Background: When dining out, I can rarely eat the dessert since I'm hypoglycemic. So I hunt for recipes that I can make myself for dessert and that are still delicious and more nutritious than most desserts. Either way it is still an indulgence. I love carrot cake. So, after several attempts in the Bond Test Kitchen, we found a version that is healthier than most cakes. It makes a big cake. I cut it into fourths, we eat one fourth that evening and freeze the rest for other nights.

3/4 cup oil (your favorite type)
3/4 cup honey
4 eggs
2 cups whole wheat flour (fresh ground is wonderful)
2 teaspoons baking powder
1/2 teaspoon salt (mol)
1-1/2 teaspoon baking soda
1 Tablespoon cinnamon (ground)
2 cups grated carrots
1 cup crushed pineapple, drained (I prefer the unsweetened variety)

1) Grate carrots (This can be done ahead. You can refrigerate or freeze the carrots in AIRTIGHT containers. until you're ready to bake the cake. See note below)
2) Grease and flour **three** 9" layer pans. See note below.
3) Preheat oven to 350˚.
4) Measure oil in cup then pour honey up to the 1 1/2 cup line. This will help you retain every drop of honey. Pour into mixing bowl.
5) Crack the eggs one at a time (see box) and drop into the honey/oil mixture.
6) Mix for 30 seconds.
7) In a bowl, stir together flour, baking powder, salt and soda.
8) Add flour mixture to the honey mixture.
9) Mix for 2 minutes.
7) Stir in remaining ingredients.
8) Pour cake batter into pans. Bake at 350˚ for 35 to 40 minutes.
9) Cool in pans for ten minutes, then turn out and allow them to cool completely on racks.
10) Ice cake between layers and on the outside with Creamy Cheese Frosting.

Creamy Cheese Frosting

16 ounces of cream cheese, softened
1 cup of butter, softened
1/4 to 1/2 cup honey (mol depending on how sweet you want it)
2 teaspoons vanilla

1) Beat cream cheese and butter until smooth and light.
2) Beat in honey and vanilla.
3) Ice cake.

> **Tip:** My mother taught me to break eggs one at a time into a cup, then to add the egg to the mix. This procedure has saved many a baking session from being a fiasco. If the egg is bad, or I accidently get some shell in, I can easily pour the one egg out. If, on the other hand, I had cracked it directly into the batter the entire batter would have had to been thrown out.
>
> **Tip:** To make shortening fall out of your measuring cup easily: before measuring the shortening, leave a thin egg film in the measuring cup by swishing a raw egg in the cup and pouring it out into another container (for later use in the same recipe).

Note:
- Whenever I can buy carrots at a bargain price, I go ahead and grate them, form them into little one-cup mounds and freeze them solid. Then I bag the carrot mounds. Whenever I need them in a recipe, I simply grab a carrot cup mound, and put it into soups, muffins, or this cake.
- You can substitute zucchini for the carrots or use a combination of the two.
- You can add in grated nuts: for the cake add in 1/2 to 1 cup, for the icing add in 1/2 cup.
- Try "flouring" your cake pans with wheat germ instead of flour. It adds a special "nutty" flavor to the cake.

Recipe: **Balmy Breezes Pie**   From: Five generations of Floridians

Background: Some recipes just go with the territory. This recipe is one of those. It'll remind you of a tropical vacation. It freezes fairly well. Admittedly, the frozen ones aren't as good as the ones made fresh that day. I'd give them an A-. So, they are worth trying. They make for a light dessert. I make at least four at a time. Depending on the size of your blender, you might have to make them one at a time, one right after the other.   In my blender I can double the recipe, so I just repeat the whole process again. Try one the first time. Freeze a slice to test it. If you like it, the next time make more pies. Note: by buying in large quantities and using generics, I can make six* pies for about the same cost as one pie buying the exact recipe size amounts.

x 1	x 2	x4	Ingredient				Personalize
1/4	1/2	1	cup cold milk				
1	2	4	envelopes unflavored gelatin				
1/2	1	2	cups milk				
2/3	1-1/3	2-2/3	cups sugar [or use fructose—approximately half the amount]				
1	2	4	packages (8-ounce size) cream cheese, softened				
1	2	4	Tablespoons lemon juice				
1	2	4	teaspoons vanilla				
1	2	4	cartons (8-ounce size) of sour cream				
1	2	4	cans (8-ounce size) crushed pineapple, drain and reserve liquid				
1/4	1/2	1	cup of the reserved pineapple juice				
1	2	4	graham cracker crust for a 8" or 9" pie (see step 7)				

Steps:

Steps that can be done ahead: make graham crackers and/or crust

1) In blender pitcher, on low, process the cold milk (1/4,1/2, or 1 cup) with the gelatin. Blend until gelatin is softened.
2) Heat 1/2 (1 or 2) cups of milk either in sauce pan or in microwave. Pour into blender container and blend until gelatin is completely dissolved.
3) Add sugar, cream cheese, lemon juice, sour cream, and vanilla. Blend until smooth.
4) Add pineapple and 1/4 (1/2 or 1) cup of its juice. Process until smooth.
5) Pour into prepared crust.
6) Chill at least three hours before serving.
7) Freeze, if desired. Note: a standard 8" pie plate will slide easily into a gallon zipper-type bag for easy freezing and sealing. Test your pans first.   *With 8" pans I can make 6 pies with 4x recipe (with 9" only 4 pies).
8) Thaw in refrigerator at least eight hours before serving.

Note:

- This pie becomes very economical when you buy the cream cheese in a 3-pound block. With a ruler, if necessary, mark off six equal sections. Cut the sections, place in airtight containers, label and freeze. They are then ready to use in many recipes and are pre-measured into the standard 8-ounce size. By doing this you cut the cost down by more than half. Note: I've had wonderful success with generic brands. You can buy a 5-pound carton of sour cream also. The #10 can of pineapple will also help cut costs.

- We make our own graham crackers, see the recipe on page 17-7. We then use our homemade crackers to make the crusts — delicious and no sugar or additives. You can crumble them and make regular graham cracker pie crusts, OR try baking the graham cracker dough directly in the pie pan. Just press the dough down with your fingers then bake (approximately 15 minutes). It makes a delicious pie shell with less calories than the traditional shell (it contains no additional sugar or butter).

Recipe: **Healthier than Thou Fruit Cake**   From: Playing in the kitchen

Background: Every recipe I could find for fruit cake called for booze and/or large amounts of sugar. I started by taking a little bit of this and little bit of that from different recipes and found this version that is booze-free and sugar-free AND yummy.

x 1	Ingredient			Personalize
2	teaspoons vanilla			
4 1/2	cups flour (I use whole wheat)			
2	teaspoons baking soda			
4	eggs			
3	sticks butter or 1-1/2 cups			
2	pints of mincemeat (store-bought or home-made)			
2 12-ounce	cans evaporated milk			
2	pounds of candied fruit (I found a brand that was not processed with sugar)			
1	cup honey			
2	cups raisins			

Steps:

Steps that can be done ahead: make your own mincemeat, or even candy your own fruit

1) Preheat oven to 300°.
2) Prepare pans by greasing well.   This recipe makes 1 large angel food cake pan-size cake and eight mini-loaves for gift giving.   Or you can make six bread loaf-size cakes.
2) In the largest bowl of your mixer (or use a handmixer and a big mixing bowl), mix together: vanilla, milk, honey, eggs, and butter.
2) In a separate bowl, mix together flour and baking soda.
3) Gradually add flour mixture to liquid mixture. Mix until well blended.
4) Stir in raisins, fruit and mincemeat.
5) Pour into prepared pans.
6) Bake mini-loaves for 1 hour. The larger sized cakes will take about 2 hours. Check your cakes several times while they are baking. Baking time will vary according to how moist a mincemeat you use. Cakes are done when they spring back in the middle.
7) Cool on racks. These cakes freeze excellently.

Salads: Having trouble getting your children to eat their salad? Put it in a pedestal bowl (like a sundae dish). We sometimes have a salad banana split. Split the banana as you would for an ice cream split, but use scoops of chicken salad, potato salad, and a boiled egg. Instead of syrup use salad dresing. Instead of whipped cream use cottage cheese. Use more fruit on top. I've never had a child turn down one of these banana splits.

Recipe: **Home-made Tortillas**   From: My mother, Zoe White

Background: While my father was serving his second tour in Germany, our neighbor was a young Spanish bride, Maria. She was very homesick and lost as how to cook her dishes with the ingredients available in Central Europe. One day a large package arrived from her mother in Mexico. It was filled with cilantro, masa, etc. Maria was thrilled. During their friendship, Maria taught my mother how to make tortillas. So, this recipe for Tortillas comes from Germany, in a round-about way. This is an Americanized version that freezes well. I make up x3 the recipe and freeze them for other meals.

x 1	x 3	Ingredient				Personalize
2/3	2	cups yellow corn meal				
2 1/3	7	cups all-purpose flour				
1/4	1/2	teaspoon salt (mol)				
3 Tblsp	1/2 cup	shortening				
3/4	2	cups warm water (Approximately — you might need more.)				
12	36	This is approximately how many tortillas you will be able to make.				
$1.00	$3.00	Savings compared to grocery store versions at 10¢ a piece.				

Steps:

1) In a large mixing bowl, mix flours and salt together.
2) With a pastry blender or two knives, cut shortening into flour.
3) Add in warm water. Stir until mixture is completely moistened.
4) Knead dough on a floured surface until it is no longer sticky.
5) Form dough into small balls (golf ball size).
6) As you work, store the dough balls in an airtight container and just pull out the one you are currently working on.
7) Roll out each ball into a circle about 1/8" thick.
8) Bake tortillas on a heated ungreased griddle or skillet one minute on each side.

Note: I roll out several, then start baking. I continue rolling while the first ones are cooking. So I'm rolling out balls into circles in between flipping the baked ones. It takes some juggling, but it is good economy of time.

Note: You can vary the ratio of corn to wheat flour, as long as the two combine to make 3 (or 9 cups). We have found that we prefer this ratio. The more corn flour the more brittle the tortillas will be.

Cake Cones: My mother-in-law, Glenna Hileman[1] gave me this recipe. She knew that it would be a hit with my children. We've made these cake cones many times with our children and visiting friends. I haven't met a child yet that hasn't enjoyed making them.

Make an oil-free cake batter, (your choice of flavor.) If you don't want to make one from scratch, Jiffy® makes a mix that works well. Pour the batter into **flat bottom** ice cream cones. Only fill cones 1/2 full with batter. Cook cone in your microwave. Test this first — but usually one minute on high is perfect. The cake batter will cook and rise up out of the cone. We then ice them with colored icing and they look like ice cream cones but are "cake cones." Children are thrilled to watch them cook. You can actually see the batter rise.

❦ *There is treasure to be desired and oil in the dwelling of the wise; but a foolish man spendeth it up.—Proverbs 21:20 (KJV)*

❦ *They joy before thee according to the joy in harvest — Isaiah 9:3b (KJV)*

CHAPTER SEVENTEEN

Quick Recipes and Easy Recipes

Admittedly, I don't freeze all the food we eat. Many recipes are best made fresh. Some are so quickly made, they aren't a burden. Here are a few quick-to-make recipes and some ideas to make meal preparation less time consuming for you. Some of these recipes aren't exactly quick, but they are easy and/or fun.

Recipe: **Quick as a Wink Coconut Pie**
From: Mama Bert

Background: We were very fortunate that my grandmother lived with us while I was growing up. She was an excellent cook and, once she discovered our favorite recipes, she'd surprise us with them. I happened to love banana pudding and this pie, so she'd often surprise me with one after a rough day or a special event. She taught me her recipes and I found this one so very easy to do that it became one of my regular desserts. Now my family loves it. Also, it is wonderful for company.

1/2 cup baking mix (See Mastermix on Page 17-9 or use Bisquick® or Jiffy®)
3/4 cup fructose or sugar
2 cups milk
1/2 stick butter (1/4 cup)
4 eggs
1 1/2 teaspoon vanilla
1 cup coconut

1) Combine all ingredients <u>except</u> coconut in electric blender.
2) Blend on low speed three minutes.
3) Pour in 9" pie pan, let stand 5 minutes.
4) Sprinkle coconut over top.
5) Bake at 350° for 40 minutes.
6) Best if chilled at least 2 hours before serving.

Note: This pie does not freeze that well. But it is so quick and easy, you can blend it up with short notice. Keep coconut ready in the freezer pre-measured in 1 cup portions.

Recipe: **Quick Monkey Bread**

Background: Like many dishes I prepare, I experimented with ingredients to try to duplicate a dish I ate at a friend's house or in a restaurant. Look for ideas everywhere you dine, both for the food and for the presentation of that dish. This dish can be made as a quick breakfast or is even attractive enough for a brunch buffet or as a dessert. I've heard it also called bubble bread. Even very young children enjoy making it.

pop biscuits in cans (see note and tip below)
cinnamon fructose or sugar mixture (approximately 1/8 cup per can of biscuits, we
     use a ratio of 1 Tablespoon cinnamon to each half cup of sweetener)
syrup, your favorite pancake syrup (approximately 1/2 cup for 3 cans of biscuits)

1) Open cans. Separate into biscuits. Divide each biscuit into three balls.
2) Roll each ball into cinnamon mixture; OR shake balls with cinnamon sugar in a
    container with a tight seal.
3) Place coated balls of dough in greased or sprayed pan (I like to use a Bundt or a
    tube pan.)
4) Pour syrup over dough. Bake according to directions on can. It usually takes
    about twice the time as the can states. But check after 1 & 1/2 times has passed.

Note: Determine the number of cans you need according to how many you will be
    serving. Since my family likes this recipe so much, for breakfast I open half as
    many cans as those eating (For our family of six, I open three cans). You could
    also use yeast roll dough instead of the canned biscuits. (Allow time for rising.)
    Buy the least expensive canned biscuits you can find.

Some other suggestions for canned biscuits:

» Roll around hot dogs for pigs-in-a-blanket.
» Divide into thirds and wrap around miniature sausages for piglets-in-a-
   blanket (a good appetizer or breakfast dish).
» Roll each biscuit flat, spread with spaghetti sauce or tomato sauce, top
   with shredded cheese and pepperoni for quick lunch pizzas. Children
   enjoy making their own.
» Turn your muffin tin upside down,
   grease or spray the bottom. Press two biscuits together, then press over the muffin
   cup. Continue with the whole can. Bake
   per instruction on the can. You'll have
   little pastry cups to fill with chicken à la
   king or other sauce-type dishes.

> **Tip:** The biscuits are easier to work with if you pop the can and allow
>   the dough to rest for five minutes before shaping.

Recipe: **Quick Quiche** From: Bell Lilienfeld

Background: The first time I met Bell, I knew we were kindred souls: two transplanted Floridians adjusting to being Army wives. Our husbands were serving in the same battalion. She served this quiche to our wives' group at a covered dish function. She shared the recipe with me. Here is a simple version of her recipe.

Vegetable Base:
2 cups of your favorite ingredients chopped — our favorites are chopped ham and broccoli. (Try bacon, chicken, ground beef, carrots, zucchini, or whatever your family likes. Use left-overs from refrigerator. Call it C.O.R.D. quiche.)
1 cup shredded cheese (we like cheddar and mozzarella)
1/2 cup chopped onion (optional)
1/2 cup chopped bell pepper (optional)

1) Arrange above ingredients in a quiche dish.

Egg mix:
1 cup milk
2 eggs
1/2 cup baking mix
1/2 teaspoon salt (mol)
1/4 teaspoon pepper

2) Beat in blender on high for 15 seconds, or one minute with a hand mixer
3) Pour egg mixture over chopped ingredients.
4) Bake at 400° about 35 minutes. Cool five minutes before serving.

Side dish suggestions: Our favorite side dish for quiche is cantaloupe. A home-made onion soup is delicious also. Add Swiss cheese to the top of the soup and melt it.

Recipe: **Fruity Tuity Stuffing**
From: A need for a quick dressing

Background: I enjoy the holidays. I even enjoy the banquets and the cooking. Yet, shortcuts or quick recipes are helpful. This stuffing grew out of a need to shorten the hour-long process of making stuffing and trying to come up with a way to use a dried out loaf of banana bread. Trent had put it in the bag, but left the bag open — it was rock-like. This can be done in minutes and is a delightful change from the usual corn bread version.

1 loaf of banana bread (fresh, stale or dried-out)
2 apples (cored, peeled, and cubed)
1 can whole cranberry sauce
2 Tablespoons Mrs. Dash® (or equivalent spices)

1) Crumble bread into mixing bowl.
2) Prepare apples and add to crumbs.
3) Mix in cranberry sauce and spices.
4) Stuff turkey and bake as usual. This makes enough to stuff one 15 to 22 pound bird.

Note: Sometimes our grocer puts bananas on sale for a dime a pound. I buy lots and make loaves and loaves of banana bread. They freeze wonderfully.

The Early Years

I laugh when I think of those early years of our marriage. I was struggling to define our family. It was an emotional battle to separate myself from being a daughter to being a wife. It really manifested itself in our entertaining. I tackled the situation trying to emulate my mother's "Southern Living-ish" hospitality. Her table would have graced any magazine cover. Do you have a mental picture of a pre-school girl playing dress-up in her mother's gown, high-heels, hat, and make-up. That's what my tables must have appeared like — form without substance and a tad bit comical. I didn't have the silver service, the linens, or the budget to match my mother's. But I stumbled along in her "high-heels" all the same. It took me a few years to grow into my own shoes and style of entertaining. Hopefully, now I'm more calm and am not out to impress anyone. I enjoy my guests and the party. I'm learning. The important thing is not how lavishly I entertain, but that I entertain — that we try to practice hospitality.

Cranberry Ice

Deb also gave me this colorful and tasty idea for a beverage. Freeze cranberry juice ice cubes. Serve these in a glass with chilled clear soda.

Recipe: **Deb's Dip** From: Deb Rodgers

Background: Deb served me this dip during our sewing group time. It is rare to find a dip that goes so well with fruit. She told me how easy it was to make. Since then, I have served it many times and am always asked for the recipe.

1/2 cup orange juice
1 small box instant pudding (vanilla, banana, or your favorite) Do **not** mix with milk.
1-8 ounce carton sour cream

1) Mix orange juice and pudding mix well, add sour cream.
2) Mix, whip until well blended.
3) Refrigerate at least an hour before serving.

Recipe: **Shawberry Dip**
From: One of my first friends, Julie Berry

Background: Julie has been one of my best friends since second grade. Recently, while her three boys and mine were playing, she and I chatted in her spacious kitchen. She served me some fresh fruit and this dip. She told me the recipe. Her maiden name is Shaw, so the boys loved that her name is "Shaw Berry" so the name stuck. By the way it is delicious with strawberries.

Whip equal portions of cream cheese and marshmallow cream together.

Recipe: **Apple Butter** From: Many relatives

Background: We love apple butter, and it is even better when you make it yourself. This is one of the easiest canning recipes I know. If you've never canned, this is a good recipe to be initiated into this rewarding cooking technique. This recipe is so simple, my children do all the work before it goes into the oven.

1 #10 can applesauce
4 cups fructose **OR** 6 cups sugar
1 2/3 cups vinegar mixed with 1/2 cup water (optional)
5 teaspoons cinnamon
1 Tablespoon ground cloves

1) Stir all ingredients together in your turkey roaster or in a baking dish. Cover.
2) Bake in a 350° oven for 3 hours, stirring occasionally.
3) Can according to your favorite method. This recipe makes 5 pints. This is the method I use.

» Sterilize and heat canning jars, rings and lids by washing in high-temp-wash setting of dishwasher. If you don't have a dishwaher, place the items in boiling water for ten minutes.
» Fill jars with apple butter, wipe off lid and rim surfaces, secure lid, and seal with ring.
» Lower into boiling water. Water must cover lids. Boil for ten minutes. (I use my large canner pot.)
» Label, include the date, and store.

Recipe: **Pizza Bread**   From: More experimenting

Background: I got the basic idea for this recipe from a T.V. program, but have adapted it and personalized it to my family's tastes. Basically, make your favorite pizza, but roll it up jelly-roll fashion and bake. Many of the ingredients can come from your freezer, from packs that you have prepared ahead. This is a real favorite when having a party with children or teens. This is also a good recipe for "hiding" good-for-you-food (the foods your children won't eat if they can recognize it.)

Use your favorite pizza dough recipe or use mine:

1/4 cup warm water
1/2 teaspoons fructose OR sugar
1 Tablespoon yeast
1 cup warm water
1 beaten egg
2 Tablespoons vegetable oil
1 teaspoon salt
1 Tablespoon fructose or sugar
4 cups flour [mol] (whole-wheat or your choice)

1) Dissolve 1/2 teaspoon sugar and yeast in 1/4 cup warm water. Set aside until frothy.
2) Mix all other ingredients <u>except</u> flour, add in yeast when frothy. Mix well.
3) Gradually add in flour. Go by feel. Mix should be very stiff.
4) Turn out onto floured board, push and knead for ten minutes. Children can knead dough and think it is fun. (Now, I let my DLX or Bosche do the kneading.) Note: When I use whole-wheat flour, I don't flour the board, I oil it.
5) Put it in a greased bowl, cover and let rise for 1 hour.

4-5 cups of your favorite ingredients
2-3 cups of shredded cheese (mozzarella, Parmesan, and/or cheddar)
1 can or jar tomato sauce

6) While the dough is rising, prepare stuffing ingredients. Use your favorites. We use some of the following: grated eggplant, zucchini, onion, bell pepper, mushrooms, pepperoni, cooked ground meat, ham, and/or pineapple. This is another good C.O.R.D. meal, just search your freezer and refrigerator for possibilities.
7) Roll out dough into a large rectangle (roughly 20" x 36"). Spread with sauce, sprinkle with ingredients and cheese. Roll in jelly-roll fashion, widthwise, sealing edges, and folding under ends. It should be 16"to 18" long, and about 4" to 5" in diameter.
8) Place roll on greased cookie sheet or jelly roll pan. It should fit if you place it at an angle. Let it rise again 20 minutes. Brush top with a beaten egg.

9) Bake at 350° for 45 minutes. Makes about 12 servings. This also warms up well.

Recipe: **Lemon Sauce**   From: Experimentation

Background: When we travel we like to take dinner breaks. Instead of the fast food rush, we stop and dine in real restaurants. The break does us all good. On one of our trips, we stopped at a delightful Chinese restaurant near Mobile Bay in Alabama. I was served a chicken in lemon sauce. I tasted it for all it was worth and have been experimenting to duplicate it. This is not exactly it, but it'll do.

1 cup fructose OR sugar
1/4 cup cornstarch
1 1/2 cups water
3 egg yolks
2 Tablespoons grated lemon rind
1/4 cup lemon juice
dash of salt (optional)

1) Combine sugar, cornstarch (and salt) in heavy saucepan.
2) Add water. Bring to a boil, stirring constantly until thickened.
3) In a separate bowl, combine egg yolks, lemon rind and juice. Beat well.
4) Add a small amount of the hot sugar mixture to egg mixture. Stir. Then combine both of the mixtures back in the saucepan.
5) Cook, stirring constantly. After about 10 minutes the sauce should be thickened and smooth.
6) Serve over chicken, vegetables (e.g., asparagus) or over cake.
7) It freezes fairly well. You might want to double the recipe and divide it into meal-size portions. Label and freeze.

Recipe: **Dragon Sauce** From: mimicking the sauce served in Chinese restaurants

Background: We love the eggroll sauces served in restaurants. Some grocers carry a similar brand of duck sauce. However, it is expensive and loaded with sugar, MSG, and other additives. So I started experimenting with peaches. It paid off. This sauce is made with the left-over peach nectar from canned peaches. Note: because we aren't adding colorings it won't be the pretty peach color like the store versions.

3 cups peach nectar/juice (Use the syrup from canned peaches. Pineapple, apricot and/or plum juice/syrup also work well.)
3 Tablespoons cornstarch (mol, more for a thicker sauce, less for a thinner sauce — we like a very thick sauce and use 6 Tablespoons)
1/4 cup fructose or 1/2 cup sugar
1/4 cup vinegar
1-2 Tablespoons soy sauce
1/2 cup pureed peaches (optional)

1) Evenly mix cornstarch into juice in sauce pot.
2) Add other ingredients.
3) Cook over medium heat until thick and transparent (about 10 minutes).
4) Serve, and/or freeze in meal-size portions.
5) Thaw and heat.
Note: I like to buy the #10 can of peaches, make a cobbler with the peaches and use the syrup for this sauce. To make it extra rich, save out some of the peaches, blend them until they're semi-liquid with small peach pieces visible. Add these pureed peaches to the sauce. This goes well with egg rolls, over chicken and duckling. It's even delicious over rice.

Recipe: **Fool Proof Sweet 'n Sour Sauce**
From: Rob Heyser

Background: Rob, a friend from college, gave me this recipe while he was a hotel and restaurant management major. He now manages a professional kitchen. It's easy and tasty. Use it with cut up franks or meatballs for a nice hot appetizer. Serve in a chafing dish. Or use it as you would any sweet 'n sour sauce. Everytime I've served it I've been asked for the secret. This is one of the most popular recipes I share.

Mix together equal parts of grape jelly and your favorite B-B-Que sauce. Heat until bubbly. Don't let it burn.

Recipe: **Graham Crackers** From: Idea from La Leche League

Background: My cousin, Kathy Brown, gave me a La Leche League cookbook as a wedding present and it is the dirtiest cookbook in my house — I use it so often. I love their whole food approach to cooking . Though I don't always agree with their child-rearing techniques, I salute them for their work in encouraging moms to breastfeed. This recipe <u>idea</u> comes from their book, though I've adapted it to better suit my needs and, I believe, have made it easier to prepare.

1 cup oil (your favorite)
1 cup honey
1/3 cup molasses
1 Tablespoon vanilla
9 to 10 cups whole-wheat flour
1 Tablespoon baking powder
1 1/2 teaspoons baking soda
dash of salt
4 teaspoons cinnamon
1 1/2 cups milk

1) Preheat oven to 325°. Grease cookie sheets with oil, butter, or spray.
2) Mix together dry ingredients in a bowl, set aside.
3) In separate bowl, mix oil, honey, molasses and vanilla in mixing bowl.
4) Alternate mixing milk and dry ingredients into honey mixture.
5) Mix until dough is stiff. Add more flour if needed. Knead.
6) Divide dough into fourths. Form into balls. Work with one ball at a time. Keep other balls in airtight container in the refrigerator.
7) Roll ball out directly onto cookie sheet 3/8" thick, With a knife, score or cut dough into cracker-sized rectangles. Repeat with other balls each on its own cookie sheet.
8) Bake 15 to 20 minutes.
9) Let cool on racks. Once cool, separate crackers along scored lines.
10) These freeze well. They also make wonderful crusts.

Note: To make them look more like the store-bought versions, before baking, prick dough with a fork for the indentions.

Tip: This recipe makes delicious graham cracker pie crusts. See page 16-36 for a variation on the standard crust.

Recipe: Wassail
From: Old hand-me-down tradition

Background: "Here we come a wassailing. . . ." This recipe is a version of that old wassail. It makes an enjoyable warm drink that is great for keeping on the stove and serving all day to family and guests as they drop in.

1 quart orange juice
1 quart apple juice
1 quart cranberry juice
1 cup fructose or sugar
2 to 3 cinnamon sticks
1 teaspoon ground cloves
1 teaspoon nutmeg
1 cup pineapple juice (optional)
3 to 4 apples cored, sliced in thin rings

1) Pour all ingredients into Dutch oven or crock pot.
2) Bring to a boil.
3) Cover and simmer.
4) It will be ready to drink after an hour. You can let it simmer all day. If you have any leftover, it freezes well.

Recipe: Merry Pop-ins
From: My needlepoint buddies at Ruthelma's Yarn Basket

Background: These make great party foods. **They freeze very well.** They are a finger food that even children enjoy. We also have them for breakfast. My children can make them — they are that easy. You can adjust the recipe to the amount you need. I like to make lots so I have some in the freezer ready for a reception at church, breakfast, or a quick party.

Basically,
use
equal
portions of
{
Cheese, grated (cheddar and/or mozzarella)
Baking Mix (Master Mix, Jiffy®, or Bisquick®)
Ground Meat (sausage and/or ground turkey/beef)

For a large batch use:

6 cups grated cheese (I like half cheddar and half mozzarella)
6 cups baking mix
6 cups of ground meat (I use 2 lbs sausage and 1 lb ground meat (beef and/or turkey).
    You can use all sausage or any combination.)

1) Mix all ingredients.
2) Form into bite-size balls.
3) Bake on prepared cookie sheets (greased or sprayed) at 325° for thirty minutes.
4) Enjoy now and/or freeze.
5) To heat: thaw and bake at 350° for 10 to 15 minutes.

Makes approximately 150 pop-ins depending on how large you make them.

Note: My family loves these served with the Dragon Sauce on page 17-6.

Ages

The shop was busy. Bins of yarn, rows of needlepoint canvas, and displays of handwork accessories festooned the neat cottage store. In one corner sat several grandmotherly women working on their latest project. A grey-haired lady and a young girl of sixteen worked together on a knitting project. A customer came over and said, "How nice you're passing on handwork traditions to this young girl." The grandmother smiled and laughed, "Oh, no! Jill's teaching me. My daughter just had a baby and I've just got to learn to knit. It's part of the package of being a grandmother." I smiled and continued to work with my pupil.

I loved my part-time job in that store. Most of my co-workers were ladies in their seventies. They taught me a great deal about grace, patience, and value. In addition to the skills my own mother and grandmother taught me, the hand skills, knitting, stitchery, and crafts these ladies taught me have given me many hours of enjoyment, years of gifts, and a ministry of sorts (the Lord has blessed my craft classes as witnessing tools). Please don't lose those wonderful skills that get passed down generation to generation. Teach your daughter.

They also gave me the recipe at right. It was called "Sausage balls." Alan gave it a kids-friendly name.

Recipe: Master Mix

Background: This recipe is a do-it-yourself version of store-bought baking mix. I like it because I can make whole-wheat or oat flour versions of popular store brands, like Bisquick® and Jiffy®.

One large batch: (yields approximately 29 cups, enough to make one of each of these recipes)
  5 pounds flour (whole-wheat, oat, or all-purpose)
  2 1/2 cups dry milk solids (powdered milk flakes)
  3/4 cup double-acting baking powder
  3 Tablespoons salt (mol)
  2 Tablespoons cream of tartar
  1/2 cup sugar (I recommend using granulated fructose for all recipes that require sugar)
  2 pounds vegetable shortening (4 2/3 cups)

Steps:
1) Sift dry ingredients together (see hint on page 16-29).
2) Cut in shortening until mix looks like cornmeal.
3) Store in refrigerator, if using whole-wheat flour or oat flour.   Room temperature storage is OK if using all-purpose white flour.
4) Use the master mix in your favorite recipes that call for a baking mix or try it in some of these:

Biscuits: 3 cups mix, 3/4 cup water, blend and knead for a few strokes. Pat out and cut. Bake at 450° for 10 minutes. (1 doz)

Pancakes/Waffles: 3 cups mix, 1 egg, 1 1/2 cups water. Blend. (18 pancakes or 6 waffles)

Muffins: 3 cups mix, 2 Tablespoons sugar (or fructose), 1 egg, 1 cup water. Mix water and egg, then add to dry ingredients, bake at 400° for 15 to 25 minutes (depending on the size of the muffins). Makes one dozen medium-sized muffins. Try substituting juices for the water. I like to use pineapple juice and sometimes add in crushed pineapple. You can add raisins and/or nuts. Another version we love is to add in one cup applesauce, reduce the water (or use apple juice) to 1/2 cup, add in 1/4 teaspoon cinnamon. Orange juice makes a delicious muffin — also add 1/2 teaspoon grated orange peel. It's hard to go wrong when experimenting with these muffins.

Gingerbread: 2 cups mix, 1/4 cup sugar, 1 egg, 1/2 cup water, 1/2 cup molasses, 1/2 teaspoon each of cinnamon, ginger, cloves. Beat egg, water, and molasses; then mix with dry ingredients. Pour into greased (or sprayed) 8" x 8" pan. Bake at 350° for 40 minutes.

Drop Cookies: 3 cups mix, 1 cup sugar, 1 egg, 1/3 cup water, 1 teaspoon vanilla, 1/2 cup nuts and/or chocolate chips; mix. Bake at 375° for 10 to 12 minutes. (4 doz)

Coffee Cake: 3 cups mix, 1/2 cup sugar, 1 egg, 2/3 cup water. Blend. Pour into greased 9" round pan and cover with topping of 1/2 cup brown sugar, 3 Tablespoon melted butter, 1/2 teaspoon cinnamon, (1/2 cup nuts and/or raisins are optional), bake at 400° for 25 minutes.   Instead of water, try orange juice and add grated orange zest (peel) to mix and topping. Experiment with other flavors you like.

Yellow or Chocolate Cake: 3 cups mix, 1 1/2 cup sugar, 3 eggs, 1 cup water, 1 teaspoon vanilla (plus 1/2 cup cocoa for chocolate cake). Blend sugar into mix. Beat eggs and water and add half mix.   Beat 2 minutes. Then add rest of the mix and beat 2 minutes again. (For chocolate cake, mix cocoa with dry ingredients.) Bake at 325° for 25 minutes (2-8" layers). If you don't like the idea of your children eating all that chocolate (caffeine, sugar, etc.) use carob powder.

Cornbread: 1 1/4 cup mix, 3/4 cup yellow cornmeal, 1 egg, 1 Tablespoon sugar, 1/2 cup water. Mix and pour in greased 8" x 8" pan or cornstick pan. Bake at 450° for 25 minutes.

Shortcake: 2 cups mix, 1/2 cup water, 1/4 cup melted butter, 2 Tablespoons sugar. Mix and knead a few strokes. Roll 1/2" thick, cut into 3-3" cakes or bake in 8" x 8" greased (or sprayed) pan. Bake at 450° for 10 minutes.

Extra Recipes

Recipe: **Bread Dough Enhancer** From: Karen Jones

Background: Karen Jones, a dear friend, was my source for fresh ground flour while we lived in Texas. She ground wheat and I'd baked loaves of bread within hours, so the flour was fresh and full of nutrients. I'd freeze loaves for later. She gave me this recipe to add to the bread dough mix to help it rise and bake better. It really works. Loaves will rise faster and higher.

4 cups powdered milk
3/4 cup Lecithin granules
3 heaping Tablespoons vitamin C powder
2 Tablespoons ginger
3 Tablespoons cornstarch

1) Blend all the above ingredients until smooth.
2) Store in airtight containers. It can store on your pantry shelf.
3) Use 2 teaspoons of enhancer in your bread dough. [I add it in when I add flour to the dough. I use 3 Tablespoons of this enhancer to each batch of bread I bake. My batches make 5 loaves. So you'd need to add 2 teaspoons to your bread dough to make it easier to handle, rise better, and bake well.]

Recipe: **Grace's Treats** From: School Experiment in the Kitchen

Background: Reed, Stuart, and I had fun in the kitchen one day. We played around making cookies for the dog. It was a wonderful time to teach the boys basic cooking, measuring, and mixing techniques. With food for the dog, I knew they couldn't go wrong. Our dog, Grace, loved them so much that she would leave the store brand dog treats alone and seek out the home-made ones.

2 cups oatmeal
5 Tablespoons beef bouillon (chicken, vegetable, or
     other flavor)
1 stick margarine OR 1/2 cup oil (This oil is wonder-
     ful for their coats and to stop itchy skin)
3 cups boiling water
2 eggs
1 cup wheat bran, or oat bran
1/4 cup honey (optional)
6 to 8 cups flour (We use whole-wheat)

1) Dissolve the bouillon in the boiling water.
2) While water is still hot, add oatmeal, margarine, wheat bran, and honey.
3) Carefully add eggs so they DON'T cook in lumps.
4) Mix in flour gradually until dough is stiff.
5) Roll out dough as you would regular cookies.
6) Cut with cookie cutters. (Note: we found a cutter that is shaped like a bone at our local craft store.)
7) Bake on cookie sheets at 325° for 1 hour. At the one hour mark turn off the oven and allow the pans to sit in oven overnight. [If you need your oven, just let them dry on the counter.] This will make them hard and crunchy.
8) Do not store in an airtight container — they will become soft. We stored them in a cardboard box that allowed them to stay hard and exposed to a small amount of air.

Note: One alternate way to prepare this is to use an equivalent amount of meat drippings in place of the boiling water and beef bouillon. Bring the drippings to a boil to mix in the oatmeal and margarine.

Every wise woman buildeth her house: but the foolish
plucketh it down with her hands. — Proverbs 14:1 (KJV)

CHAPTER EIGHTEEN

Whole Home Management

As wives, mothers, and ladies, we're interested in more than just eating. I know I need help in more than my kitchen, I need it from the front edge of the lawn to the back yard fence. In this chapter we'll look at a few areas in your whole home management: personal care; children's projects and gift-giving; laundry management; health matters, organizing; and household cleaning.

Personal Care

While Alan and I were courting, I spent more money on manicures in one month than I have spent on my entire family's personal care items for a whole year. I prided myself on having ten perfectly-manicured nails. My fingers looked delicate and slim with long healthy nails. Now I look down at my hands and it's hard to believe they belong to the same person. My priorities have done a 180 degree turn. Cuts, scars, broken nails, wrinkles, and just worn (that "they've-seen-better-days" look) is how you'd describe my hands now. Thank you. I've worked hard to earn this look. I'm funny — I insist on washing my hands each time I change a diaper. I insist that my family eat off clean dishes, walk (and crawl) on clean floors, wear clean clothes, etc. So my hands reflect my values.

Yet, I still can do what I can to look my best. There's a balance between being a "fashion plate" and going to pot. With that in mind, I've learned a few ways to save you some money and time with your personal care expenses:

Models' Facial

I learned this "trick" from my modeling days. Separate a regular egg and then do both steps a few minutes apart:

1) Warm: Apply yolk to clean face. Let dry, or better yet, dry with heat (e.g., blow dryer). Rinse face with warm water.
2) Cool: Apply white of egg to face, let dry (use cool/air setting on dryer, fan, or natural air).

Feels great and leaves skin shining.

Nail Treatment

As I stated earlier, I'm rough on my nails. To have any nail on my fingers, I watch my diet and use this treatment from "The Formula Book" by Norman Stark[1].

Mix 3 Tablespoons water, 1 teaspoon powdered alum (available at drug stores), and 1 Tablespoon glycerin. Pour into a child-proof container and label it appropriately. Each night brush it on your nails to strengthen them. Wash off with water, and/or rubbing alcohol (denatured, type 40 or isopropyl). Don't allow your hands in your mouth. **This is not for consumption.**

Soap Management

If you're using bar soap, you could be sending half of the soap down the drain just from the water hitting it while you shower. So to cut your soap expense in half, keep the soap in a covered dish. Only allow it to make contact with water when you are actually sudsing-up. Then return it to the dish while you rinse.

Use a wash cloth or sponge to apply the soap. This will not only cut down on your soap use, but it is better for your skin. Your pores need that rubbing for proper cleaning.

And/or use liquid soap. I buy a large container (40 fl. oz) of a liquid soap (I like Rainbath®). By using a sponge, that one container lasts me for two-and-a-half years!

Hair Care

How often do you wash your hair? I know I'm getting personal with you now, but only because it might help you. The more you wash your hair the more you'll have to wash your hair. You are training the oil glands. Could you skip a day? I'd recommend that you gradually wean yourself from daily shampoos. I'm one that washed, blow dried and hot rolled my hair daily. In case no one has ever taught you this, the key to having clean hair is not in washing the hair, but in washing the scalp. Use your nails and wash every area of your scalp. Your hair will automatically be cleaned with this regimen of rubbing the skin on your head and will stay clean for days. If all you've been doing is washing the hair then you'll have to wash daily.

Now I shampoo once a week, then let it dry naturally. My hair is healthier now than when it received the daily treatment. You not only save the money on shampoo, water, and electricity, but look at all the time you save. I prefer to use the old-fashioned rollers and/or let my hair dry naturally — time. This saves quite a bit of electricity. Admittedly, sometimes I do use my electric curlers when I've failed to plan ahead.

Go to your bathroom and read your shampoo bottle label. I read through the shampoo section at the local store. The leading ingredient on most of the bottles was water. That means the main ingredient in your shampoo is water. I don't need to buy their water. So I buy concentrated shampoo. Look in your phone directory for a beauty salon supply store. One bottle of concentrated shampoo (you mix with your own water) lasted me for over five years. I figure that one step saved me more than $50. And that shampoo was a better grade than the mass-marketed version. This same idea applies to other personal care products (e.g., cream rinse).

I have long hair. The charge for a trip to the beauty parlor costs me at least $40, just for a trim. That's about $350 a year. Our barber bill would be around $300 a year. We keep that money for spending elsewhere. We cut each other's hair. We bought a low-cost pair of electric dog clippers and my mother gave us a pair of hair clipping scissors. Alan and I cut the boys' hair and do each other's. It takes some work, some time, and some practice. I was terrified at first cutting Alan's hair. Admittedly, I gave him a few cuts that fortunately grew back quickly. But with each time, I'm getting better. I purposely wear a hair style that is not one that requires hours of styling each day. I have better things to do with my time than to fuss over myself.

Aside: We love our Airedale terrier, Grace. She is one of the few breeds that doesn't shed (a big plus in house cleaning), but her fur needs to be clipped regularly. We use the same low cost pair of electric dog clippers and save $45 each time. Alan made a quick adjustment with the clippers (added a washer between the motor and the blades to offset the cutting for her thick fur) and they clip as well as the high-priced pair at the pet store ($26 compared to $165).

Miscellaneous Personal Care

The same principles of reading labels, buying the product (not the advertising) can be applied to other personal care items. The toothpaste you buy only costs a tiny portion of the total price of the box, tube, and promotion. Are you just buying "sex appeal?" Besides all the negative reports concerning fluoride, do you want the Madison Avenue version of tooth abrasives? It's the brushing and flossing that benefits your teeth the most.

**Graying-
and Proud of it**

During a solemn, quiet moment in our Sunday School Assembly program Alan burst out LOUD, "A gray hair- your first gray hair!" He says it with as much excitement as a miner finding the "mother lode". Of course, our entire Sunday School Department heard him and burst out laughing. Wouldn't you?

Contrary to the condemnation from the media and our society, growing old is not horrible. I'm proud of each of my gray hairs. (By the way I'm getting more every day.) I have no plans to buy a bottle and dye them. Instead of fretting about not being beautiful with salt and pepper hair, I get my encouragement and attitude from Scripture:

"The hoary head [gray hair] is a crown of glory, if it be found in the way of righteousness." Proverbs 16:31 (KJV)

Grow gray with His grace and you'll save money on rinses, dyes, and beauticians and look at all the time you'll save in treatments and in fretting.

Chronic bad breath is not a result of what you just ate — usually it's a result of what you ate 24-hours ago. Your tongue acts like a sponge. Study your digestive system and you'll discover that body odor and bad breath are more dependent on your colon's condition than on which mouthwashes, fragrances, lotions and creams your apply to the surface. Don't treat the symptom — treat the cause. And, in the process, you'll not only save money, you'll be healthier.

Children's Projects/Gifts

Children like to get involved. I strongly dislike gifts or toys that "do it all" for the child. What good is a toy that doesn't require the child's interaction, involvement, and imagination? We love to make our own toys. We rarely buy anything at a toy store. We don't need them or want them for that matter. So many of the so-called toys are demonic in nature, prey on a child's sin nature, advocate violence, greed, or selfishness, and/or stifle their own God-given talents. Here are just a few ideas of projects that children can do that get them involved, are wholesome, and FUN! In the resource section are some other resources for you to check into for more ideas.

Children's Modeling Clay

> » 1 cup flour (use cheapest you can find)
> » 1 cup water
> » 6-7 drops food coloring depending on the intensity you desire
> » 1/2 cup salt
> » 2 teaspoons cream of tartar (don't substitute)
> » 1 Tablespoon cooking oil
> » 1 or 2 drops of oil of cloves, cinnamon or wintergreen (optional, for scent)

Mix food coloring in water. Add other ingredients in a saucepan. Cook over medium heat for three minutes. Mixture will pull away from the side of the pan and usually within this time frame it will look like finished playdough-type dough. Dump onto pastry sheet to cool. When it has lost some heat, you may knead out any little lumps of flour that didn't blend while it was cooking. Store in an airtight container.

Easy Bake Clay

>   » 4 cups flour (use inexpensive white)
>   » 1 cup of salt
>   » 1-1/2 cups of water

Mix flour and salt. Slowly add water, mixing while you pour. Dough should be very stiff for best results. Add more water, a tiny bit at a time, if needed. Knead for 10 minutes until soft and smooth.

Be creative. Use your favorite shapes and cut out like cookies, or mold with hands. Since dough dries out quickly, keep dough in airtight container and work with portions of it at a time. This is an excellent project for little ones. Bake at 325° on a flat smooth baking sheet. Baking time will depend on the thickness of the dough. As a rule of thumb allow 1/2 hour for each 1/4 inch thickness.

Scented Soap Balls

>   » 2 cups IVORY SNOW® detergent
>   » 1 Tablespoon extract (any scent you desire)
>   » 1 teaspoon food coloring (more or less depending on desired intensity of color) added to 1/4 cup water

Mix together water and food coloring and extract, add to detergent. Knead with hands until well mixed. Shape into balls or other desired shapes. Let dry 24 hours.

Example: use red dye, strawberry extract and shape into 2-inch strawberries. Color some green and form the strawberries' leaves. OR use lemon extract, yellow dye and shape into lemons. OR mix colors to customize for your bath and use a floral scent and shape into balls, shells, etc.

This is a great project for children and makes for great gifts. Compare these that you can make for 5¢ to 10¢ apiece to those found in stores for more than 75¢ a piece.

Cinnamon-Applesauce Ornaments

These ornaments smell wonderful and look very attractive. Three years ago, my children made several and those still have their wonderful smell. We store the Christmas tree ornaments in an airtight container when they're not on the tree.

Coat a pastry sheet/board/cloth with cinnamon. In a mixing bowl, start with 1/2 cup to 1 cup cinnamon. Add warm applesauce, 1 Tablespoon at a time (warm in microwave or on stove top). 3 Tablespoons is a good amount to start with. Mix well. Roll out with a rolling pin. Use your favorite cookie cutters and cut shapes as you would cookies. While moist, use a plastic straw to poke holes in the tops for threading a ribbon through. To microwave, lay the ornaments on a paper towel on top of a flat microwaveable dish (or use a sturdy piece of cardboard). Dry on LOW power for about 20 seconds to a minute, depending on how many ornaments you are drying. Then turn them over and dry a few more seconds. Don't try to dry them on high power, they might bubble.

OR let them dry overnight on a paper towel. Paint them if desired, but only on one side so as to allow the aroma access to the air.

These also make lovely refrigerator magnets. Don't make a hole in them. Decorate them with dried flowers, paint, and/or ribbon.

Gift Ideas

Purchase all your birthday cards once a year and have them on hand to send out. Keep sympathy, congratulations, baby, wedding, get well cards, etc., on hand for quick sending without having to rush to the store to buy one. There are many mail-order sources that will save you money.

Buy all your wrapping paper and bows once a year also.

OR get a roll of newsprint from your local newspaper and make your own paper (end of rolls are usually free and last for years in home use) .

Example: for one Christmas, we rolled out 20-foot lengths of newsprint across our patio, poured red and green paint in some flat dishes, had our then 17-month-old and 3-year-old step in the paint and then walk on the paper. They also did hand prints. We received more rave reviews from the wrapping paper we sent the presents in than for the presents themselves. Since then, we've been decorating our own wrapping paper with markers, paint, crayons or whatever. It gets the children involved and people love the personal touch.

Example: for a shower gift, we cut a sponge into the shape of a teddy bear. Reed sponge-painted brown bears all over plain brown wrapping paper. I made little red bows from ribbon and we glued them to the bears' necks. The lady that received the gift took special care of the paper and was going to make a wall hanging of it to decorate above the baby's crib.

Wrapping

Try unusal things for present wrappings. I've found many of the following suggestions are about the same price as printed wrapping paper and ribbon, and yet, they are something that can still be used:

- For a gift for a cook, wrap the gift in a dish cloth and use kitchen twine for the ribbon.
- For a gift for a seamstress or quilter, wrap the gift in a remnant of cloth and use a tape measure for the ribbon.
- Use computer printouts for a high-tech look on a package. (Or flip it over and let children decorate it like newsprint.)
- Try wrapping a personal gift in a bath towel or wash cloth. Use a hair ribbon for the bow.
- Put a small gift inside a balloon and then inflate it, tie securely with a long ribbon.

Let your imagine create even more ideas and cleverly wrapped packages. Just remember to give a gift as you would love to receive it yourself.

So, be creative. You have great ideas. So do your children.

Our boys make our Christmas cards each year. Even small children can stencil. One year, they stenciled a row of candy canes over a photocopied message on green paper. We're still receiving compliments on those cards.

The Christmas of 1990 was my favorite Christmas yet. It was our "cheapest" Christmas, too. Since I was still bed-ridden and in the middle of recuperating from complications with Bethany's birth, I couldn't go out shopping. So, we had an old-fashioned Christmas of home-made gifts from things we could find around the house. It was grand.

» My mother and I knitted the children slippers out of many lengths of left-over yarn. The children loved the multi-colored footwear.

» The boys made a rattle for Bethany that is by far her favorite toy. With an old plastic 2-liter bottle, they cut and tore paper, ribbon, yarn and foil into small shapes and stuffed the bottle three-fourths full. They glued the cap back on. She has a silent rattle of colors, shapes and textures that entertains her for hours.

» Reed, with help from Magah (Grandmother), made a magnetic fun kit for Stuart. He painted an old rusty cookie sheet blue. Then with electric tape, he stripped down the matrix for a tic-tac-toe board. Out of wrapping paper, he cut two different pictures (6 of each picture), glued them to cardboard squares, and affixed a magnet to the back for a spill-proof game. They included a funny faces set. They drew nine different faces, cut them in thirds horizontally (cardboard and magnets, too), so Stuart could mix and match foreheads with eyes/noses, and mouths for all kinds of comical combinations. They also made other similar magnetic games from things around the house. It was a big hit!

» Stuart and Reed made sock puppets for Trent.

» The children made a pencil holder for Daddy (the old wooden popsicle sticks glued around an orange juice can, stained walnut, and stenciled a duck design on them.)

I'll stop the list here because I'm sure you get the idea and have even better ideas of your own. I mention this to encourage you to teach your children the attitude you want them to have about gift-giving. Is it to be a trip to the toy store filling a shopping cart with plastic (soon to be broken) toys that are advertised on Saturday-morning cartoons? Or is it to be a quiet time of being creative, using their minds, skills, talents and their own money to make gifts for each other? Or, a combination of the two? What's right for your family?

Do you have any out-of-town relatives? In an attempt to "spend" more time with them. We decided to have breakfast with aunts, uncles, grandparents every morning — the children made placemats for them. We cut out a placemat shape from poster boards. They glued, drew, cut, stenciled, or placed photographs on each side of the placemats. They were then reversible. We had them laminated. To give you some ideas, here's the colors and themes we came up with:

Christmas 1990

I must include, to be truly honest, that we did have some toys under the tree for Christmas morning. With the monies given to us from loved ones and the great people at The Timberdoodle (quick handling) the children had some wonderful, sensible toys that aren't advertised on T.V. — like a marvelous set of Fischertechniks engineering systems (worth your looking into), a child-size quality broom (Trent's favorite "toy"), bee's wax (marvelous material for young sculpters), etc. See Appendix C for their address.

Gifts don't have to be a waste of your child's intellect. They can be fun, exciting and educational.

Color	Side One/Front		Side Two/Back	
	Holiday/ Season	Concept/Art	Holiday/ Season	Concept/Art
Red	Christmas	We used religious Christmas card pictures and stenciled candy canes.	Valentine's Day	On white paper doily placemats they glued a rainbow of colored hearts and wrote a message of love.
Orange	Thanks-giving	They made "hand" shaped turkeys, painted the tail feathers and glued them on the placemat and printed the words: "Dear God, Thank you for . . .".	Fall	They cut out leaf shapes from fall colors of construction paper and pasted them down — "Falling in love with you."
Blue	American (e.g. July 4th, Flag day, President's birthdays, etc.)	They cut strips of red and white paper and glued them down to form the stripes of our flag leaving the upper-left corner bare. In this box they pasted little gold star stickers. With colored markers they drew curves from the stars, giving them the appearance of fireworks.	Springtime	They cut out of construction paper three large flowers, stems and leaves: tulip, rose bud, and daisy. They pasted these down for a very bright springtime picture.
Green	Easter	The youngest child cut two white strips of paper and glued them to form a cross. He printed, "He is Alive."	Summer-time	Out of different sheets of colored paper, the boys cut a sailboat and sun. They drew a face on the sun and decorated the boat with: "S.S. Summertime."
Yellow	Birthday	This one was a picture of a large construction paper cake with the words "Happy Birthday, name & date."	Anyday	We cut out all sorts of shapes from a variety of colored paper. The children then made pictures with these shapes glueing them down . For instance, they made pictures of people and boats, in a sort of "pop art" style.
Black	Anniversary	They cut two large bells out of Silver anniversary wrapping paper.	Winter	They made standard snow-flakes, and stenciled snowmen on the poster board. They wrote with a white paint pen: "May your day be warmed with love"

Those were just some samples of ways you can involve your children with their gift-giving. I've always felt, probably a spirit taught me by my parents, that gifts are even more wonderful when they cost the giver something. Something more than a flip of a credit card. Even if it is a store-bought gift, the giver can pour love into the package. Not all people are crafty, but I know of people who will spend hours hunting in stores for just the right color of an item, or just the perfect what-not for that niche in your home. It's a giving of yourself that makes the gift special.

I was "complaining" to a friend about some gifts we had received from a few out-of-town relatives that read children's clothing labels logically, I suspected. They had sent clothes the sizes of my children's ages! Which really is the smart thing to do, if you think about. Why isn't sizing accurate? For the un-initiated in today's children's clothing market, a size 18-months doesn't fit a child 18 months old. In our case, it would have fit my hulking babies at age 6 weeks. Size 4 fits an 18-month-old. But if you have small children now, you know that. Bless our out-of-town relatives' hearts, they really tried to send appropriate gifts. We gave Stuart, Reed's outfit, and gave Stuart's outfit to a friend who had a preemie. As we were both laughing, my friend said "Oh, my husband's family sent the right sizes. The outfits fit perfectly today. But tell me what-in-the-world are we to do with Wisconsin Snow Suits during our three-year-long tour here in Panama?" Sometimes, it's best just to send cash.

A check can be a family's answer to prayer. Many of our relatives send us checks. We pool the checks and are then able to buy the children presents that otherwise we'd never be able to afford like a play-gym for the yard, a VCR, or a bicycle.

One trick to gift-giving that my Mama Bert (maternal grandmother) taught me was to never wait till the last minute. It's in the last minute that we tend to spend more than we can afford and buy something that will more than likely end up in their garage sale next spring. She would begin Christmas shopping December 26. She'd shop all year long and store the presents. That's how she was able to give gifts like a vase that matched the custom wall-paper to an Aunt, a sweater the exact shade of blue to go with a skirt for a granddaughter, etc.

Gifts are such personal things. We must be careful about investing too many emotional attachments to our gift-giving. With each pull of the needle I stitch in love, I also stitch in hours and hours of time (or paint, or craft, or . . .). Especially when we make a gift, we can set ourselves up for a let-down. After logging over one hundred hours on a quilt for someone once, I felt unappreciated because she didn't fawn all over it. She probably could have done backflips and I still would have thought she didn't like it enough. I'm learning to **give** gifts. Give. That means the gift becomes theirs. I ask myself if the focus is on them or on my gift-giving? Have you ever been given a gift with strings-attached — meaning: for the next twenty years that person will point out that they gave you the gift? Have you ever given a gift and been disappointed with the reception? My advice for all that it is worth: Don't set yourself up for disappointment. If you focus on the person you are giving to and want

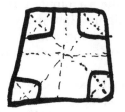

them to be happy, you shouldn't care if **you** scored any points.

I've blown it in gift-giving; and I've shone. I've been heart-broken with gifts I've received and thrilled beyond measure. Never did it have to do with the amount of dollars spent. It always had to do with the love that was included in the gift. Remember every good and perfect gift comes from the Lord. We can only pass on the joy — even if it's in packages with ribbons and bows.

Money Laundering

Are you laundering your money? Have you ever looked at how much you are spending on laundry, not to mention the hours and hours of labor? Some of the same concepts we've applied to meal preparation can work with laundry. No, we can't pre-prepare six months of clean laundry over a weekend. Well, at least, I can't. Not with this tribe. So I sought help. First with my attitude.

I don't get excited about my laundry. I don't even get dull about my laundry. It just <u>exists</u>. I knew I'd have to be writing this section soon. I couldn't put it off anymore. I just couldn't get motivated to write about dirty socks. So I took my attitude to the Lord. I was reminded of all the pointers and tips of this section, but what about my attitude? Then just last night He bowled me over.

As Alan read through chapters in Mark's gospel during our nightly read-aloud time, I folded and sorted the last basket of that day's mountain of laundry. I smoothed yet another tiny shirt and placed it in the appropriate stack, when I did a double take.

There it lay — ruffles, and a little flower appliqué on the tiny blouse. Bethany had looked so precious in it. My heart felt like it went up into my throat. I have been wanting a daughter all my life, and now the Lord has given us Bethany Kay. I thought of the little girl, Joy, who had been visiting us that day. Joy had played dress up with Bethany adorning her in her lace and frilly dresses, her rumba-bottomed tights, and ribboned hats. Joy was delighted with her "live baby doll." I though of how much I enjoyed dressing Bethany, too.

Then I reached in the basket and pulled out yet another pair of big-boy pants. I held them a minute as the Lord doubled the size of my heart. It wasn't a chore, but a delight. How many times had I been praying for a break-through in Trent's potty-training, and just that day he had two successful trips. He'll be out growing big-boy pants soon, off and riding a bike, then off to college before I know it.

I matched socks with the typical problem of lonely-onlies. Our dryer is eating socks at the rate of three per load now. I found a match for my husband's yard socks. The Lord reminded me of my prayers to Him to nag Alan to always wear his shoes when he mows. It terrifies me that he'd do something so dangerous as mow without the safety of shoes on. So instead of bugging Alan I bugged the Lord. As I look down at the green stain that didn't come completely out, I thank the Lord instead of cursing the stain. I pray this revival in my own heart stays. I like it.

Soap, Suds, and Duds

What is really getting your clothes clean?

☐ 1) The miracle soap with the sparkle of power?
☐ 2) The agitation of the water?
☐ 3) Or a little of one and a lot of the other?

Did you check box number 3? You're right. But it's a little of the soap and a lot of the water agitating. Most all laundry detergents are similar. Some companies just dye a portion of their granules to give them that "extra action" look. Basically, soaps make your water wetter, or they help the water to penetrate the fibers of the fabric. So, you might as well use the cheapest stuff you can find and then only use a tiny bit of it.

First of all, why pay good money for more soap than you need?

Second, why put more soap in your fabric than your machine can rinse away? I don't want my baby sucking soap into her system when she gnaws on her bib.

Third, why wash more soap into the city's water system? We buy a 40-pound container with the catchy name: "Laundry Soap" three times a year for about a total of $30. That $30 is not being used to fund "soap" operas, or other questionable fare. That $30 is being used conservatively. We only use about an eighth of a cup per load. If I used the popular brands in the amount they recommend, I'd be spending more than $200 a year on soap and my family's clothing wouldn't be any cleaner.

For those tough stains, I use a product called "Simple Green." The way I figured, if Alan is buying this product at the automotive supply store to clean his hands when he changes the oil in the car and to clean hard stains in his workshop, why wouldn't it work with my jobs. So I tried it on an old tablecloth that was so badly stained that my Aunt gave it to my father as a plant covering for cold nights. For years my father dragged this cloth out and draped it over his azaleas. When we were moving, he wrapped it around a mirror to protect it. This cloth had been through it. So, I sprayed the stains that had been put in 15 years ago. They came out. We are using

Alan Clarifies:

Whiteners are often added. Plus some surfactants (water wetters) work better than others.

Guess-timates

Have you seen the "pros" on television able to exactly pour out the right amount of any ingredient? They can pour out exactly 4 tablespoons. But may I caution us to measure out our soaps. I thought I could guess-timate 1/8 of a cup. I was over — almost double. Take the time to measure. That overage of 1/8 of a cup adds up over time.

This idea of exact measures applies to the kitchen also. For example, I'm stretching my children's abilities regularly. I allow the older ones to pour their own cereal out. However, they were continually pouring more that than they could eat. The dog loved it —she received the left-overs. We solved this problem by leaving a half cup measuring cup in the cereal container. They could pour out one half cup at a time. If they were still hungry then they could scoop out another cup (and in some cases another). We have less waste and they also use less milk. They are also better able to match their appetite to the amount of food they serve themselves.

that cloth on our dining room table now. It only takes a quick spray, and it works great. I don't know if you'll have such success, but I've been thrilled. You might want to test it first if you're trying it out on a delicate fabric. We bought one gallon of "Simple Green" and it's lasted us almost two years.

We have several different friends that own dry cleaning firms and we asked what they use for stain remover. One of their top "secrets" was to use either "409," "Fantastic" or "TnT." They've worked for me, too. Try putting lemon juice on a baby's stain and hanging the item out in the sun for days. The lemon juice safely "bleaches" away the stain.

So the real dud in laundry suds is expensive soaps.

Wrinkles Beware

Mother's law was clear. "If you buy it, you iron it." So, at an early age in my clothing selection, I learned to read labels. Permanent Press was a must. I didn't like ironing any more than she did. Once in a while, I have to pull the ironing board out for something besides sewing, but it's rare. I also use a little steam machine that is quick and works well.

Once when we were moving (by the time we were married seven years, we had moved over ten times), my neighbor allowed me to use her washer and dryer while she wasn't home. I opened her dryer and it was full of dry clothes all wrinkled. She had told me to just dump them into a basket. She later told me that she ironed everything, even permanent-press things. She spent more than two hours every day ironing! I asked around and found out that most of my friends spent more than an hour a day ironing! I was amazed, I didn't think I spent two hours that whole year ironing. I think it was their excuse to watch their television shows while they HAD to iron. Why spend all that productive time doing something that could be avoided? It seemed wasteful, not only for time, but for the energy loss — both the ironer and the iron.

I checked around and found some tips that I grew up knowing. Having an Ironing-loather for a mother has its advantages:

» First, buy wrinkle-free clothing and fabric. Test it yourself, don't depend totally on the label. While in the store, whether it is ready-made clothing or fabric for you seamstresses, crinkle a section of the cloth in your fingers. If it stays wrinkled, you know what it will look like out of your dryer. If it evens out and returns to its original smooth surface, then you probably have a winner.

» Remove your perma-press clothing from the dryer while they are still damp. Let them completely dry on the hanger. Be sure to smooth them by hand and shape them correctly on the hanger.

» If you get tied up and your clothes dry too long or they sit in a still dryer (this happens during at least one load a day for me), just wet a wash cloth and throw it in the dryer with the dry clothes. Turn your dryer back on for a few minutes, and presto, smooth clothes again. This is a quick method for Sunday mornings when your child wads up his best pants in the back of his closet — they're clean, but wrinkled beyond hope. Instead of spending fifteen minutes of precious getting-ready time dragging out the ironing board and melting your hair, toss the pants in the dryer with a wet cloth. While it tumbles, you can re-braid your daughter's hair for the fourth time. Most all of my "experiments" with this work well.

» Sometimes you can't avoid buying clothes that have to be dry cleaned — husband's suits and some dresses. Just when you're choosing clothes, keep in mind that those dry cleaning bills add up quickly and are a real cost. So even if this blouse is $10 less than that one, but has to be dry cleaned at $5 a shot, that means if you wear it twice you've loss your savings.

» Teach your children to hang up their clothes. Simple, but effective. Many times clothing can be worn again without being washed again. Just hang it up to air out the "woofyness" (those horrible smells). The more often you wash, the sooner it will wear out.

» Don't teach your children to wad their clothes up and stuff the laundry basket as tight as they can. This sets in wrinkles. Teach them (and maybe hubby, too) to gently fold their clothes and lay them in the hamper — never to cram the hamper full. The pressure combined with the moist clothing just presses in the wrinkles. Warning — this translates into ironing.

Scheduling

Save money, water, energy — only run full loads in your washer. One way to get a headstart in the morning is to have loaded the washer ahead of time. I try to get all my laundry done by 10 a.m. so I'm not bothered with it while we have school, or with my other activities. Or in other words, I try not to start a load unless I also have the time to dry it, fold it, and put all the clothes away. If I still have more laundry to do when my schedule is up, I go ahead and load the washer and have it all ready except for turning the washer on. The next morning, Alan will just click the switch and by the time I stumble out, it's ready to go into the dryer. By doing this I'm an hour ahead with the laundry in the mornings. There are other scheduling tricks like this if you examine your own schedule.

The Immaculate Order of Perpetual Folding

It seems that every time a close friend, Martia DeMore, comes to my home, she finds me folding yet another load of laundry. We joke about my home being "The Immaculate Order of Perpetual Folding." I average three to four loads a day, sometimes doing as many as 10 (sheets, rugs, curtains, etc.).

In the early years of our marriage it was easy to separate the clothes — there were Alan's and mine. Then Reed's little socks entered the fray, but it still was simple. He had the shirt with the red caboose on it, Alan's had the polo player. Then came two more boys, and I needed a better system. As I stated earlier the size on the tag has very little relationship to real life. Trent has shirts sized 2, 3, 4, 5, 6 and they all fit him. Stuart has sizes 5 to 8. So, when sorting the first two boys' clothes started getting confusing, we started dotting the clothing. The way they grow, a pair of pants that fit last month are hand-me-downs now. Writing "Reed" then scratching it out to write "Stuart" was impossible on a one-inch tag. So we use a permanent pen and make dots. One dot for the eldest. Then when it goes to Stuart we add a dot. And then three dots for Trent. Sorting clothes is now easy. They can even do it. Just look for the dots. No erasing, marking out, or confusion.

My team helps me. If you haven't guessed it by now, I'm a mommy that needs help. One of the first tasks they learned was sorting socks. It became a lesson in classification (Good Science, lesson # 1). Think about it. It takes mental ability and reasoning skills to match socks, what with all the different sizes, colors, and patterns. It also takes mental deduction, the type Sherlock Holmes is keen about, to solve the case of the "lonely-onlies" while searching through a basket for "matchie-atchies" (we use highly technical terms here). We don't know yet if the perpetrator of this grand larceny is the dryer, washer or laundry hamper, for surely it couldn't be one of us.

Mending

Stay looking neat and tidy. Have your children ever ripped off a button on your way out the door?

Keep two needles threaded and knotted (one with white thread, one with dark thread). Hide them up high on the back of your drapery (in the edge seam) — ready to use for quick mending.

For other than emergency mending, keep a basket or box. Label it "mending" and put all the mending chores there. Then once a month take an hour and stitch them up. Load your sewing machine with clear thread and you can mend all those split seams quickly. It sure beats pulling out the machine and stitching each time it happens. It takes me fifteen minutes to just set up and put away my machine. (We don't have a huge house with a room for me to leave it permanently set up). When I mend once a month, I usually have 15 to 20 needy items. By doing it all once a month, instead of each time, I save three to five hours a month. By using clear thread you not only save the threading and re-threading of the machine, you save in having to buy all different colors of thread, plus you re-enforce the seam because the clear fiber thread is sturdier than most common sewing threads. Or use quilting thread for white stitching on pant's inseams. Do some preventive stitching and re-stitch the crotch seam again right next to the first stitching. It does help with those raucous young-uns. A stitch in time does save nine.

Health Matters

It really does.   Your diet and lifestyle can do much to assist you in having a healthy life and in avoiding many illnesses/diseases that are linked to stress and improper eating. My quality of life is excellent, though I've been diagnosed with a string of chronic conditions that, if I let them, could cripple me and depress me. Asthma, Irritated Bowel Syndrome (IBS), deep-venal thrombosis with valve damage, trick hip, vertigo (inner ear condition), allergies to everything I've ever been tested for, and hypoglycemia are some of the diagnosed conditions I have. Yet, with proper care from my current doctor, Sheila Horsley, a Christian physician who stresses diet and exercise interwoven with Divine healing, I'm taking no medications now. And this from the same lady that had to have three allergy shots a week, take steroids and massive amounts of pharmaceuticals just to breathe enough to pick up her own child. And this from the same lady that became unconscious and almost went into a drug-induced coma from following the exact instructions of a physician (to be nameless) in taking precisely the medication she prescribed. (That case was investigated and it was proven the doctor was in error.) I don't say all that to say "Hey, poor me." I say it to empathize with whatever conditions you're battling with now. I know a source of hope. Real Hope. If you interested in knowing more about this Hope, please read Appendix A.

Sickness robs us of so many things. Pursue health. Yet, when you are stricken, don't lose your praise. There have been several times in my life when I've been bed-ridden for months at a time, not knowing if I'd be alive a week later. So, I cherish each day and jump on my soapbox in support of the family and motherhood. Time is precious. Sickness robs us of that time. It destroys your family budget. We're still digging our way out of the hospital bills from a recent emergency. So, we do all we can not to help sickness along.

There are some new books with old ideas of preventive medicine, of home remedies and of wise-mother's tales from back before the answer to every complaint was "take a pill." The other night while we were watching a news show there were back-to-back commercials—take a pill to go to sleep, drink caffeine (coffee) to wake up. It would be humorous if it weren't so sad.   Here are just five simple home-con-coctions.   Maybe, they'll get your mind headed toward a more simple approach than what some people (never us, of course) have of popping over-the-counter, under-the-counter, and prescription drugs for every complaint. If you have any home remedies, I'd love for you to share them with me and my newsletter readers, please write me with them. By no means am I giving you any medical advice, as I'm not a medical doctor. These are only suggestions and methods that work for my family.

Diaper Rash

At one time or another it happens and it must be very painful — diaper rash. Both my nephew and my son were suffering from horrible bouts of it. Between ourselves, my sister and I tried dozens of "cures." Nothing seemed to work except for this treatment given to Kay from a wise old mid-wife. It struck me as down-right

Notes:

odd at first, and if anyone else besides my trusted sister had told me to do this, I would have thought it was a practical joke. Yet, I've used it with all four of my own children and nothing (including prescriptions galore) works as well:

Alternate on your baby's red bottom: Milk of Magnesia® and basic shortening (e.g., Crisco®). The next time you change their diaper, after the clean up, gently apply M.O.M. to their rash. Then diaper them as usual. At the next changing and cleaning, gently apply the shortening to their bottom. Alternate back and forth between the two until it clears up. (It's usually within a day.) I just keep a tiny container of shortening and one of M.O.M. in the changing table.

Diarrhea

How rude of me to mention, huh? But it happens. Here's a cure that my family has been using for more than 20 years. My Aunt Pearl, originally from Australia, learned this remedy from her father who was an M.D. and specialized in herbal/natural treatments. She taught it to us. It works very well and gently.

Take two 8-ounce glasses. Fill one with orange juice. Add to it a tablespoon of honey and a pinch of salt. Fill the other glass with boiled and then cooled water (or distilled). Add to the water 1/2 teaspoon of baking soda. Drink from one glass then the other, back and forth, until you've downed all 16 ounces.

Swimmer's Ear Treatment

This idea also comes from my sister. She uses it with her son, who's in and out of pools quite often living in Florida. My children rarely swim here in Texas, so it's not a problem for us. This helps to prevent the situation from developing.

Solution: 1/2 ounce of white vinegar and 1/2 ounce of rubbing alcohol

» One half hour before swimming: drop a few drops of solution in each ear.

» After swimming: dry ear out and repeat drops in each ear.

Sore Throat Gargle

As a child, my parents had me gargle with hot salt water. More recently, a friend, Kathryn Sleigh told me about also adding the vinegar and the cayenne pepper. These two make the gargle even more unpleasant, but the cure comes quicker.

At the first sign of a sore throat, gargle (one mouth full at a time) with as much of this liquid mix as you can tolerate for as long as you can:

Mix:

- » 8 ounces of water as hot as you can take it (you might not be able to gargle all 8 ounces, but try).
- » Add 2 to 3 Tablespoons of salt
- » 1 teaspoon of vinegar (optional, use to seal off the infection)
- » dash of Cayenne pepper (optional, use to bring additonal blood to area of soreness)
- » Repeat this every hour. This will not only ease the pain, but in many cases, stop the progression of the sore throat and retard the development of an infection.

"Mom, where's my _____?"

"Mom, where are my church shoes?"

"I don't know. The last time I wore them, I put them away."

"Mom, where's the tape?"

"Stuck to the dispenser."

"Mom, where's my _____?" You fill in the blank.

Do you have conversations like this in your home?

I've been accused of being organized, but we still have these grades of conversations in my home. Yet, there are a few closets that I have conquered. Maybe there are a few tricks that we're doing that could help your family. Perhaps, things that work here in this zoo can help you with your cages and wild animals, too.

Control or KAOS?

Did you ever watch the old sixties television show, "Get Smart"? Maxwell Smart was a secret agent for a secret government agency called "CONTROL." The arch enemy was an organization called "KAOS." Max (agent 86) would risk life and limb, guffaws and slap-stick humor in his weekly adventures of trying to stop KAOS's latest attempt to undermine "CONTROL" and, consequently, the civilized world.

Sometimes I have to look at my home in the same light. Without CONTROL(control), KAOS(chaos) would indeed overtake our world (home). Sometimes my handling and savvy is par with the bumbling of Agent 86, so I must adopt the same light-hearted attitude. And likewise receive some canned laughter.

Control, organization, Gestapo tactics, however you want to look at them, do have their benefits. It's easier and healthier to cook with clean dishes. Have you ever had to let a sauce become lumpy because you had to crawl into your child's sandbox, dig out the whisk and wash it before you could continue cooking? Have you ever had to change clothes at the last minute because you didn't have the time to untie 3, 416 knots in your belt? (The one your son had been using to plug the tub because he lost the real tub stopper using it to make "neat" shapes with his clay.) Have you ever had to call the doctor's office three times to find out when your next appointment was because your daughter kept eating the paper scraps you were writing the notes on?

"A place for everything and everything in it's place." That sounds reasonable on the surface. But if you really analyze it, you'd have to have the Library of Congress to have a place for everything. I don't have a house that's all closets. Though that might be nice. We don't have that luxury. What we have done to make up for it is buy more than one hundred boxes and a Rolodex® card system. (We took an idea from Emily Barnes[2] and adapted the concept to our Bonding Place.)

Simply, we have a box for each general category of items. We label the boxes with an alphanumeric code. We do not write the contents on the box. For one thing, the boxes aren't that large, and two, we change the contents around. Then on a Rolodex® card we write the letter-code and number and list the contents of the box. **For instance,**

- » X- For all Christmas items
- » H- For all other holiday items
- » C- For craft items
- » S- For schooling and educational items
- » G- General household
- » Special boxes: one for each family member's keepsakes, garage sale items, mending needs, etc.

Examples:

- » C-23 is for all my quilting supplies (templates, thread, books, etc.)
- » S-2 is geography supplies (postcards, souvenirs, posters from other countries)
- » X-4 is the mantle decorations for Christmas
- » H-5 is some of our Easter decorations

We have a wall of these boxes (they're all the same size and shape) neatly stacked in our attic. If I need anything, I simply flip the Rolodex® until I find the box number for the needed item, and pull out that box — simply and easily.

We do have a few boxes in the garage. These contain frequently used items or items that would be ruined in the extreme heat of the attic (e.g., C-8: glues and adhesives holding all different types of craft and school glues, tapes, and my hot glue gun and glue sticks). Those boxes were one of the best buys I've ever made. The boxes are the type that offices use as extra file drawers. They are cheap but effective, with lift-off lids. Admittedly, there are a few items (e.g., our Christmas tree) that are too large to fit in the 12" x 16" x 12" boxes. For these we have a few larger boxes, but labeled in the same manner.

An Ounce of Prevention

One way to make money go farther is by taking care of what you already have. Teach your children good stewardship of their and your belongings. For example: we want our children to appreciate books as much as we do. We want them to enjoy looking at the pictures and reading them. Yet, we don't want the books damaged or to have to spend money on replacing torn books. We seal our paperback book covers with clear contact paper. We have the hardback book jackets professionally laminated. You could also coat the hardback books with a plastic laminate sealant. Notice how your local library takes care of its book. Ask your librarian for advice. I've elaborated on books, but the same principle applies to all our possessions. (Idea: coat your belt buckels and metal barrettes with a coat of clear finger nail polish to keep the metal from flaking.) Think of ways to make things more durable and train your children to act with them responsibly.

Like my mother always told me — it is easier to prevent a mess than to clean it up AND it costs less to take care of something than to replace it.

I'm really big on bins, hooks, baskets and racks. The alternatives of piles, stacks and heaps aren't pleasant. I gradually buy different organizational aids to help turn those "drawers" into work centers; those "closets" into clothing terminals [where shirts(trains) really do move in and out smoothly without any crashes or scheduling delays]; and those "pantries" into works of art. A great deal can be done without buying anything. Just cut down empty cereal boxes to make magazine holders; arrange some small boxes to separate drawer clutter; and wash out laundry soap tubs to stack other items in the corner. There are books available with all sorts of wonderful ideas for using your space for organization and methods to use. See Appendix D for some suggestions.

The point is — start! Why spend time hunting for something over and over again. Find someplace to put it back to each time you use it. Teach your children this. Their future spouses will love you for it. Consider your material possessions — could you throw anything out? Oh, it's hard for homeschoolers, Vacation Bible School teachers and/or crafters to toss anything. "Why, you could paint it red and make it into a _____." I know, I know. That's why I use the box system for the really good stuff. One woman's garbage is another woman's treasure. Be sure it really is treasure.

The First Mate's Log

Have you ever seen what all went into a Captain's Log on board ship? Everything. Reports of seaweed. Reports of storms. Reports of mutiny. Reports of sightings. Reports of reports.

Instead of a Captain's Log, I have a First Mate's log. It's simple. But it works. It's the old basic spiral notebook — 200 pages, ruled, cheap. Here's how it works and why it works.

» First of all, on the first available line I write the day's date. Then as the day progresses, I jot down anything and everything. For instance: all phone calls out: name, number, subject of call (be brief, one or two words)

» The pages are blank except for the lines. I can write in two lines one day, and take up five pages the next day. It's flexible that way. Some professional message systems work well if every day's the same, or every call's the same. For instance, one day I have the "distinct privilege" of calling every appliance center in a 60 mile radius for quotes on a dishwasher gasket. So I write down the store name, number and price. Then I'm to call for directions to a friend's house for a meeting that night. Then I call to reconfirm a doctor's appointment. The first task covered a page and a half, the second took up half a page, the third was only one line.

» The pages don't fall out. This has saved my neck a number of times. I keep these notebooks and I can't tell you how many times I've had to refer back to them for information I never dreamed I'd ever need again. For instance, a year after getting the gasket replaced, we needed another one. Instead of recalling all the places in the Yellow Pages®, I flip back and use all my previous notes. I now know the way to my friend's house, but Alan has to stop by on his way home from work to pick up something for me. I have to give him directions, so I flip back to the notes. (I can drive there, but I can't remember the name of a single street.)

» The pages stay put. Loose notes get lost. They get eaten by babies. They're written on the back of envelopes never to be seen again. How many times have you lost the phone number of someone? By writing it down at the time of the call, when you hear it, the information is always there.

» It's a real bargain — usually under $2. That speaks for itself.

» It lets me keep track of the mail. I jot down letters out and letters in. That way time doesn't slip away unnoticed between letters. ("I just wrote Amy last week," I think — turns out it was six weeks ago.]

» It has a "photographic memory." It recites whatever I write down. In this notebook, I jot down when I order something and who I talk with. It's so easy to forget when I placed an order, or made a call. That way I can say that "I called your company on June 1 and talked with your Miss Smith, and she said. . . ." It's those calls that you think solved the problem that seem to keep coming back again and again.

You can make this a multi-purpose notebook and include all your goings-on or keep separate notebooks per item. (One for prayer requests, one for phone calls, one for mail, etc.) I personally like to keep one master list (I receive many prayer requests during a call).

Note: there are some wonderful household organizer notebooks on the market. I like them to some extent. I use them as reference books to fill with important household data, (account numbers, etc.), but for everyday activities (appointments, calls, etc.) I like the First Mate's log approach.

Mrs. Clean

Mrs. Clean I could be called. Not because that's my name, but because I'm married to Mr. Clean.

I know the Lord has a sense of humor. He matched a West Pointer, Alan, with Miss Asthma, me. Alan had lived with white glove inspections for four years. I, on the other hand, had been shooed outdoors when it came time to dust so I wouldn't have an attack. He had to maintain an equal distance between the hangers in his closet (they were actually measured for accuracy). I would shove all my clothes from side to side looking for something. His uniforms were spotless and immaculately pressed. I was allergic to bleach.

We were married. We had to cut short our honeymoon to the Florida Keys to elude an approaching hurricane. That must have been a subtle hint of the approaching storm to hit within our marriage.

Alan knew more about cleaning than I had ever known. He had run the vacuum cleaner a hundred times more than I had. Compared to the pristine West Point, my housekeeping looked like the ravages of a hurricane. Ignorant would be an understatement to describe me.

We struggled along for two years with his frustration coupled with my "I tried" routines. My mother had been a marvel, and I hadn't appreciated her. I had never known that one has to dust the tops of the doors. That is until she came to help when Reed was born and wiped up black junk from my doors for days. She gave me a lesson. And more lessons. I started asking for tips. There had to be ways to work smarter and quicker.

One man that can help immensely in this area is Don Aslett. Read anything he writes. Watch his tape. Not only is it entertaining, but it's a real help. He's a professional janitor that turned cleaning into a successful writing, speaking and business career. As with laundry, buy quality products for cleaning. Don't mess with the standard household products fanfared in the mass-media. Save money, elbow grease and heartache — buy industrial cleaning stuff (cleaners, brooms, mops, etc.). Don Aslett does such a great job in teaching you professional techniques. I can't improve on his advice here. If you hate housework like I do, get one or more of his books.[3]

I'm not great. I'm not even good. But I have improved. Our house is "healthy." Alan still does more cleaning than I do. But at least it's not 99 to 1 anymore, but more like 60:40.

Wrap-up

The question I get asked more than any other by friends and readers, is "How do you have the time to do so much?" I don't have 25 hours in my day. I just don't spend hours ironing, cooking, cleaning, etc. I use that time to do things I think are more important, like rocking my baby to sleep. . . .

Dutch Clean

Genetic codes can totally skip a person. I know. My maternal grandmother, Mama Bert, was 100% Dutch. She enjoyed cleaning! She actually derived pleasure from dusting, scrubbing, and vacuuming. I never understood. Her home and, then when she lived with us for nine years, our home appeared as if the cameras for a home magazine had just left. The Dutch are famous for being clean-aholics. I believe it, but still it skipped me. My mother used to joke with Mama Bert that I was afraid to get up in the night to go the bathroom because she'd probably come back and make my bed. Then one night I did get up and heard a strange whirling sound. I tiptoed down stairs and there she was. Three o'clock in the morning and Mama Bert was deep cleaning the family room and was running the hoover behind the couch. She couldn't sleep so decided to do something she enjoyed — cleaning! I went back to bed . . . wondering if I had been adopted.

Through wisdom is an house builded; and by understanding it is established: — Proverbs 24:3 (KJV)

CHAPTER NINETEEN

Graduation

The mailman drove off. My mother made the sound of a pretend trumpet and tossed the envelope on my desk. She gave me a hug. That was my college graduation ceremony. We opened the manila envelope and saw the parchment from the university.

The school had offered very little pomp and a very short circumstance. The learned administrators had decided that allowing each student to walk on to the platform for a handshake was too time consuming. So it was decided that all the business majors would stand. There would be 2 minutes of applause. All the business majors would sit. Then the math majors would stand, etc. Diplomas would be mailed to everyone.

Some ceremony, I thought. A four-year degree and I don't even get a handshake. I decided not to attend, which is precisely the reaction for which the administrators hoped most of the graduating seniors would opt. But then I was just graduating.

Hours of preparation and planning . . .
Details, logistics, and particulars . . .
Meals, banquets, and balls . . .
Receptions, parades, and spectaculars . . .
Dinners, parties, and cruises . . .

. . . all went into a week-long extravaganza around Alan's graduation.

For me, it was like a fairy tale. My dashing young cadet, immaculately dressed in his gray, double-breasted, full-dress uniform, escorted me around his domain. I was finally seeing the great gray halls of West Point. He had been writing me from these historical edifices for three years. At last I was seeing it.

The grounds were beautiful, all in bloom at the end of May '81. Flirtation Walk was breath-taking. The cruise down the Hudson was idyllic. The Tea at the Superintendent's home was posh.

The parades were stirring with a distinct brand of patriotism. The graduation banquet in the dining hall was solemn and filled with flair, pride and years of tradition.

Ah, the graduation ball in Eisenhower Hall was like a scene from Cinderella. The young ladies in the arms of their cadets added splashes of color against the starched Dress Whites as they all waltzed across the floor to the music from the orchestra.

How could I but fall in love all over again with my soon-to-be husband?

All these ceremonies were but precursors to the big event.

Graduation.

The stadium was filled. On the football field, cadets stood at attention facing the platform awaiting the arrival of their commander-in-chief.

President Ronald Reagan was to give the commencement address. He gave an encouraging message to his troops. In wisdom he was beginning a military build-up and emphasis on the troops that history would bear out.

It was the most extravagavant, pomp-and-circumstance college graduation I had ever seen. I thought back to a few months before to my "graduation." "Well, look," I thought, "I just graduated from XYZ U. Alan is graduating from The United States Military Academy."

I listened intently as my betrothed was called and he crossed the podium to shake the President's hand and receive his diploma. It was a beautiful diploma with carved etchings and hand-written lettering, larger than most — 18" x 24".

Then the ceremony changed directions.

This wasn't just a graduation.

It was a commissioning.

The graduates stood and took the oath and became 2nd Lieutenants.

Then overcome with joy, they launched their hats into the air. It was over. Yet, it was just beginning.

As I searched through the sea of people on the field, he found me. It was definite, I would marry this guy. Then he received his first salute. He gladly forked over the traditional silver dollar. He wasn't a kay-det anymore, he was a "Sir."

When I think back to that week more than ten years ago and contrast it to "normal" graduations, I'm impressed with the idea that it wasn't just the end of something. All other graduations I've seen are that — graduations, a good-bye. Yet, Alan's was a commissioning. A launching.

Whenever I attend a church service, I like to think that it is not just an information exchange, but that the real service begins after the instruction, after the sermon.

Just as Alan's graduation wasn't the acknowledgement of having jumped so many hoops during four years, it was the authorization to begin to serve. In his case, it was to serve in the military.

But in our case it's to serve our families.

Now, it is official! You've "graduated" from the "Dinner's in the Freezer!" kitchen management system.

I hope you don't perceive the reading of this book as just more knowledge obtained, but will look at it as a sort of commissioning. This system only works if you use it.

The Disciples didn't graduate from three years of ministry training to be able to hang accreditations on their walls. Their education was for using.

I hope that you value your education, especially the informal kind you gather through living life, that you value the talents the Lord has given you, that you appreciate your station (i.e., mission field) in life, and that you accept the Great commission in life.

❦ *And Jesus came and spake unto them, saying, All power is given unto me in heaven and in earth. Go ye therefore, and teach all nations, baptizing them in the name of the Father, and of the Son, and of the Holy Ghost: Teaching them to observe all things whatsoever I have commanded you: and lo, I am with you always, even unto the end of the world. Amen. — Matthew 28:18-20 (KJV)*

Appendix A

I have hopes that this book will fall into the hands of someone that can answer yes to one of these questions:

- ☐ If you are interested in knowing more about this relationship I repeatedly referred to in the book — The Lord's touch on my life . . .
- ☐ If your idea of Jesus is wrapped up in attending church and religious ceremony . . .
- ☐ If you desire to know Jesus in a personal way . . .
- ☐ If your life needs hope and meaning . . .
- ☐ If you are troubled with guilt . . .
- ☐ If you are not 100% sure that you'll arrive in Heaven when you die . . .
- ☐ If you are looking for something else besides worldly affirmation . . .
- ☐ If you desire a closer fellowship with Almighty God . . .

Read on . . .

Perhaps you've attended church all your life, but really feel like an outsider. Perhaps you feel that Christians are odd, stuffy and no fun at all. Perhaps you've never even heard the answer to all your problems. Perhaps you know all about Jesus.

There is a difference between knowing about someone and knowing someone. That's where I was more than 25 years ago. I knew all the answers in Sunday School, but I didn't know Jesus in a personal way. Then one beautiful bright and glorious Sunday, Jesus remade me. The process was instantaneous and an amazing miracle. I became a new person. He erased my sins and began a work in me that has given me a peace that is hard to understand.

The God that created this breath-taking planet and wove together every cell in your body has the power to do anything He wants to do. And what He wants to do is pick you up in His strong arms and cradle you like a child. What keeps all of us from the comfort of being His child is the sin in our lives, in our personalities, in our very nature. If we're honest and look inward, we all must admit we are not perfect, that we haven't met God's divine standard. If you can admit this, you're under the conviction of the Holy Spirit. That's a miracle in itself. If you can realize that you can't stand in front of God and plead that you're innocent — there is hope! Deep inside of yourself you know you've been wrong, that you've sinned. It's a hard thing to admit because of the pride we, as humans, have. But if you can now admit it, then you realize you need help.

Christ is perfect. To qualify as our saviour He had to be. Yet, He willingly died for YOU. On the cross, He took on all the sins you've done and will do. He crucified them. If you would like to start fresh, clean and innocent, you must recognize, in addition to acknowledging that you're a sinner, that Christ died for you and your sins. Accept the fact. Then open your heart and believe Jesus is Lord and Saviour of your life. The second you do this, He will pour out Himself into you. You'll never be the same again. You'll begin to really live.

What I've written here is the plan of salvation spelled out in the Bible. I've tried to use everyday language that would make sense to you. If your heart is hungry, please pick up a Bible and read it. If you ask the Lord to reveal Himself to you, He will.

Appendix B

Education and Homeschooling Resources

The following is written specifically to those who are interested in the education of their children or grandchildren. Even if you can't homeschool, many of these resources are helpful in supplementing other educational programs. Some of these are also excellent resources for adults (e.g books, etc.).

Now, when I mention that I homeschool our children, I'm flooded with questions. So many mothers are considering it for their families. If you're interested in homeschooling, I'd like to refer you to some resources for more information. "What curricula do you use?" is one question mothers repeatedly ask me. So I'll answer that here, also.

If you contact any of these companies, PLEASE mention that you heard of them through this book. Some of the companies will give you a discount on your material or special handling if you mention us. It will help us to substantiate the impact we're having and will help us be able to offer YOU more discounts in the future.

When I was pregnant with Reed, I started researching homeschooling and curricula. I was sold on the idea. Alan thought it was wonderful, but surely wondered if I could handle the physical work. Then we read the book, "The Peanut Butter Family Homeschool" by Bill Butterworth. Alan was encouraged that if Bill's wife could homeschool while sick with the pregnancy of their fifth child, then he figured I could do it, too. His book is delightful, funny, and helpful. It's published by Fleming H. Revell Company, Old Tappan, New Jersey, ISBN 0-8007-5244-9.

We firmly support the Home School Legal Defense Association. They are on a constant vigil in our behalf. They defend members and homeschooling in general in many legal cases. Contact them for more information in Paeonian Springs, VA 22129, (703) 338-5600.

Ray Ballman has written an excellent resource for homeschoolers: "The How and Why of Home Schooling" (Westchester, IL: Crossway Books, 1987— soon to be updated.) I especially appreciate his chapter on homeschooling and grandparents' impact. His latest book is "How Your Family Can Flourish." You can contact him about his books or for speaking engagements at Foundation For Family Development, P.O. Box 1267, Burleson, TX 76097 or call 817-447-9673.

One resource that is very helpful is Gregg Harris' Christian Life Workshops. If you write his organization at PO Box 2250, Gresham, OR 97030, they will send you a catalog and his itinerary.

Mary Pride researched supplies, curricula, books for homeschooling families and printed up her reviews in a series of books. She is a wealth of encouragement and solid information. Contact her through Home Life, PO Box 1250, Fenton, MO 63026.

There are a few homeschooling magazines I enjoy and recommend: *Christian Home Educations News* (12847 66th St N, Largo, FL 34643-1806 — 1-800-878-1973); *The Home School Digest* (Wisdom Publications, PO Box 575, Winona Lake, IN 46590); *Homeschooling Today* (PO Box 1425, Melrose, FL 32666); and *The Parents' Review* (71 Farah Dr, Elkton, MD 21921; $20 per year — focusing on Charlotte Mason's approach).

There are many wonderful programs available. There's one to fit your teaching style. I highly recommend that you research before you buy. Talk to someone that actually uses the program you're considering buying before you spend your money. I've talked with so many parents that have programs that looked great, but didn't fit their family, so these curricula just sit on the shelf gathering dust. Spend time before you spend money.

The following are materials that we use in our home. After years of research, we chose these programs that first, didn't compromise the gospel. Next, we looked at the approach to children, teaching, style, applicability to our family goals. We considered what we wanted to teach our children and then researched to find the best match. I wanted age-intregrated programs because want to school as a family. Being a budget watcher, I did a great deal of real cost comparisons. I like programs that are non-consumable. I can use the book with all four of my children. I wanted programs that I could look forward to teaching. I also am a tad bit independent so we use these resource as guides but still do our own studies. I am not saying that programs we are not using are bad. I am saying that the programs we are using are good, they work wonderfully for our family and that they are economically sound. We use the public library often. Note: Our most important resource is the Bible.

Phonics and reading:

- **Play 'n Talk**, Dept: 389/016; 7105 Manzanita Street, Carlsbad, CA 92009.

- **Accelerated Reading Program**: (800) 755-9818.

- Reading materials from many, many sources including books ordered from the companies on the next pages. I confess I'm a book-aholic. Our home is decorated in a style I laughingly call: Library Revival. Some of our favorite early readers for the children are:

  » **To Grow by Storybook Readers**, written by Janet Friend. This set is a wonderful accessory to the PLAY'n Talk phonics program. Published by Huntington House, Lafayette, LA.

  » **The 1838 McGuffey Readers** published by Mott Media. We ordered our set through the Conservative Book Club, 15 Oakland Ave. , Harrison, NY 10528-3739.

  » **Bible Stories for Early Readers** by Lavaun Linde and Mary Quishenberry. This series is excellent first readers. Bradshaw Publishers, PO Box 277, Bryn Mawr, CA 92318.

  » **A Beka Book Publications**, a ministry of Pensacola Christian College, Box 18000, Pensacola, FL 32523.

- And hundreds of books from the library, other ministries, garage sales, swaps, etc.

Math:

- **Saxon Math**, available from several companies see pg B-3.

- **Mortensen**, PO Box 98, Hayden Lake, ID 83835

- **CalcuLadder, The Providence Project**, 14566 NW 110th St, Whitewater, KS 67154

- **Cube-It! Manipulataive Math**, PO Box 1534, Waldport, OR 97394-1534.

- **Skip Count Kid** and **Bible Skip Count Kid**, obtained from Lifetime Books and Gifts — address on pg B-3.

- **Home-made math** — our own ideas including using milk caps, giant math numbers made from grocery sacks, real-life math exercises like balancing the bank book, budgeting, home improvement projects.

- **ABC Arithmetic Bible Concepts** — our own program. If you'd like a free flyer on what we do, send a #10 SASE, plus 25 cents, The Bonding Place, ABC Math, PO Box 736, Lake Hamilton, FL 33851.

Overall:

- **Self-designed.** After using Konos for more than a year, we decided to branch out and design our own studies and it has been a joy. Konos is excellent for beginners to the unit-study idea and for those teachers who want more ideas. **Konos,** PO Box 1534, Richardson, TX 75083.

- **Konos Helps!** (A magazine for Konos users), 2285 Pleasant Valley Rd, Newark, DE 19702-2105. We've found that we used the newsletter more than we used the curriculum itself. We regularly refer back to issues of *Konos Helps,* while, if I'm honest, the curriculum book hasn't been used in two years.

Art and Music:

- **The Cornerstone Curriculum Project,** 2006 Flat Creek, Richardson, TX 75080.

- **Vic Lockman,** 233 Rogue River Hwy #360, Grants Pass, OR 97527

- Private art classes locally, and a variety of music lessons (pianos and choirs).

Science:

- **Good Science,** Institute for Creation Research, PO Box 2667, El Cajon, CA 92021.

- **Creation Resource Foundation,** PO Box 870, El Dorado, CA 95623.

- **Backyard Scientist,** PO Box 16966, Irvine, CA 92713.

Current Events:

- **World Magazines,** Box 2330, Asheville, NC 28802.

Writing:

- <u>Writing to God's Glory</u>, by Jill Bond (me). I could never find a writing curriculum I could fully endorse, so I've written my own. For more information on the concept and ordering information send an SASE to The Bonding Place, WGG, PO Box 736, Lake Hamilton, FL 33851.

- **C.H.E.R.I.S.H.,** Rt 1 Box 267, Dodge Center, MN 55927. "A publication for those who use home as the base to make disciples of all nations." Subscriptions are $10 per year. They print articles written by children. Submit your work to them.

- <u>Market Guide for Young Writers,</u> by Kathy Henderson. Book orders: 1-810-648-5102 (Writer's Digest Books).

- **His Writers, and His Writers, Jr.** Why not start a writers' fellowship in your area to encourage adult and/or children to write to God's glory? It is a rewarding ministry. For more information, contact Jill Bond.

Special Needs: (Our third son, Trent, is autistic)

- **Nathhan,** (NATional cHallenged Homeschoolers Associated Network), 5383 Alpine Rd, SE Olalla, WA 98359. This support group ministers to me and our Trent. Worth the dues a thousand times over ($15 per year).

- **N.A.C.D.** (National Association of Child Development) 1-801-745-6179, PO Box 380, Huntsville, UT 84317. A wealth of help for anyone with a special needs child (advanced or challenged).

- **Family & Education Consulting Service (FAm Ed),** 6900 Office park Cir, Knoxville, TN 37909 (615) 584-6144. Bob Beninger uses the whole family approach as he ministers to those of us who need extra help.

- **PREACCH** (Parents Rearing and Education Autistic Children in Christian Homes) PO Box 736, Lake Hamilton, FL 33851. My (Jill's) ministry to other families walking the Christian walk with a child with autism. We publish a newsletter.

Miscellaneous:

- **Audio Memory,** 1-800-365-SING We appreciate their "Sing Around the World" Geography Kit.

- **Fischertechnik,** available through Timberdoodle (see listing on next page), are engineering toys that are far superior to other building sets we've seen.

- We also use a variety of games (card, board, & homemade) to reinforce the lessons we are studying, (e.g., *Journey Through Creation*).

- **Spanish Made Fun** is a delightful program written by a lovely lady with a heart for the Lord. The program is excellent! PO Box 35832, Tulsa, OK 74153.

- **HoneyWord** offers a program that is wonderful. My children love their creative approach to Bible study. It is even helping me with my Bible memory work. This program is well worth you checking into for churchs, schools, home Bible study, and for anyone who could benefit with help in Bible study. Call them at 1-800-HoneyWord (1-800-466-3996).

- **Discovery Toys.** We appreciate Discovery Toys very much. We like many of their products, but there is one toy set they carry we highly recommend: Think-It-Through. We like it so much we have two sets. It is a fun way to reinforce what you're teaching.

I can't emphasize enough that we use the Bible as our main text. The more I study and the more I teach, the more I use the Bible. Some day our Bible study goes on for more than four hours. Math, science, history, language, reading, writing — they all can and should be taught out of the Bible.

For example, one day we started reading about Hezekiah's Tunnel and that led us through engineering, math, history, geography, archeology, language development, science, water displacement, water management systems, escape routes, geology — well, as you can tell, we had a very interesting day and we used our Bible as the cornerstone of our lessons.

We, as a family, spend a goodly amount of time memorizing scripture — entire chapters. Everyday we add a verse and review previously learned verses. We not only memorize them, but seek to make them a part of who we are. We study the verses and internalize them.

Be sure to check the bonus page — several of these companies are offering discounts to DitF! readers!

We use a variety of additional teaching tools and books. Most of these companies offer products at substantial savings. Remember, never pay retail unless you don't have any other choice. This list is not conclusive. Send a postcard to these companies to receive their catalogues filled with products for your children and for yourself:

Christian Book Distributors
508-977-5000
Box 6000, MA 01961-6000
(Adult and children's books and tapes at discount)

Christian Teaching Materials Company
14275 Elm Avenue, Glenpool, OK 74033-0639
(Carries teaching material and curricula)

Best to You
Highway 16 East, PO Box 1300
Siloam Springs, AR 72761-1300
(501) 524-9554
(An economical source for Christian-themed gifts and cards)

God's World Book Club
1-800-951-BOOK
PO Box 2330, Asheville, NC 28802
(Books at excellent prices and we thoroughly enjoy their line of newsmagazines for different ages)

Lifetime Books and Gifts
3900 Chalet Suzanne Drive
Lake Wales, FL 33853
1-800-377-0390
For a catalogue send them $3 along with your name and address.
(Entire line of educational materials — more than 5000 items. They are a literacy-raising company)

Christian Book Bargains
Po Box 1009
Dover, OH 44622
1-800-221-2648
(Tapes and books at discount prices.)

Concordia Publishing House
1-800-325-3040
3558 S Jefferson Ave
St Louis, MO 63118-3968
(Books, gifts, Precious Moments®)

The Timberdoodle
East 1610 Spencer Lake Road, Shelton, WA 98584
(Educational "toys," books, teaching aides, etc. We love and highly recommend the line of Fishertechnik they carry. They also have a video tape on sign language that is excellent. Our children want to recommend their line of beeswax.)

Great Christian Books
PO Box 8000, Elkton, MD 21922-8000
1-800-775-5422, and fax 1-800-291-6341
(Books, video, and tapes at reduced prices. They also carry this book, if you want additional copies.)

Baker Book House
PO Box 6287, Grand Rapids, MI 49546
(Books, video, and tapes at reduced prices.)

Shekinah Curriculum Cellar
967 Junipero Drive, Costa Mesa, CA 92626
(Books, video, and tapes at reduced prices. They carry Ruth C. Haycock's "Bible Truths for School Subjects" which is a wonderful study-tool to coordinate lessons with the Bible.)

Berean Christian Stores
East of Mississippi: 800-944-8121
West of Mississippi: 800-237-3267
8121 Hamilton Ave
Cincinnati, OH 45231
(Christian gifts including games, figurines, books, and tapes.)

Impact Book Shop
800-755-3848
PO Box 1201
Lebanon, PA 17042
(Good selection of Christian books on tape, books, t-shirts, gifts.)

Today's Family Times
1-800-441-0511
PO Box 140990
Nashville, TN 37214-0990
(Books and tapes at discounted prices.)

> There are other wonderful companies with products. This list is just a sampling of resouces for your use. I'll gladly expand my list. Please contact me with your favorites. In the End Notes are listings of additional resources for you. Don't forget to look at the Bonus Page for about $150 worth of samples & discounts from some of these companies.

I would be remiss if I didn't also mention these next items. We're "new" to them but from what we've seen and have already used, we're impressed.

- When Bethany is older (she was born in 1990) I'll be using the Dorcas Series by Ellen Lyman to begin her sewing skills. Ellen's work is a marvelous program for teaching sewing in an enjoyable and productive way. Write her for more information at "Right at Home Productions" 7206 N Claney Ct, Spokane, WA 99208. (Referenced on page 7-8)

- We've started teaching our children foreign languages. We're using **"Spanish Made Fun"** see the Bonus page for the special offer on this program.

- Don't we all want to learn Greek? We are looking to Dr. Mal Couch of the Tyndale Theological Seminary and Biblical Institute at 6800 Brentwood Stair, Suite 100, Fort Worth, TX 76112 to help us with **Greek on Video**. Call 1-800-886-1415. He has programs for children and adults.

Appendix C

Miscellaneous Resources and Suppliers

If you contact any of these companies, PLEASE mention that you learned of them through The Bonding Place or this book. Some of the companies have offered to give donations to our "Kids Write" scholarship fund for referrals from us. Some of the companies will offer you a discount on your material or special handling if you mention us. It will help us to substantiate the impact we're having and will help us be able to offer YOU more discounts in the future through our newsletter.

Alltrista Corporation, Consumer Products Division, 310 South High Street, Muncie, IN, 47305. THE resource for canning. If you mention this book, they will send you a newsletter filled with information and coupons. I highly recommend that if you're interested in canning, order their "Ball Blue Book® Canning Guide" offered in the newsletter.

California Tree Fruit Agreement, PO Box 255383, Sacramento, CA 95865-5383. They are offering a packet of information including healthful recipes and directions, all free of charge. They even sent us a coloring book for the children free of charge. The offer changes from year to year.

Cornerstone Services, Inc.: For a free issue of *The Bread Lady Nutritional,* call (703)339-6467, or write Greg and Donna Spann at 9005 Macsvega Court, Lorton, VA 22079. They carry a full-line of kitchen machines and non-toxic household and personal products.

GVS Distributors: 1-800-398-2494. This company has a thick catalog filled with values. With them you can mega-shop for clothes (socks, underwear, etc.) and other household needs. They operate their company with Christian principles. I've been impressed with their excellent selection. Call them for a free catalog. Don't forget to mention us.

Joyful Living Distributors: Kristy Bell is a homeschooling Mom who helps families in the Texas, mid States region with bread making equipment, homeschool supplies, books, and other products. You can reach this fascinating mom at 817-441-7074 or by writing to 1601 Kelly Rd, Aledo, TX 76008.

Speciality Equipment and Supplies for the Kitchen: Vicki Schellhase is a national discount distributor for the Magic Mill DLX breadmaker/mixer, home-flour mill and other appliances. She also carries the well-known Watkins line of high-purity spices and hard-to-find extracts and seasons. She and her husband, Robbie, are Christian parents of seven, who practice my mega-cooking system, and who have a desire to help others save money and improve their nutrition. For information on any of their products, you can write to them at 3810 Archer Place, Kensington, MD 20895, or call them on their home business line, 1-800-726-6200.

PLAY 'N TALK ABC's of Nutrition, Carlsbad, CA 92009 or call 800 Vit-amin (Outside CA) or call 800 848-2636 (From CA). They have a line of quality vitamins and dietary supplements that our children love. No sugar or dyes. They're all natural. I had recommended their "Quiet Tyme" capsules to a friend who's children had been treated for hyperactivity. Nothing had worked. My friend tried "Quiet Tyme" and she said within hours she saw a postive change in her children. She thanked me again and again for pointing her to the ABC's of Nutrition. Their Herbal C is worth your checking into. This is a Christian company. If you mention this book on your order blank, you can take a $1 off your first order.

Posy Collection: Posy Lough, a godly lady, carries a line of craft patterns with Christian themes. Write her for a free brochure. Her work has been featured in *Focus on the Family Magazine* and many other publications. The Posy Collection, Box 394, Simsbury, CT 06070. Posy and Tom view their business both as a way to fulfill their Christian family responsibilities and as a way to minister to other families.

For rubber stamps try: Home on the Range, 5912 24th Ave S, Tampa FL 33619-5463, 813-622-8153 and **Jews for Jesus** 60 Haight St, San Francisco, CA 94102-5895, 415-864-2600

Christian Health Care Ministry, The Christian Health Care Ministry offers a Biblical alternative to medical insurance. Although we are not subscribers (Alan's company provides adequate insurance), we realize many families don't always have company provided insurance. After reading through the literature from Christian Health Care Ministry, we want to recommend this program to anyone in need of an alternative to medical insurance. Write to: Christian Health Care Ministries, c/o Samaritan Ministries International, P.O. Box 413-J, Washington, IL 61571-0413 or call: 309-698-8765 (Ext. 10).

For the organization boxes call **Viking Office Products** for a free catalog: 800-421-1222. Or check your local office supply store. We found Viking had the best prices for ordering several at a time and free shipping.

Appendix D

Miscellaneous Reading and Support Teams

There are many wonderful books/videos on the market to help you get organized in specific area of your life. In addition to the books listed in the endnotes, the following books make a brief list of available resources for you:

*Don Aslett: A cleaning expert. All of his books are helpful. His video, <u>Is There Life After Housework?</u> is not only a timesaver, but very entertaining. I order most of my cleaning products for one year at one time through his company and I know I save more than one hundred dollars per year. 1-800-451-2402.

*Rhonda Barfield: Rhonda, a dear Christian lady, has written a super book: <u>Eat Well for $50 a Week.</u> It is only $12.00 from Lilac Publishing, PO Box 665, St Charles, MO 63302-0665. This book is packed full of cost saving ideas. I've known Rhonda for several years and can personally testify: she's terrific! (See bonus page for more information.)

*Emilie Barnes: An organization expert. She surely can add "More Hours in My Day" and for you also. She has several books on the market and has trained representatives that give seminars. They are a wealth of information on getting your act together.

Cheapskate Monthly: I love Mary Hunt who produces this great newsletter. Mary loves the Lord. I've been a guest in her home and can agree that she "brings dignity to the art of living within one's means." Worth the subscription price again and again. $12.95 per year. Write to the Cheapskate Monthly, PO Box 2135, Paramount, CA 90723-8135. If you're serious about cutting costs, you "have" to get the Cheapskate Monthly.

*Cheri Fuller: <u>Christmas Memories</u>, <u>From Crayons to Careers.</u> I like Cheri and I like reading her work. Her books are brimming with practical ideas and real motivation. Publisher: Honor Books, PO Box 55388, Tulsa, OK 74155-1388.

Christian Home Swapletter. This monthly publication is ideal for anyone trying to make ends meet on a tight budget. Why not swap for those books, crafts, supplies, home products you need? This is the idea behind the swapletter. It is a newsletter that prints families' ideas for swaps. I've enjoyed it. I've been able to swap my book for so many things I've wanted. Write 118 Brighton Rd. Akron, OH 44301. Subscriptions are $10 for ten issues. (See bonus page for more information.)

*Gloria Gather and Shirley Dobson: <u>Let's Make a Memory</u> experts. Their book is packed full of great ideas, you'll have more than enough to fill all your new spare time.

Eliason, Harward and Westover: I don't have their book, <u>Make-A-Mix-Cookery</u>, yet I've seen it and have a friend who raves over it.

*Ann Hibbard: A family expert. She has written a very helpful book, <u>Family Celebrations</u> that is loaded with ideas to make holidays so very special.

Heart & Home, is a delightful magazine for Christian Home-Centered Families. Subscriptions are $15 a year for 6 issues or a sample copy is $2.50. Contact Tim and Teri Powers at Heart & Home, PO Box 531-B, St. Louis, MO 63032.

HomeWork has a slogan: *"The Home Business Newsletter with a Christian Perspective."* Contact them at H&FBFI, PO Box 2250, Gresham, OR 97030.

*Mimi Wilson and Mary Beth Lagerborg: GO get their book, <u>Once a Month Cooking,</u> and learn more mega-cooking. They are lovely ladies who share this mission-field to help us all in the kitchen. Their book is available by calling 1-800-AFAMILY. *Focus on the Family* publishes their book- it's that good!

*Raymond and Dorothy Moore: Their work is so extensive and all-encompassing that I decided to list them here. I could have just as easily listed them in the educational appendix since their work is a welcome addition to any library. They write on homeschooling topics, home business concerns, child-rearing issues, and over-all home management themes - all with a Biblical perspective. Everything I've read of their work has been encouraging, informative, and inspiring. I highly recommend their work.

M.O.M.S. and P.O.P.S.: Mothers of Many Siblings and Papas of Plenty Siblings - This non-profit Christian organization provides ideas, encouragement, fun, fellowship, support and service to large families with 5 or more children. Write M.O.M.S. at PO Box 57392, Webster, TX 77598-7392 and send a LSASE. They publish a periodic newsletter called "Legacies."

Moms, Inc. Newsletter: Family and Home Business Ideas for Christian Moms. Contact the Gibsons at Fast Forward, 3890 Cone Ave., Rochester Hills, MI 48309-4374. Subscriptions are $16 for one year. A FREE sample issue is available.

MOPS: Mothers of Preschoolers is a ministry bound to encourage any of us with little ones. Contact them at 1311 S. Clarkson, Denver, CO 80210 for more information.

Lindsey O'Conner: <u>Working at Home: The Dream That's Becoming a Trend.</u> Lindsey is the founding editor of the HOMEWORK newsletter listed above. She is a talented author with so much to say and to give you tools and good advice on the ins and outs of working at home. Publisher: Harvest House Publishers, Eugene, OR. Revised in 1994. You may have heard her on Focus on the Family, Point of View, or other shows.

The Officer's Wive's Club of Fort Campbell, KY: These highly motivated and delightful ladies have compiled a cookbook called "Air Assault and Pepper." The sample recipe in this book is printed with permission from their cookbook. Copies may be attained by addressing: "Air Assault and Pepper" Officer Wives' Club, PO Box 106, Fort Campbell, KY 42223. The books cost $7.50 each. Add $1.50 for postage and handling.

Patriarch: An excellent magazine for Christian Men. Patriarch, PO Box 725 Rolla, MS 65401. ($18 per year in print, or $24 on tape.) Sample print $3 or sample tape $4.

Quit you Like Men: "Quit you Like Men" magazine is an excellent monthly resource for the family provider. The name is taken from 1 Cor. 16:13-14, and is full of things of interest to godly men: integrity, self-discipline, loving one's wife, rearing our children, family worship, providing good government and much more. It also has strong interest in land-based lifestyles, home-based business, family farm and homesteading, with monthly columns on gardening, etc. For more information see the bonus page or write to PO Box 1050, Ripley, MS 38663.

The Proverbs 31 HomeMaker Newsletter, providing the homemaker with encouragement and information. Write Jennifer McHugh at PO Box 17155, Charlotte, NC 28270; 1-800-337-0031. $14 for one year 12 issues. One FREE sample available.

*Starred (*) titles are also available from Great Christian Books, most at a discount. Call 1-800-775-5422 for more information!

End Notes

Chapter 1: More Mary and Less Martha

1. Charlie Shedd, *Promises to Peter*. I like the way Charlie Shedd writes. His book *Letters to Karen* was my favorite reading during my engagement. He wrote these books as open letters to his children. (Nashville, TN: Abingdon Press, 1965).

2. *McGee and Me* is a video tape series from Focus on the Family. They are a delightful blend of cartoon and live action set in a tale of Biblical Truth. My children adore them. Yours will, too. Focus on the Family is one of my prime suppliers of entertainment in our home. Contact them for a free copy of their magazine and for more information about their ministry. Focus on the Family, Colorado Springs, CO 80995.

3. Vic Lockman has written a book on cartooning that our son Reed is devouring, *"The Big Book of Cartooning."* It is well done. You can order this artbook directly from Vic Lockman at Box 1916, Ramona, CA 92065. ($10.00 plus $2.00 shipping.)

4. This situation really happened. I've tried to disguise the participants because I don't want to continue with the labeling. The mother enrolled the child in a private Christian kindergarten. He is doing great in school, by the way.

5. I have to keep a tight rein on my thoughts now as I did then. In this situation, which I've tried to disguise to protect the innocent, I dwelled on Philippians 4:8 — *"Whatsoever things are true, whatsoever things are honest, whatsoever things are just, whatsoever things are pure, whatsoever things are lovely, whatsoever things are of good report, if there be any virtue, and if there be any praise, think on these things."* (KJV)

Chapter Two: The Logic Behind the Program

1. This statistic is calculated from facts from several sources. *The World Almanac and Book of Facts* was a source for some of the figures. Primary resource was another. This figure is a representative figure. In some cases the figure might even be higher. The mark-up on groceries on the average is 100%. Advertising budgets (e.g., commercial air time) can run as high as 50% of a manufacturer's/producer's budget.

2. This graphic illustration was told to me by my friend and healthy-living specialist, Elaine French. Her husband served in Vietnam and knows the details first hand.

3. This figure is common knowledge in the industry. I checked with several middlemen to see if my figure was accurate. It was confirmed. Names withheld for business reasons.

4. My mother cherishes this story of a dialog between my brother, Gary and my sister when they were pre-schoolers.

5. If you appreciate word pictures as I do, or need help in developing them, you'll enjoy reading *"The Language of Love"* by Gary Smalley and John Trent, Ph.D. published by Focus on the Family. This book discusses the advantages of using emotional word pictures. (ISBN # 0-929608-16-X)

6. This is a truthful story told to me by a friend. She prefers to be anonymous.

7. Since the writing of that section of the book, we have moved to Florida.

Chapter Three: Benefits Worth Considering

1. One of our family's favorite set of books are the *Chronicles of Narnia* by C.S. Lewis. I highly recommend them for your read aloud time.

2. Ron Blue has written several helpful books. We have three of his books and have enjoyed listening to many interviews with him: *The Debt Squeeze* (Pomona, CA: Focus on the Family Publishing, 1989), *Money Matters for Parents and their Kids* by Ron and his wife Judy (Nashville, TN, Oliver Nelson, 1988), *Master Your Money* (Nashville, TN: Thomas Nelson Publishers, 1986)

3. We advocate home or family businesses. I'm often asked to recommend sources and resources for those interested in home business. We've read dozens of books on topics relevant to our business. The most important being the Bible. The rewards are many. We have a "Family Business" section in our newsletter to answer specific questions.

4. The Lord has truly blessed me with this Godly friend, J.J. Howe. She writes a regular newspaper column in South Carolina. She also is one of the editor's of this book. She has not only checked the words of this book, but has worked the system and is one of my strongest supporters and encouragers.

Chapter Four: The Recycling Revolution

1. The Research Station in Lake Alfred gives tours to groups. On one of these tours my mother was fascinated with this information on their work.

2. We enjoyed offering a "Good News Club" to the neighborhood children. Five children became believers during our club meetings. Child Evangelism Fellowship sponsors this ministry. They have a wealth of Bible teaching resources: songs, learning aides, visuals, mission stories, books, and support classes. You may contact them in Warrenton, Missouri 63383.

Chapter Five: C.O.R.D.

1. I'm not advocating baloney sandwiches. I can't stomach them. I highly question the ingredients in regular baloney. I have found a turkey substitute that is better than the regular.

Chapter Six: Equipping the Professional: YOU

1. Though I don't look it, I am "Irish" — so may tell this anecdote as a family hand-me-down story. Way back at the time of the American Revolution, my great,-great . . . great-grandfather was drafted into the Revolutionary Army right off the boat from Ireland.

2. Air pans are sometimes called "insulated." Different companies make them. The ones I owe are made by Wilton, the company that is famous for cake decorating supplies. The pan is made of two levels of metal separated by a cushion of air. I'm impressed with their performance.

Chapter Nine: Personalizing Your Plan

1. We thoroughly enjoy Chuck Swindoll's ministry. This quote is from his book, *"You and Your Child,"* © 1977 ISBN #0-8407-5616-X pbk. Published by Thomas Nelson Publishers, Nashville, TN. His writing is always a delight to read, and this book is very helpful with child-training advice. You can contact his ministry, Insight for Living at PO Box 69000, Anaheim, CA 92817-0900.

Chapter Ten: The Mega-trip: Shop — pppiiinnnggg

1. We like Sam's Wholesale Club for our bulk shopping. Small business owners may join this private shopping club. This is one more reason to look into starting your own home business — you can join Sam's and benefit from their great prices.

2. We're members of the United Consumer Club which is a club that pools the buying power of individuals to enable its members to buy items at wholesale prices. Depending on your plans for major purchases (appliances, furniture, carpeting, etc.) you might find this club benefits your budget. For example: we ordered our sons' bedroom furniture (high quality) with a savings that more than paid for the membership fee. For more information contact them at their National Headquarters, 8450 Broadway, Merrillville, IN 46410. If you do contact them, please note us as the point of contact with the reference number 286504-R.

3. My grandparents enjoyed radio dramas. I like that radio allows for more input from the listener than does T.V. In the same creative vein of the old radio dramas, Focus on the Family produces the "Adventures in Odyssey" series. This series is a favorite not only of our children but of Alan and mine. This series weaves a Biblical truth into a fun drama. Check into it. They air it over many radio stations and also sell the audio tapes separately. Contact them in Colorado Springs, CO 80995.

4. If you are concerned with the horrors of Saturday morning television, I'd recommend you read the work of Phil Phillips. For instance his books "Turmoil in the Toy Box" and "Horror and Violence, the Deadly Duo in the Media" [published by Starburst, Inc., PO Box 4123 © 1986 Starburst, Inc Lancaster, PA 17604] are very helpful and eye-openers.

Chapter Eleven: The Mega-cook

1. This story reminds me of the title of one of my favorite devotions: *"When the Handwrtiing on the Wall is in Brown Crayon."* This book by Susan L. Lenzkes is noted as "Devotions for the Harried Homemaker." I've given many copies as gifts because I can definitely

relate to this author's perspective and I have many friends who do also. If you'd appreciate an insightful book from someone down in the trenches with us, I'd recommend you check this book out. Daybreak Books; Zondervan Publishing House; 1415 Lake Drive, SE; Grand Rapids, MI 49506; ISBN # 0-310-42631-1.

Chapter Twelve: Storing It All Away

1. I read this fact in the *Farm Journal's Freezing & Canning Cookbook* (page 4). This is a wonderful resource for your home. It is filled with recipes and techniques for even more freezing and canning then this book could cover. I recommend you read it as you delve more into freezing and preserving your food. (Garden City, New York: Doubleday & Company, Inc., ©1978) ISBN # 0-385-13444-4; Library of Congress number 77-81787.

Chapter Fifteen: Hospitality

1. I have recomended the Rainbow cleaning system to many families and have talked with many owners. I haven't met one yet, that wasn't glad they bought it. This system is different from regular vacuum cleaners. It does the work of a regular vacuum cleaner better than any vaccum I've seen, AND it cleans the air, deep cleans cushions, scents the air, and with an extra attachment, deep-cleans your carpets as well as professional equipment can. It even works well on wood or tiled floors. If anyone in your family has asthma or allergies this system is wonderful. It is so good that my physician even wrote a prescription for it. It is worth checking with you doctor and insurance company. Some might help pay for it because it is so beneficial for anyone with respitory or dermicalogical problems. The national office can put you in contact with a local distributor who will give you a free demonstration. Call (313) 643-7222 or write 3221 West Big Beaver, Troy, MI 48084. When you contact them please mention us as your referral.

2. If you are into camping, you might be interested in some of my father's inventions. He is the creator of the HOLD-AWN Secure Awning Systems. His company, HOLD-AWN Manufacturing, Inc., produces a line of accessories for campers to use with their awnings. For more information call 1-800-235-1631, or write 117B Lee Jackson Hwy, Haines City, FL 33844.

Chapter Sixteen: Freezer Recipes

1. Clarification: Yes, I have more than one mother-in-law. My husband has mothers of the wives of his father, adoptive father, and step-father. All are close to us. So we tell our children — more grandparents to love you.

Chapter Eighteen: Extras and Whole Home Management

1. Norman Stark's *Formula Book* was a real find for me in the public library. It is filled with the formulas of many household products. We've made many of our own solutions from inexpensivve chemicals available from the local drug store for fractions of the cost of prepackaged versions. We appreciated the real-life chemistry experiments. Try your library as the book is no longer in print. Library of Congress number 75-17054, ISBN: 0-8362-0629-0.

2. Emily Barnes is listed in Appendix D.

3. There are only two things I'd like to add about cleaning as a supplement to Don Aslett's work:
    a. He recommends a good commerical quality vacuum cleaner and says basically don't waste your money on more expensive cleaners. I agree with him if all you need is a "dirt picker-upper." But if you have a need more extensive cleaning (allergies, asthma, crawlers, pets, etc.) I still stand with my recommendation for a Rainbow. See endnote 15-7 above.
    b. He teaches us, when cleaning the toilet bowl, to use the cleaning brush and drive out the water. It is easier to clean a dry bowl than one half filled with water. Now, Alan can force the water out just as Don shows on his tape, but I can't. I've talked to many women who can't either. So I just grab a standard plummer's helper and force the water out that way. It's almost as quick and for we "weaker" vessels, it certainly is easier.
    His address is listed in Appendix D.

BONUS SPECIAL OFFERS!

The following companies are generously offering special incentives for you, our "Dinner's in the Freezer!" readers. To qualify for these special offers, you must mention "Jill Bond - Dinner's in the Freezer" when you contact these companies. Enjoy! There are about $150.00 worth of free samples, free catalogues, discounts and other incentives available to you. *Please note that these items are listed in no particular order.

The Posy Collection - FREE brochure on Christian family craft projects. Make memories and build traditions in your family with these kits. Send long, stamped, self-addressed envelope to: The Posy Collection, Posy Lough, Box 394, Dept. DF., Simsbury, CT 06070.

Hearthside Family Enterprises - Wholesome books, games, videos, and toys for all ages. We've previewed them so you can relax and know you are giving the best. Over 300 choices. We gift wrap and mail for you too! We are a small family business that cares about our customers. Call for our catalog only $3.00, 1-800-876-0309, or send check to: Hearthside Family Enterprises, 3673 Cragsmoor Road, Ellicott City, MD 21042. All Jill Bond customers identify yourselves for 10% off on all books and games.

Accelerated Reading Program - A phonics based software program for IBM compatibles. Enables you to successfully teach your child to phonetically read through a college level vocabulary. This program is proven to be very effective with children who have reading problems and /or learning disabilities. Call for a FREE information kit: (800) 755-9818.

HoneyWord - FREE Book - GOD HAS EYES IN THE BACK OF HIS HEAD ($5.00 value), with a purchase of "The HoneyWord Way through John," a fun and exciting book to help children retain spiritual values and key concepts of the Bible, along with their book and chapter locations for $14.95. Call 1-800-HONEYWORD, available 24 hours a day.

Great Christian Books - Monthly catalog with more than 12,000 titles, 4,500 directly related to homeschooling. All at big discount. FREE MEMBERSHIP with mention of this listing. A $5.00 value, Call 1-800-775-5422.

Harvest Health Foods - Sells vitamins, herbal supplements and natural foods. Offer: $1.00 off the price of the cookbook: "Home Cooking." Regular price: $7.29. call Jerry Rauch at 800-292-1392 or write to him at: Harvest Health Foods, Villa North Mall, 915 N. Main St., Bluffton, IN 46714.

Christian SwapLetter - One of Jill's favorite publications. Please send $1.00 & a 32 cent stamp, mention DinF!, and get a sample issue & a $1.00 coupon good on a later subscription. Value $.60 . Please note their new address: 118 Brighton Rd., Akron, OH 44301

Eat Well for $50.00 a Week - Rhonda Barfield has written a winner of a book. Save $1.00 off her publication "Thrifty-Lifestyles" (an 8 pg. over-sized special report) regular $3.00, for DifT! readers: only $2.00. Her book is available for $12.00. Contact Rhonda through Lilac Publishing, Dept. DF, PO Box 665, St. Charles, MO 63302-0665.

Cheapskate Monthly - If you're serious about saving money, this 10-page publication full of money saving tips is just for you. Mary Hunt writes it in a fun, yet very helpful style. For a sample and $1.00 coupon off a yearly subscription, send $1.00 to POB 2135, Dept. DF Paramount, CA 90723-8135.

NATional cHallenged Homeschoolers - Do you know anyone with a child that has special needs? NATHHAN is a Christian Non-Profit Org. for families homeschooling special needs children. Get your FREE sample copy of NATHHAN News. Just send $1.00 to help with postage costs to NATHHAN, 5383 Alpine Rd. SE, Olalla, WA 98359. (Value: $3.75.)

Education Systems 2000 - The only company specializing in software for the home education market. They are offering a very generous 10% discount on your first order. Call 1-800-706-9506 for more information.

Cornerstone Services, Inc. - which has published "The Bread Lady Nutritional", has changed the name of the publication to "The Family Matters". Ministering to the family on health and nutrition, household management, & home businesses with humor! (Proverbs 17:22) Sample copy $1.00 that can be applied to later subscription. $2.00 value. Call (703) 339-6467, or write: 9005 Macsvega Ct,. Lorton, VA 22079.

C.H.E.R.I.S.H. - This delightful publication features homeschooling children's work. For a FREE copy send the postage of $1.00 to: Rt 1, Box 267, Dodge Center, MN 55927. Value $2.50

Kim Schimmel - A sweet, Christian women who sells Mason shoes. These shoes are a wonderful, smart investment. They have all adult sizes available, She's offering a $2.00 discount on all orders. Send a LSASE for a catalog to: 4404 Bewcastle Ct, Greensboro, NC 27407-6458 or call 910-547-0090.

GVS - This company carries a wide selection of clothing and other supplies for families. Bulk quantity prices on just about everything. It's megashopping for clothes! They will send you a FREE catalogue, just call 1-800-398-2494. Value $1.00.

Christian Health Care Ministry - offers a Biblical alternative to medical insurance. I fyou or someone you know needs a low-cost alternative to medical insurance, you will want to find out more. If you become a part of their medical need-sharing ministry, or refer someone to them who becomes a subscriber, they will give you a $50.00 gift certificate for ordering books and materials from a Christian company. For more information and/ or brochures to give to your friends - call 309-698-8765 (Ext. 10).

Spanish Made Fun - The name says it all, Jill has met the creator of this program and has seen a demonstration of it. The program is teacher-friendly. $45.00 w/binder, $40.00 without, testing kit (includes written and oral exams) for $10.00. Mention this listing and get FREE shipping!

Home School Digest - "The magazine that no serious homeschooler can afford to be without!" Offer: Order your subscription today and while you're at it, you can enter a gift subscription for a friend absolutely FREE! Your subscription is $15.00. Theirs is FREE. Wisdom's Gate, P.O. Box 125, Sawyer, MI 49125. Value $15.00. Be sure to mention "Dinner's in the Freezer" as this is a special for our readers.

ABC's of Nutrition - As offered in the book. Call 1-800-VITAMIN or write to: 1185 Linda Vista Dr., San Marcos, CA 92069; mention this book and receive $1.00 off your first order.

Innovative & Quaint - A source for healthy books, Lorraine Mabbet is offering you a 1% discount per book ordered to a maximum of 20% off and no freight charges - FREE shipping! Write: P.O. Box 4873, West Hills, CA 91308-4873.

Moms, Inc. - is the only tax tips newsletter specifically for Christian women who work from home, or are considering it. Learn how to reduce your income tax from 20%-40% to 5%-10% legally using IRS guidelines, earn extra income, and still stay at home. Topics include all aspects of home businesses from how to choose and run a profitable business, to balancing family and business, Christian parenting and marriage, homeschooling, and more. Tax saving column in each issue. Sample issue - $2.00. SPECIAL OFFER to "Dinner's in the Freezer: readers - Get $3.00 OFF the regular subscription rate of $16.00/10 issues. Write to: Moms, Inc., Dept. DF, 3890 Cone Avenue, Rochester Hills, MI 48309-4374.

Staff of Life Products - Robbie and Vicki Schellhase run this family business from their home. They offer deep discounts on milling and breadmaking equipment, dehydrators, and water distillers. They also sell the high-quality line of Watkins spices, baking supplies, and household products. Call them at 1-800-726-6200 to receive product literature, or information about starting your own home business. Mention Dinner's in the Freezer to receive a free gift of Watkins products with any appliance purchase, or a discount on your first order of any size.

D. P. & K Productions - "BIG Ideas/small Budget" is a newsletter written by homeschoolers for homeschoolers - full of money saving/making tips! Discover how to eat out for FREE, get paid to SHOP, Make money at other people's garage sales, Start your own home-based business, and much, much more. For a FREE sample, send $1.00 to help with postage and a LSASE to: 2201 High Road, Tallahassee, FL 32303

Quit You Like Men - A magazine that is an excellent resource for the provider: Manliness, encouragement, loving the family, family worship, home business, homesteading, monthly gardening, etc. Write to: P.O. Box 1050, Ripley, MS 38663. Mention Dinner's in the Freezer, get a FREE issue - $3.50 Value.

Color Coded Greek - Don't we all want to learn Greek? We are looking to Dr. Mal Couch of the Tyndale Theological Seminary and Biblical Institute at 6800 Brentwood Stair, Suite 100 - Dept. DF, Fort Worth, TX 76112 to help us with Greek on VHS Video. Call him at 1-800-886-1415. He has programs for children and adults. Mention "Dinner's in the Freezer" and receive $30.00 off the first course.

Right At Home Productions - Ellen Lyman, author of Celebrate with Dorcas is offering $1.00 off your first order of beautiful patterns of modest Victorian-style clothing for women and children. Just mention Dinner's in the Freezer! when you order. Also, to get a FREE brochure about Celebrate With Dorcas send a LSASE to: 7206 North Claney Ct., Spokane, WA 99208.

> Since some discounts are stated as percentages, the total (about $150.00) reflects savings based on sample orders. Please note - these were the special offers as of printing of this book (February 1995). The offers and prices might change over time. These companies are making these special offers for you, the reader of this book. Be SURE to mention this listing to receive these offers. LSASE is a long, business-sized self-addressed stamped envelope - 9 1/2" X 4 1/4".

Recipe: _____   **From:** _____
Background:

x1	x____	x____	Ingredient	x 1	x____	x____	Measurement

Steps:
Steps that can be done ahead _____
1)

2)

3)

4)

5)

6)

7)

8)

9)

Notes/Comments:

Side dishes:

Servings:

Menu

tested	re-written recipe	shop-ping list	tasks list	Entree/Dish	# of meals	Comments

Shopping List for _____   Page _____ of _____

done	Place	Ingredient	1- 8-	2- 9-	3- 10-	4- 11-	5- 12-	6- 13-	7- 14-	Totals

Pricing Chart for Comparison Shopping

Item	Store			Store			Store		
	size	price	compare	size	price	compare	size	price	compare

Tasks to be Done:

✔	Task	Priority	Who?	Before Recipe	Note

Pricing Chart (Farmer's Market)

Item					Item				
Apple					Okra				
Apricot					Onions - white				
Artichoke					Onions - yellow				
Asparagus					Onions - Green				
Avocado					Onions - purple				
Banana					Orange				
Beans - green					Peach				
Beans - lima					Pear				
Beans - pinto					Peas - field				
Beans - wax					Peas - green				
Bell pepper					Pecans				
Blueberries					Pineapple				
Broccoli					Plum				
Brussel Sprouts					Potatoes - white				
Cabbage					Potatoes - new				
Canteloupe					Potatoes - sweet				
Carrots					Prune				
Cauliflower					Pumpkin				
Celery					Radish				
Cherries					Raisin				
Coconut					Raspberries				
Corn					Rhubarb				
Cranberries					Rutabagas				
Cucumber					Spinach				
Dates					Squash - Fall				
Eggplant					Squash - yellow				
Garlic					Squash-zucchini				
Grapefruit					Strawberries				
Grapes					Tangerines				
Honeydew					Tomatoes - reg				
Lemon					Tomatoes-cherry				
Lettuce					Turnip greens				
Lime					Watermelon				
Mushroom					* Honey				
Nectarines					* Herbs				

Timing Chart

Item:	Start time:	Approx cooking time:	Check progess at:	Estimated ending time:	Comment/ done

Shopping List for _____

Page _____ of _____

done	Place	Ingredient	1- / 11-	2- / 12-	3- / 13-	4- / 14-	5- / 15-	6- / 16-	7- / 17-	8- / 18-	9- / 19-	10- / 20-	Totals

Jill Bond & Speaking Engagements

Are you planning your next ladies retreat, book-fair, or special events schedule for your church, support group, or organization? Jill has traveled across the country encouraging families through Biblical presentations. Jill's style is friendly, humorous, and practical. When Jill started this ministry she saw it as equipping the saints. God's vision is so much clearer and broader. He's been using these presentations for evangelism. While a lady might not feel comfortable visiting a Bible study with you, she is open to a cooking class.

Jill has spoken to small Bible study groups and to thousands at conventions. Our main prerequisite is prayer. We try to be faithful to God's direction. Jill has a range of pre-prepared presentations and has developed custom talks for special groups. Some of her topics include: "The Power of Positive Parenting," "Mega-cooking," "Writing to God's Glory™," "Purpose," "Another Professional Mommy™," "Handicapped or Blessed," "Nutrition - The Bible Connection," "More Mary and Less Martha™," and "Why Math?"

For more information about Jill's speaking ministry, write to her at: Jill Bond c/o GCB Publishing, 229 S. Bridge Street, P.O. Box 254, Elkton, MD 21922-0254.

Dinner's in the Freezer!™ Video Seminar

If you want to have a Dinner's in the Freezer!™ workshop at your church, but your group isn't large enough to be able to fly Jill in - we understand. We now have a full six-hour DitF! Workshop on four video tapes. These tapes were professionally recorded and duplicated.

We are offering them with 2 different options: 1) for personal home use. You would buy the tapes licensed for private showing and use only; or, 2) you would rent the tapes for public showing and host a DitF! Video Seminar. Contact our office through GCB Publishing for full details and pricing. We work with groups to make the fees very reasonable. The rental arrangement would include written permission to publicly show the videos. Books are available with bulk discounts from GCB Publishing.

If you are interested in hosting a video seminar write to: Jill Bond c/o GCB Publishing, 229 S. Bridge Street, P.O. Box 254, Elkton, MD 21922-0254.

Dinner's in the Freezer!™ Seminar Featuring YOU!

Dinner's in the Freezer!™ will change your life for the better and many of you will want to share this concept with others. We salute you. Regularly, we are contacted by ladies who want to present these ideas to their support and church groups.

We encourage you and have handouts available. **We ask that you contact Jill first** so that we can assist you in your presentation and coordinate with you to have books (or order forms) available. Please include your phone number so that we may call you. In their presentations, some ladies utilize the video and audio tapes we have available. Let us help you minister to your friends in the best way possible. Depending on your plans, we can provide you with written permission to copy some pages from the book.

Also, some readers are organizing "Dinner's in the Freezer!™" support groups with the idea of team cooking, co-op buying, recipe-swapping, and encouragement.

If you'd like more information about hosting a seminar starring you write to: Jill Bond c/o GCB Publishing, 229 S. Bridge Street, P.O. Box 254, Elkton, MD 21922-0254.